A Human Right to Culture and Identity

Studies in Social and Global Justice

Series Editors:
Ben Holland, Lecturer in International Politics, The University of Nottingham
Tony Burns, Associate Professor of Political Theory, The University of Nottingham

As transnational interactions become more prevalent and complex in our interconnected world, so do the questions of social justice that have often featured in political discourse. From new debates in human rights and global ethics to changing patterns of resistance and precarity in the global economy, Studies in Social and Global Justice features books that grapple with a broad array of critical issues faced in the world today.

In partnership with the Centre for the Study of Social and Global Justice at the University of Nottingham, the series comprises both empirical and theoretical studies that critically address issues of social justice using a wide array of approaches, providing a vital space for the interdisciplinary interrogation of issues. The series draws upon diverse work from international relations, political theory and philosophy, as well as utopian studies, urban studies, gender studies, queer studies, postcolonialism, critical animal studies, disability studies, or theology, amongst other fields of study. It problematizes the dualisms between explanation and evaluation, theory and practice, the academy and activism, universities and the local communities in which they are situated, and between the Global North and Global South.

Titles in the Series

Labour and Transnational Action in Times of Crisis, edited by Andreas Bieler, Roland Erne, Darragh Golden, Idar Helle, Knut Kjeldstadli, Tiago Matos and Sabina Stan
A Human Right to Culture and Identity: The Ambivalence of Group Rights, by Janne Mende

A Human Right to Culture and Identity

The Ambivalence of Group Rights

Janne Mende

ROWMAN &
LITTLEFIELD
———— INTERNATIONAL
London • New York

Published by Rowman & Littlefield International, Ltd.
Unit A, Whitacre Mews, 26-34 Stannary Street, London SE11 4AB
www.rowmaninternational.com

Rowman & Littlefield International, Ltd. is an affiliate of Rowman & Littlefield
4501 Forbes Boulevard, Suite 200, Lanham, Maryland 20706, USA
With additional offices in Boulder, New York, Toronto (Canada), and London (UK)
www.rowman.com

Copyright © 2016 by Janne Mende
First paperback edition published 2018

Translated by Jochen Gahrau

All rights reserved. No part of this book may be reproduced in any form or by any electronic or mechanical means, including information storage and retrieval systems, without written permission from the publisher, except by a reviewer who may quote passages in a review.

British Library Cataloguing in Publication Information Available
A catalogue record for this book is available from the British Library

ISBN: HB 978-1-7834-8678-6
ISBN: PB 978-1-78348-679-3

Library of Congress Cataloging-in-Publication Data

Names: Mende, Janne, author.
Title: A human right to culture and identity : the ambivalence of group rights / Janne Mende.
Other titles: Kultur als Menschenrecht? English.
Description: Lanham : Rowman & Littlefield, 2016. | Series: Studies in social and global justice | Based on author's thesis (doctoral - Justus Liebig-Universitat Giessen, 2013) issued under title: Kultur als Menschenrecht? | Includes bibliographical references and index.
Identifiers: LCCN 2016020902 | ISBN 9781783486786 (cloth : alk. paper) | ISBN 9781783486809 (electronic) | ISBN 9781783486793 (paper : alk. paper)
Subjects: LCSH: Indigenous peoples--Legal status, laws, etc. | Group rights. | Culture and law.
Classification: LCC K3247 .M4613 2016 | DDC 342.08/72--dc23 LC record available at https://lccn.loc.gov/2016020902

∞™ The paper used in this publication meets the minimum requirements of American National Standard for Information Sciences Permanence of Paper for Printed Library Materials, ANSI/NISO Z39.48-1992.

Printed in the United States of America

Contents

Tables	vii
Acknowledgements	ix
Abbreviations	xi
Introduction	1
Part I: Decisive Approaches to Collective Rights, Culture, and Identity	**15**
1 Liberalism and Communitarianism	19
Part II: Rethinking the Key Themes	**47**
2 Society and Culture	49
3 Identity	63
Part III: Indigenous Human Rights	**87**
4 Indigenous Rights in History and the Present	89
5 Indigenous Demands in the United Nations	107
6 Indigenous Rights: Culture, Identity, and Beyond	147
Conclusion: Culture and Identity as Collective Human Rights?	161
Appendix: UNPFII Documents	177
References	187
Index	205

Tables

Table 1.1	Communitarianism and Liberalism: Four Lines of Argument	20
Table 6.1	Dimensions of Demands for Indigenous Rights	148

Acknowledgements

Financial support for the translation to English was granted by the International Center for Development and Decent Work (ICDD), which is one of the five Centers of Excellence for Exchange and Development programs managed by the German Academic Exchange Service (DAAD) with funds from the German Federal Ministry for Economic Cooperation and Development (BMZ).

Abbreviations

ASEAN	Association of Southeast Asian Nations
CoE Doc.	Council of Europe Document
DESA	Department of Economic and Social Affairs
ECOSOC	Economic and Social Council
EMRIP	Expert Mechanism on the Rights of Indigenous Peoples
FPDN	First Peoples Disability Network (Australia)
FPIC	Free, prior, and informed consent
ICCPR	International Covenant on Civil and Political Rights
ICEDAW	International Convention on the Elimination of All Forms of Discrimination Against Women
ICESCR	International Covenant on Economic, Social and Cultural Rights
IFAD	International Fund for Agricultural Development
ILO	International Labour Organization
IM	National Socialist Council of Nagalim (Isak-Muivah)
IWGIA	International Work Group for Indigenous Affairs
MILF	Moro Islamic Liberation Front
NDFP	National Democratic Front of the Philippines
NGO	Non-governmental Organization
PINGO	Pastoralists Indigenous NGO's Forum
PM	Permanent Mission to the United Nations
POPs	persistent, organic pollutants
RCIADIC	(Australian) Royal Commission into Aboriginal Deaths in Custody
UDHR	Universal Declaration of Human Rights
UN	United Nations Organization
UNCHR	United Nations Commission on Human Rights
UN Doc.	United Nations Document

UNDRIP	United Nations Declaration on the Rights of Indigenous Peoples
UNESCO	United Nations Educational, Scientific and Cultural Organization
UNHRC	United Nations Human Rights Council
UNPFII	United Nations Permanent Forum on Indigenous Issues
WGIP	Working Group on Indigenous Populations

Introduction

In the twenty-first century, the idea to codify culture and identity as a collective human right is gaining momentum and substance. It becomes most visibly manifest in the development of indigenous rights and their preliminary climax within international law: the United Nations Declaration on the Rights of Indigenous Peoples (UNDRIP). However, even after decades of discussion, the question remains whether a collective human right to culture and identity should exist at all, and, if so, in which form and to what effect.

The terms *culture, identity,* and *cultural identity* are placeholders that can be defined in many different ways.[1] In demands for collective human rights, their meanings often intersect and multiply. The field is complexly structured and sometimes contains contradictions, stark contrasts, and interchangeable terminology for and against identical demands. This gives reason to analyze patterns and arguments of demands for collective cultural human rights. These will be scrutinized in order to evaluate which aspects of culture and identity are being related to which justifications and functions in collective human rights demands. The goal is to answer the question whether and how collective cultural human rights equate to a meaningful enhancement of international human rights. In other words: is it true that "human beings have a right to culture—not just any culture, but their own" (Margalit/Halbertal 1994: 491)?

Before outlining this study's structure and line of argument, I will give an overview of the development of international human rights, and concepts of group rights and minority rights, in order to facilitate access to the field of research.

HUMAN RIGHTS: DEVELOPMENT AND CONTROVERSIES

In the "common narrative of the history of human rights"[2] (Menke/Pollmann 2007: 12), human rights are associated with three steps of development in the history of ideas. The first phase, in the seventeenth and eighteenth centuries, is characterized by the philosophy of a natural law that argued the case of certain rights every human being holds naturally (it was not, at the time, enforced in the political realm). During the second stage, represented by the bourgeois revolutions starting in the mid-1800s, civil rights became law. They lost, however, their universal, valid-for-every-human-being character. The third stage is marked by the Universal Declaration of Human Rights (UDHR), which, finally, united the universalism of the first phase and the juridification of the second. To Christoph Menke and Arnd Pollmann, this narrative of succession is a result of a foreshortened terminology that, above all, does not recognize the decisive break preceding the development of today's human rights (Ibid.: 12ff.). "An essential precondition of today's human rights politics is . . . the experience of a political-moral catastrophe so fundamental it also shook the history of human rights to its foundations. This catastrophe is political totalitarianism" (Ibid.: 16). This break is described even more clearly as a "rupture in civilization," manifested in the Holocaust (Diner/Benhabib 1988).[3]

This rupture plays a decisive role regarding content, normativity, and (international) law. Additionally, it prohibits equating pre-modern and modern declarations of human rights. The French Declaration of Human Rights of 1789, for example, or the US Declaration of Independence of 1776 can, with limitations, be conceptualized as historical predecessors of the Universal Declaration of Human Rights. It makes no sense, however, to discuss, assess, or criticize modern human rights only in reference to their antecedents.

At the same time, acknowledging the rupture can be compatible to the model of different phases if focus is not put on a harmonious, linear succession, but on the main differences of the three stages of human rights. In the course of this book, the term human rights will exclusively refer to the modern system of human rights that developed after the rupture of 1945.

The foundation of the United Nations (UN) in 1945 and the passing of the UDHR in 1948 constitute the sensational beginning of an international system of human rights. The International Covenant on Civil and Political Rights (ICCPR) and the International Covenant on Economic, Social and Cultural Rights (ICESCR), both of 1966 and effective since 1976, together with their protocols, not only specify and extend human rights but make them legally binding and provide parts of the UDHR with the strength of customary international law. Together, these documents constitute the International Bill of Human Rights. Compared to older human rights approaches, the modern human rights system is characterized mostly by the fact that

> on a domestic level, the individual used to be dependent on the freedom or lack of freedom provided by the political system in which he or she lived while the internationalization opened up a completely new way: the state submitted to a twofold necessity of legitimation: to the inside, a traditional-constitutional justification is still mandatory, and to the outside control was added by means of a "forum of world consciousness" and the possibility of criticism by other states and international organizations like the UN. (Riedel 2004: 12)

A complex and growing system of contracts, conventions, declarations, and resolutions on state, regional, transnational, and international levels is designed to support demands for human rights.

Due to different mechanisms of control and the lack of international executive sanctions institutions, international human rights are characterized by an interlocking of political, moral, and legal mechanisms of implementation. This allows for heterogeneous forms of human rights' enforcement not limited to the legal process. There are forms of enforcement based on customary international law, *ius cogens* (peremptory norms), *erga omnes* (law toward all), UN declarations, human rights contracts, as well as universalized standards and moral norms (Clapham 2006: 85ff.). This diversity results in gray areas and leeway that might be used for opposing purposes. The background for this is a general trait of international (human rights) law that will be present in the following discussions and that will make it sometimes hard to draw a clear line between normative and legal claims: International rights and norms are characterized by (the possibility of) debates on their interpretations (Ibid.: 70f.). International law is based on, and at the same time influences, social realities, institutions, and balances of power (Reus-Smit 2004: 279f.).

Therefore, the development of international human rights law, like the interpretation of human rights norms, has never been uncontroversial. Rather, it has been orchestrated by different criticisms that can be summarized under four central aspects.

The *first* controversy revolves around the relation of international human rights and state sovereignty. The founding document of the UN, the Charter of the United Nations from 1945, is the first example of this uneasy relation: In Article 2.7, on the one hand, it protects domestic affairs from foreign intervention. However, the UN Security Council can, on the other hand, initiate far-reaching measures "in order to contribute to the maintenance of international peace and security," as stated in Article 43.1. Additionally, all UN member states oblige themselves to "universal respect for, and observance of, human rights and fundamental freedoms for all without distinction as to race, sex, language, or religion" (Article 55c). These human rights were specified and filled with content by the UDHR while at the same time their development was fought against (ultimately in vain) by pointing to the sovereignty of states guaranteed in Article 2.7 of the Charter of the UN (Lauren 2011: 199ff.).

The contradiction between state sovereignty and international human rights remains unsolved even in today's discussions, especially regarding international humanitarian interventions. Nonetheless, the perception of sovereignty has changed due to the establishment of a binding human rights system and its reinforcement at the 1993 United Nations World Conference on Human Rights in Vienna (UN Doc. A/CONF.157/23). Responsibility for human rights (not only in the more recent responsibility-to-protect approaches) is seen as an important component of sovereignty and statehood (Human Rights Council 2008; Weiss 2005: 72f.; Chandler 2002; Deng et al. 1996). At least formally, "there is no longer any such thing as 'domestic affairs' when it comes to human rights" (speaker at the Peace Implementation Conference on Bosnia in London, 1995, cit. in Lauren 2011: 303). How and to what extend this claim is put into practice depends on further strategic, political, moral, and economic considerations. Pointing to the paradigm of sovereignty remains a common argument in this context.

In a *second* line of argument, the perception of the human rights system and the UN's task "to resolve conflicts peacefully and change people's lives for the better" (Ban Ki-Moon, cit. in United Nations Department of Public Information 2011: v) is criticized as an idealistic narrative and contrasted with political and power constellations. A pragmatic weighing of national reservations against human rights in general and against rights for colonized and domestic minorities in particular, as well as strategic considerations of domestic interests and Cold War conflicts are at the center of a critical view of the development of human rights (see Neier 2012: 93ff.; Lauren 2011: 211ff.; Morsink 1999). Sixty years after the passing of the UDHR, the human rights system and the UN system are often used only as a means to domestic ends and marked by huge gaps between pretension and reality. The United Nations receives criticism for its bureaucracy, ineffectiveness, passivity, and insider relationships that undermine the protection of human rights (see, for example, Bandow 2008).

Most critics, however, do not question human rights per se, but rather their effectiveness and their sustainability. These implementations in their various forms, as well as the development of human rights, remain the topic of controversial discussions and interpretations, which in turn relate to complex questions regarding the legal and moral status of human rights, their justiciability, and their legitimacy (Sen 1999: 227ff.; Lohmann 1998).

A *third* complex of criticism is marked by culture-related, cultural relativistic, and particularistic objections. They outline the character of values, needs, morals, and dignity as strictly cultural. A 1947 statement by the American Anthropological Association regarding the UDHR draft is paradigmatic for this argumentation: It denounces the demand for an international human rights project as Western and highlights instead the particularity of each culture (American Anthropological Association 1947; for more details, see: Mende 2011a: 19ff.). This cultural relativist argumentation was adopted by authoritarian states in the 1990s and used to legitimize their domestic human rights violations (see Yasuaki 1999: 105; Sen 1999: 228; Nagengast 1997: 353).

The ensuing, and even today ongoing, association of human rights with Western states and cultural relativistic demands with non-Western states is shortsighted, though. During the drafting and development of modern human rights, colonized and non-Western countries insisted on their universality in order to push back the then-existing colonial powers. Contrary to the common narrative of "Western human rights" and without relativizing international power relations, it can be stated that so-called non-Western actors contributed significantly to the universalization and effectiveness of international human rights (Yasuaki 1999: 111; Lauren 2011: 200ff.; Reus-Smit 2001: 529ff.).[4]

Meanwhile, critiques of universalism have largely changed. Human rights and culture are not considered mutually exclusive anymore, and critics predominantly advocate particularistic or culture-sensible rights (An-Na'im 1999a) by formulating a human right to culture (Rorty 1993; Bobbio 1996; Cowan 2006) or by establishing concepts of culture, identity, groups, and society *within* the framework of human rights.[5]

A *fourth* field of criticism focuses on who or what should be the subject of human rights. "In this context, the question to be answered by society is no longer about relativism or universalism, but whether *groups*, however constituted, or *individuals* should be the decisive legal entity of society" (Reese-Schäfer 2000: 299; italics in the original). Traditionally, human rights hold the individual as the legal entity and the state as the duty bearer (Donnelly 1990: 43). However, this understanding is questioned increasingly, especially in light of different concepts of the individual, (former) colonized states, and the global imbalance of power. Demands for collective human rights point to the right of peoples to self-determination, to different forms of societies in terms of their history, culture, and religion, and to the fact that parts of the existing human rights only make sense in a community (Stavenhagen 1995; VanderWal 1990; Crawford 1988b; Etzioni 1993). "The formation of the right to self-determination, of minority rights, and of the protection of indigenous peoples by international law shows that this law is not only for states with inviolable sovereignty" (Pritchard 2001: 31).

It becomes clear at this point that the four dimensions of critique do not stand independently for themselves but can overlap and intersect. The fourth aspect is shaped by specific ideas of community, culture, and identity. These ideas and concepts sit at the center of the study in hand.

Every one of the four critiques has both the potential to strengthen and to weaken the human rights system. The direction to which it moves—stronger or weaker—is determined by each critique's respective shaping of it and by the basic assumptions the argument is built on. Because the issues of criticism mark far-reaching differences and discrepancies, a general consensus on human rights cannot simply be presumed—despite international agreements, forums of cooperation, and tight networking. At the same time, the four areas of critique neither fundamentally question the idea of universal human rights, nor do they aim to reverse the development of the past decades; on the contrary, they want to advance human rights development by using the possibilities given by the dynamics and contingencies inherent to human rights.

Against this background the following remarks will focus on demands for collective rights within the framework of international human rights that allows for intrinsic and semantic changes.

MINORITIES, GROUPS, AND COLLECTIVES IN HUMAN RIGHTS

Demands for collective rights are sometimes summarized as the third generation of human rights. The term *generation* is, however, confusing because it implies succession, constant improvement, and linearity (Flinterman 1990: 75). Rather, the first two generations developed simultaneously and the third generation is not meant to supersede, but to supplement them.

The first generation sums up traditional civil and political rights whose goal is, above all, to guarantee freedom from state-imposed limitations. The second generation comprises economic, social, and cultural rights that demand active support by the state. The Cold War block confrontation led to the two separate UN covenants: The states of the Eastern bloc highlighted the collective aspect of economic, social, and cultural rights while the Western states considered liberal freedoms, guaranteed by civil and political rights, more important (Ibid.: 76).[6] Because of this division, the indivisibility of human rights, as reinforced by the 1993 United Nations World Conference on Human Rights in Vienna, was, and partly still is neglected today—just as is the insight that both generations contain positive as well as negative rights (Krennerich 2013).

The idea of collective rights gained momentum when the concept of the third generation was introduced at a 1978 UNESCO conference. Third generation human rights focus on rights that can be achieved only by common efforts, such as with regard to peace, environment, and development (Vasak 1979; Flinterman 1990: 77; Tomuschat 2008: 48ff.; Rosas 1995b). They are not limited to demands for collective rights. Conversely, demands for collective rights go beyond the third generation of human rights.

Collective human rights focus on groups. Groups have already been the subject (if not the legal subject) of human rights in some individual human rights concerned with family, the "community" (UDHR, Article 29.1), religious, ethnic, and language minorities, or the "will of the people" (UDHR, Article 21.3; Pritchard 2001; Donnelly 2006: 614). The various definitions of groups differ widely, both diachronically and synchronically, as a short overview of the evolution of group rights will show.

At the end of World War I, a group concept based on ethnicity evolved. With the rearrangement of national borders, minorities emerged on "foreign" states' territories. The idea was to establish general minority rights, which, in a reduced and democratic fashion, were later included into the Covenant of the League of Nations. In this context, inhabitants of the territories Germany had to cede were characterized as so-called *Auslandsdeutsche* (Germans living in a foreign country). To strengthen a collective German identity, they were to be supported and later to be "fetched back." This racial interpretation of minority rights gained lasting influence in Germany and became the momentous subject of National Socialist politics (Stapleton 1995: xff.; Pritchard 2001: 51ff.).

During the debates on the development of international human rights law after 1945, this appropriation of minority rights by National Socialism led to a decisive refusal of concepts based on collective rights. The formation of the modern framework of human rights marked a clear distinction between anti-democratic theories of ethnic groups, on the one hand, and group-focused human rights theories, on the other. In the mid-twentieth century, an understanding of groups prevailed in the latter according to which groups are neither biological nor ethnical-traditional determinants but rather formed because of social imbalances. Negative freedom rights, equality, and freedom from discrimination within the framework of *individual* human rights were at the center of these ideas (Stapleton 1995: xxvii; Pritchard 2001: 114).

The understanding of groups in the context of human rights changed profoundly in the last third of the twentieth century. Among other things, decolonization processes initiated a different legal approach to the group concept, containing "first, national minorities who have been forcibly integrated into a dominant culture and, second, 'disadvantaged' groups who identify with the national culture but whom society is held to have stigmatized or 'marginalized' or discriminated against on racial, cultural, or sexual grounds" (Stapleton 1995: xxix). The new minority politics gained momentum internationally in the 1990s in light of Eastern and Southeastern European transformations and worldwide efforts for self-determination.

A second dimension was added to the freedom-from-discrimination component of liberal minority rights. It was indicated that minorities might need special protection in order to preserve their characteristics and flourish (Pritchard 2001: 114) — a need that could not be accommodated by traditional, negative liberties. In a similar way, the United Nations Sub-Commission on Prevention of Discrimination and Protection of Minorities[7] differentiated as early as 1947 between equality of minorities and the majority, on the one hand, and "differential treatment in order to preserve basic characteristics which [minority groups] possess and which distinguish them from the majority" on the other (UN Doc. E/CN.4/52 1947). According to this distinction, "securing and developing the characteristics of certain groups" (Pritchard 2011: 43) serves the cause of preserving their unique culture and identity (Ibid.: 200). Developing this dimension of group rights within the framework of human rights leads to the crucial question of how to weigh individual and collective human rights, respectively, what their relation is like, and what the consequences are.

The tension between the two dimensions of collective and individual human rights is also reflected in minority rights based on human rights. They can be characterized by a "point of view, centered on individual rights, that understands a minority as the sum of distinct human beings, linked by conviction and life circumstances" and also by a "point of view, centered on collective rights, that understands minorities as mostly super-individual entities defined by objective features" (Ibid.: 23). Article 27 of the International Covenant on Civil and Political Rights is regarded as the founding principle of minority rights in the modern human rights system. It states: "In those States in which ethnic, religious or linguistic minorities exist, persons belonging to such minorities shall not be denied the right, in community with the other members of their group, to enjoy their own culture, to profess and practise their own religion, or to use their own language." It remains unclear, however, whether Article 27 should be interpreted from a collective or from an individual rights perspective, or from some point in between. This shows very clearly the ambiguity of international law.

The principle to characterize minorities based on ethnicity, religion, and language continues to be decisive for any further discussion of group and minority rights based on human rights. The Special Rapporteur of the United Nations Sub-Commission on Prevention of Discrimination and Protection of Minorities, Francesco Capotorti, confirmed these criteria a few years later in his report, saying that a minority was a

> group numerically inferior to the rest of the population of a State, in a non-dominant position, whose members—being nationals of the State—possess ethnic, religious or linguistic characteristics differing from those of the rest of the population and show, if only implicitly, a sense of solidarity, directed towards preserving their culture, traditions, religion or language. (Capotorti 1979: § 568)

The United Nations Declaration on the Rights of Persons Belonging to National or Ethnic, Religious and Linguistic Minorities, of 1992, substantiates Article 27 of the ICCPR and counts as a decisive breakthrough for minority rights. Nonetheless, the question whether it should be interpreted from a collective or from an individual rights perspective, or if a balance between individual and collective rights is possible, remains controversial.[8]

The sense of minority rights based on collective rights is seen in securing the minorities' existence and identity, in bridging gaps and, finally, in promoting world peace (Heintze 1998b: 19). Unlike the protection from discrimination based on individual rights, minority rights are not so much trying to achieve equality for disadvantaged groups but rather aiming at long-term and continued stabilization, support, and reproduction of their distinct existence. This, it is assumed, is the only way to achieve actual equality with the majority group in a society (Pritchard 2001: 49f.; Sanders 1991; CoE Doc. H/Coll 90). Since human beings only exist in cultural, linguistic, and religious groups and because these groups are not protected sufficiently on an individual basis, human rights principles of individuality need revision, the argument goes (Thornberry 1991: 12). Otherwise groups would dissolve or be forcefully assimilated (Chapman 2011: 253; Heintze 1998b: 20ff.; also see Pritchard 2001: 25; Brölmann/Lefeber/Zieck 1993). This is why ethnic, linguistic, religious, and/or cultural rights are deemed necessary for so-called autochthonous minorities.

The decisive distinction between autochthonous and allochthonous minorities assumes that only the former need collective rights for the protection of their culture because the needs of the latter can be satisfied by individual rights.[9]

The distinction of protection from discrimination based on individual rights, on the one hand, and self-preservation based on collective rights, on the other, gives decisive importance to the concepts of culture and identity. This makes it necessary to somewhat restrict the subject of the modern understanding of groups, as described by Julia Stapleton,[10] because groups disadvantaged because of their gender do not fall into its scope. Although important discussions exist that are concerned with the implementation of women's rights and that led, among other things, to the United Nations Decade for Women, from 1976 to 1985, to the International Convention on Elimination of All Forms of Discrimination against Women (ICEDAW), adoption in 1979 and entry into force in 1981, to the "Women's Rights Are Human Rights" campaign, kicked off in 1991, and to follow-up agreements, these efforts can be subsumed neither under the collective rights aspect nor under the demand for a distinction in terms of culture and identity.

In demands for collective rights, a group is a legal entity in a strictly defined sense: "By collective entities I mean groups that exist as units and not simply as aggregations of individuals" (van Dyke 1982: 22). Vernon Van Dyke suggests eight criteria to determine the strength of a group's demands for collective rights (Ibid.: 33ff.):

1. A group has a self-confidence and a shared heritage that separates and distinguishes it from others.
2. A group's structural chances to maintain its existence are good.
3. A group has clear and visible membership criteria, including race, language, religion, nationality, and shared cultural norms. The possibility to leave the group (exit option) can be, but does not have to be, a criterion.

4. The group offers its members a specific identity that distinguishes it from other human beings.
5. The group's demands correspond to its members' interests and are of low cost to the state.
6. The group is effectively organized and highly responsible.
7. There is a tradition to treat the group as a collective.
8. The group's demands are compatible to the principle of equality (this is the criterion hardest to meet).

These criteria can hardly be applied to groups marginalized on social or gender grounds. Although interpretations of group definitions differ in detail, van Dyke's classification is paradigmatic for the justification of demands for collective rights. With the focus on culture, identity, and distinction, it names central and constantly recurring criteria.[11] Accordingly, culturally justified collective rights should be distinguished from individual minority rights and from individual cultural rights (e.g., the individual right to participate in cultural life).

The recognition of cultural groups as subjects of collective human rights is controversial. There is disagreement whether cultural groups can be adequate legal entities both morally and legally (see Xanthaki 2007: 30; Jones 1999). From political science and philosophical points of view, it is feared that they might undermine the foundation of individual human rights:

> Demands for *"collective"* human rights are, firstly, confusing in their terminology, and, secondly, cannot be justified, since the universal, egalitarian, and categorical claim of human rights cannot be justified in the same way for collectives as for individual human beings. (Lohmann 2004: 106f., italics in the original; see also Donders 2002; Donnelly 1990)

From a state's perspective, the granting of collective human rights is seen as a threat to market economy, national sovereignty, and state borders (see Heintze 1998b: 15).

In contrast, arguments in favor of collective rights stress the indivisibility of certain collective goods and the discrimination of disadvantaged collectives (see Jones 2000). To justify the prioritization of collectives over individuals, threatening scenarios for a group's demise or the nonuniversality of concepts of individuality and freedom are cited.[12] "Indeed, not all cultures perceive autonomy as important" (Xanthaki 2007: 32; for a more general account, see Berting et al. 1990). Another important argument for collective rights lies in the communitarian understanding that "human beings establish a healthy identity and a (tellable) unity of their lives only if they remain embedded in the interactions and recognitions of their respective community" (Lohmann 2004: 100, criticizing the communitarian MacIntyre 1984).

A consensus-oriented approach declares the whole conflict between individual and collective human rights a pseudoconflict, based on the assumption that collective and individual rights do not necessarily collide; on the contrary, both legal forms complete each other, are in a "dialectic, reciprocal relationship" (Stavenhagen 1990: 255), and are "simply concurrent" (Crawford 1988a: 167). If individual rights are violated, this does not happen because of the nature of collective rights but because of their abuse, the argument goes (UNESCO 1995: 15). Similar to the practice in other cases of conflicting (human) rights, a fair balance (Pritchard 2001: 223) needs to be found in a case in which collective and individual rights collide. To achieve this, the leading criteria for such conflicting human rights issues as developed by the Human Rights Committee, which consist of objectiveness, reasonableness, necessity, and proportionality, can be consulted (Xanthaki 2007: 285).

There are, indeed, possible subject areas in which individuals and collective rights could complete each other; or at least could coexist. Regional and international human rights courts have, actually, developed criteria and operationalizations for principles like objectiveness, reasonableness, necessity, and proportionality. Nonetheless, there are plenty of subject areas in which the two legal forms collide and limit each other, and in which the guiding principles are so open for interpretation that they can be equally used by conflicting demands—depending on the interpretation of the terminology and on the normative criteria used.

In conclusion, it can be stated that demands for collective human rights contain heterogeneous concepts that leave plenty of room for interpretation and great potential for conflict. The book at hand aims to further outline and define these and to question their conceptual and normative basic assumptions.

OVERVIEW OF THE BOOK

The subject of this study includes the scope, limits, and the means and problems of the justifications of demands for collective cultural rights within the framework of human rights. It discusses the field of debate, central terminology and concepts, and the concrete example of indigenous rights.

Part I gives a detailed account of the conceptual, analytical, and normative presuppositions and basic assumptions of demands for collective cultural human rights. To systematically analyze the controversies, it is necessary to first examine the crucial constellation of communitarianism and liberalism. Next, Charles Taylor's, Will Kymlicka's, and Susan Okin's respective paradigmatic argumentations will be analyzed because they play an important role in the discussion of collective rights (chapter 1). This analysis will form the basis and point of reference for the discussion in the following chapters.

Chapter 1 will show that concepts of the individual, society, identity, and culture are core points of reference for the debate. In the course of the argument, they are used both as criteria for criticism and categories of analysis. The terms *culture* and *identity* are used in many ways and almost excessively. This makes it harder to analyze them, and it weakens their normative capacity. To meet these difficulties, chapters 2 and 3 of part II will give detailed accounts of their conceptual and normative meanings and content. To support an understanding of the different concepts, their inherent and contradictive dimensions will be discussed. Their contradictive character is, as will be shown, constitutive for the analysis of the terminology and, at the same time, a good example for why identity and culture are not sufficient normative criteria in debates concerning human rights.

Part III will empirically examine and substantiate these conceptual thoughts in light of demands for indigenous rights, which play an equally prominent and controversial role within the human rights system. Indigenous rights are seen as paradigmatic, collective-rights-based extensions of human rights norms. Today's furthest-reaching declaration that is focused on the collective protection of identity and culture of distinct groups is the United Nations Declaration on the Rights of Indigenous Peoples (UNDRIP), which passed in 2007 after many years of debates, revisions, and compromises (see chapter 4). Demands for indigenous human rights are, at the same time, highly diverse, which has effects and implications that demand a closer look. The interpretations both diverge and complement each other, which can be shown through the examples of the blurred term of indigeneity and the international indigenous movement. This culminated in the United Nations Permanent Forum on Indigenous Issues (UNPFII). An interpretative and a content analysis of the statements and objections made in the Forum will illustrate the manifold meanings, interpretations, and applications of collective cultural rights (chapters 5 and 6).

The conclusion will jointly discuss the theoretical and empirical results by asking what collective cultural rights and concepts of culture and identity inherent to them can contribute to human rights. The oppression of domestic minorities and the production of hypostatized, statically set identities—not least by international law itself—point to problems in concepts of collective rights. This should not, however, lead to the conclusion that collective human rights cannot have emancipatory effects.

To understand the repressive and emancipatory aspects of collective rights more profoundly, a moral philosophical discussion will be included whose influence is growing not only in political theory, but also in the study of global governance and international relations. Carving out the determinants for explicitly or implicitly used criteria shows that neither individual nor collective approaches to human rights operate beyond normative ideas of culture and identity.

But neither culture nor identity can be consulted as unambiguous normative criteria, if all their emancipatory and repressive aspects are to be kept in mind. Therefore, alternative or supplementary criteria need to be found. International human rights deliver the framework for a normative discussion. They contain, apart from the legal dimension, a moral one that holds up the perspective of something different, something "better." Morality is, however, repressive when (metaphysically) claimed or imposed from above. Then again, neglecting the moral dimension altogether would mean to be stuck with the status quo. A normative yardstick for criticism of the status quo is necessary, but, at the same time, impossible: It is necessary in order to criticize and transcend the status quo, and it is impossible to operationalize because, as a set category, it would become static, reified, and repressive. In the following, this conflict will be solved by mediating immanent (internal) and transcendent (external) criticism, building a substantial form of critique.

The analysis of a mediated constellation of the individual, culture, and society, of normative and conceptual utilizations of culture and identity, and of preconditions and expectations of collective human rights allows for a substantial approach to collective human rights. No individual element can be singled out and used as a normative yardstick, because emancipatory and repressive aspects appear in all elements and dimensions. Every element can be bent and utilized to an extent where emancipatory efforts have repressive (side) effects and vice versa. At the same time, it is possible to speak about "emancipatory" and "repressive" effects in the first place—as long as they are open to scrutiny and discourse.

Examining these interdependent yet conflicting constellations as well as the theoretical and empirical ambivalences of collective human rights will show the complexity of the emancipatory and repressive dimensions of culture and identity as a part of collective human rights.

NOTES

1. This has led to a struggle among political science and social-philosophical approaches to complicate, expand, substantiate, or waive these concepts. Examples of this can be found in the approaches discussed in the following chapters as well as with Benhabib (2002); Phillips (2007); Honig (1999); Bassel (2012); Brubaker/Cooper (2000).

2. The translator has translated this and all following sources of other languages.

3. The foundation of the United Nations and the passage of the Universal Declaration of Human Rights were marked by further conflicts, interests, and functions. Frank Schimmelfennig (2008: 266ff.) offers a summary of different explanations and critiques of their respective reaches.

4. Moreover, the dichotomous constructions of "Western" and "non-Western" can themselves be criticized (Hall 1992b).

5. For discussions of cultural human rights, see Cowan et al. (2001a); Donders (2002); Stamatopoulou (2007); Francioni/Scheinin (2008); Borelli/Lenzerini (2012); Nafziger et al. (2010). Nicole Deitelhoff (2009: 192ff.) describes different approaches to "cultural fragmentation" that can range from ignorance to exploitation to deliberate

processes of understanding. A comprehensive survey of the relation between cultural relativism and universalism and a concept of a mediated universalism can be found in Mende (2011a).

6. But see Whelan and Donnelly (2007), who oppose this idea of political motives for the two covenants and instead assume pragmatic reasons.

7. In 1999, this subsidiary body of the United Nations Commission on Human Rights was renamed Sub-Commission on the Promotion and Protection of Human Rights.

8. Further documents dedicated to the protection of cultural, religious, and ethnic minorities are: United Nations Convention on the Prevention and Punishment of the Crime of Genocide, of 1948, Article 5 of the UNESCO Convention against Discrimination in Education, of 1960, the UNESCO Declaration of the Principles of International Cultural Co-operation, of 1966, and many regional human rights covenants as well as international, but not legally binding, declarations. See Dinstein (1976); Stavenhagen (1995); Rosas (1995b); Bloch (1995); Berting et al. (1990); Riedel (2004); Heintze (1998a).

9. Kymlicka (1995b); for a more critical account, see Horowitz (1985: 209ff.); Pogge (1997: 209ff.); see also, for example, UN Doc. E/CN.4/1992/SR.38, § 30, and the discussion in chapter 1.

10. See above: To Stapleton, the term group refers, among others, to "'disadvantaged' groups who identify with the national culture but whom society seemingly stigmatizes or 'marginalizes' or discriminates against on racial, cultural, or gender grounds" (Stapleton 1995: xxix).

11. Dinstein's prior definition of a people as a subject of human rights is similar. It connects the objective factors of shared traditions with the subjective factors of a shared identity. See Dinstein (1976: 104).

12. This is the point where arguments based on collective rights and on cultural relativism overlap. See Mende (2011a).

Part I

Decisive Approaches to Collective Rights, Culture, and Identity

Discussions on legal, political, and moral dimensions of collective human rights are highly controversial, and, in particular, their relation to individual human rights is up for debate. The spectrum of the discussion includes, on one side, the argument that collective human rights are not only important, but also necessary as a counterweight to individual human rights often perceived as Eurocentric. Since the connection of individual identity and cultural group is not of free or voluntary choice, the protection of collective, cultural identity is the basis of a just society (McDonald 1991: 219). "For it is the welfare or interests of the community that is at stake and not just the welfare of a given member" (Ibid.: 232).

On the other end of the spectrum stands the assumption that collective human rights are self-contradictory, that is, since human rights can only apply to individuals, collective demands would undermine them. "Individual human rights and group rights are, at their core, incompatible, since individuals need to be protected not only against assaults by national authorities, but also against those groups that try to forcefully include or exclude them" (Reese-Schäfer 2000: 354). Participating in a cultural, sub-state community can, however, be understood as part of human dignity, but only if it is rooted in a free and individual decision, the argument goes. According to this perspective, the rights and the freedom of choice of group members are best protected by individual human rights—even if this choice means being part of a traditional society negating individuality (Donnelly 1990: 52ff.).

And, finally, there are positions that promote the possibility of the compatibility of individual and collective human rights. "Cultural freedom . . . is a collective freedom. It refers to the right of a group of people to follow or adopt a way of life of their choice. . . . It protects not only the collectivity but also the rights of every individual within it" (UNESCO 1995: 15).

Important for this third approach is the form of the underlying mediation. It can take the form of mutual complementation, dialectic supplement, hierarchical integration, or overlapping of individual and collective human rights. "Collective rights neither trump nor supplant nor justify abuses of individual rights. They are rights *in addition* to individual rights" (Thompson 1997: 788; italics in the original).

The integration and disintegration of these positions show the heterogeneity of the discussion, which is marked by contradictory and supplementing axes of argumentation. This constellation demands an in-depth analysis in order to develop a differentiated view on collective human rights. Chapter 1 will outline the scope of the conflict, referring to decisive debates, essential terminology, concepts, and contradictions.

Crucial to the controversy on collective human rights is, first, the confrontation of the individual and the group and, second, the criterion of voluntariness. This constellation is closely tied to a debate held under the terms *communitarianism* and *liberalism* in the late twentieth century. Since then, many approaches, positioned within and outside the dichotomy of the two schools of thought, have emerged. Therefore, communitarianism and liberalism are today seen as outdated. "There is no reason to go back to them" (Bedorf 2010: 18). "The dichotomization and false labeling of the 1980s was, however, stimulating, because it triggered a debate on the highest intellectual level" (Reese-Schäfer 2000: 27). The same is supposedly true for the once highly controversial concept of community. "Today, *community* thinking is consistently understood as a necessary and desirable complement of the liberal society. Additionally, worldwide discussions on communitarian thinking flushed away every particularism of communities" (Reese-Schäfer 2001: 144; italics in the original).[1] The dichotomy of communitarian and liberal positions has been transformed into more mediated approaches. International and domestic discussions on collective human rights nonetheless show that decisive controversies remain unanswered. The concepts of the individual, culture, and identity are still disputed. Above all, there is no definite answer yet as to who should, could, or may be the subject of collective human rights and if (or in what form) such heterogeneous and undetermined concepts as culture and identity should be part of international law.

To zero in on these questions, the theories that are at the core of the debate on communitarianism and liberalism can be (re-)considered. They contribute to the fact that, in demands for collective human rights, one cannot just resort to a "collective ideology tending to be totalitarian" (Ibid.: 142) or to radical moral relativism. Communitarians do not aim at suspending any given aspect of liberal individualism, but rather at correcting it (Ibid.: 134). This is a central criterion used to distinguish collective human rights from ethnic collective rights, the latter being part of right-wing and nationalist arguments. This study discusses only the former, that is, demands for collective rights within the framework of modern human rights. Therefore, the scope of the debate can be sketched around the tension between communitarianism and liberalism. This tension is firmly represented by the theories by Charles Taylor, Will Kymlicka, and Susan Okin. They establish ways to justify collective human rights as well as to examine their limits. The following chapter shows why their arguments are paradigmatic for premises within the current discussion on collective human rights.

NOTE

1. The development of the concept of community as part of the liberal society is reflected in the German terms *Gemeinwesen;* as opposed to *Gemeinschaft*.

ONE
Liberalism and Communitarianism

As the discussion on individual and collective human rights intensified in the last decades of the twentieth century, two positions, summarized under the names liberalism and communitarianism, stood in (seemingly) inextricable opposition. Based on John Rawls's *A Theory of Justice* (1971), the liberalist idea of individual, civil liberty was discussed in contrast to the concept of a substantially "good," a collectively defined liberty. Isaiah Berlin (2002) classifies the former as negative liberty—freedom of something—while the latter calls for the content of positive liberty. From a communitarian point of view, the content of positive liberty can only be determined by considering the respective cultural context that provides an inevasible "normative horizon" (Forst 1994b: 14). With regard to the scope of this study, liberal theorists assume uncircumventable individual rights while communitarians prioritize collective goods, values, and/or rights. The different forms of liberalism are sometimes subsumed under the term individualism because every person should develop his or her own concept of a good life while public politics and morality are legitimate only if voluntarily agreed to (see Etzioni 1997). Liberals are confronted with the argument to only abstractly apprehend the individual, as a monad not dependent on society (MacIntyre 1984; Sandel 1982). Communitarians are, in turn, accused of hypostasizing the community that, in their view, produces the individual, which is why the community should be given priority. Both positions are accused of either "forgetting the context" or "being obsessed with context" (Forst 1994b: 15; see also Shue 2004: 220).

During the 1980s and 1990s, both sides began to include the criticism directed at them into their respective theory-making. Ultimately, it became clear that "not only the assumption of the both sides' homogeneity, but also of the general incompatibility of particular liberal and communitarian arguments was wrong" (Forst 1994b: 13f.).[1] As a consequence with regard to collective human rights, the lines of argument can be depicted as a four-pole constellation along two axes.

Along the horizontal axis of differentiation separating opponents and supporters of collective rights, both liberal and communitarian positions can be found on both sides. Across lies the vertical axis of differentiation, on which either the individual or the collective serves as the explicit or implicit criterion (see table 1.1).

Four lines of argument result from this constellation, which will provide orientation throughout the study. In a *liberal line of argument opposing collective rights* (1), interests of individuals are rated as more important than a collective's possible interests. These individual interests are considered to be endangered by collective rights, which is why collective rights supposedly are a threat to individual rights and human rights.

A *liberal line of argument supporting collective rights* (2) aims at strengthening collectives when they serve the individual. This is established in different ways, for example by assuming that groups help to constitute, orient, or give sense to individuals. Peter Jones's concept of collective group rights falls into this category. A collective group right is a right that all group members share: "The group has no existence or interest that cannot be explicated as that of its members. In particular, the collective conception does not require us to give a moral standing to the group that is separate from the moral standing of each of its individual members" (Jones 1999: 85). The moral claim of a group is legitimated by stating that it serves the interests of the individual (see also Raz 1996). As for the first line of argument, the individual is the normative criterion for the second line as well.

The traditional *communitarian line of argument for collective rights* (3) focuses on the well-being of the collective that needs to be protected and acknowledged in its autonomy. Jones distinguishes corporate group rights and collective group rights and doubts that the former fits into a

Table 1.1. Communitarianism and Liberalism: Four Lines of Argument

(1) Liberal opponents of collective rights: • The individual is more important than the group. • Criterion: individual	(4) Communitarian opponents of collective rights: • The group is protected by individual rights. • Criterion: collective
(2) Liberal supporters of collective rights: • The group serves the individual. • Criterion: individual	(3) Communitarian supporters of collective rights: • The group/culture is a good in itself. • Criterion: collective

Source: Author

human rights framework. The communitarian, or corporate group rights, line of argument attributes collectives a discrete moral claim that basically exists independently of its members and their interests. To achieve this moral claim, "a group must possess a morally significant identity as a group independently, and in advance, of whatever interests and rights it may possess" (Jones 1999: 87f.). Such a group is characterized by its distinct collective identity.

Though it hardly exists, a *communitarian line of argument opposed to collective rights* (4) could, in theory, be outlined. It would see a group's well-being best protected by individual rights because individuals constitute the group and because community life regulated by liberal rights would stabilize and reproduce the group.

In human rights debates, communitarian and liberal positions most often overlap in argument (2), supporting collective rights on the grounds that individuals are constituted by groups.[2]

Based on this scheme, the implicit preconditions, relations, and limits of theoretical approaches to collective rights as represented by Charles Taylor, Will Kymlicka, and Susan Okin will be analyzed in more detail. None of the three authors can be classified as purely communitarian or liberal, and all of them claim to overcome the dichotomy and to productively connect relevant aspects of both sides. Their results differ greatly. Taylor and Kymlicka represent "the most advanced theorists of the social-theoretical debate on multiculturalism since the 1980s" (Reckwitz 2001:181) who justify the need for collective rights from a coherent theoretical perspective. In contrast, in her controversial essay "Is Multiculturalism Bad for Women?" Okin resolutely rejects the demand for collective rights from a liberal and feminist perspective (Okin 1999a). The discussion of these three authors cannot cover the whole field of communitarian and liberal debates. Nonetheless, it reflects a wide and at the same time profound spectrum of the chances and challenges of collective human rights.

CHARLES TAYLOR'S COMMUNITARIANISM

Taylor is seen as one of the central authors of the communitarian line of argument (3). He himself rejects being called a communitarian (Taylor 1994b: 250)[3] and, rather, aims at describing the debate in all its complexity and multidimensionality (Taylor 1989a: 182). Taylor's approach is significant for a discussion of collective human rights in multiple ways. His argumentation develops from different starting points that become important by the way he interrelates them. Although no direct and linear justification of collective rights can be drawn from Taylor's work, he nonetheless suggests one.

The following passage is central to Taylor's argumentation:

We can argue 1) that the conditions of our identity are indispensable to our being full human subjects; 2) that, for people today, a crucial pole of identification (in some cases, *the* crucial pole) is their language/culture and hence their linguistic community; thus 3) the availability of our linguistic community as a viable pole of identification is indispensable to our being full human subjects. Now 4) we have a right to demand that others respect whatever is indispensable to our being full human subjects (for example, life and liberty). Therefore, 5) we have a right to demand that others respect the conditions of our linguistic community being a viable pole of identification. The conditions mentioned in 5) can be spelled out to include the health and expressive power of our language, a certain realization in crucial sectors on the part of our linguistic community and some degree of international recognition. (Taylor 1993: 54f.; italics in the original)

Two central premises in Taylor's argument are the importance of an identity as constituted by language and culture, (points 1 and 2) and the right to recognition of the constituents of human personhood (point 4). The first premise contains far-reaching assumptions on the concepts of identity, culture,[4] and the individual. What are the implications and consequences that develop from these concepts?

Following symbolic interactionism, Taylor works with a dialogic concept of identity according to which identity is not developed from inside the individual, but by interacting with significant others (Mead 1979), by dialogue of the "rich human languages of expression" (Taylor 1994a: 32).[5] It is only against the background of a dialogically and intersubjectively formed identity that preferences, wishes, opinions, and efforts make sense (Ibid.: 33f.). Taylor's understanding of identity is based on his earlier studies of Hegel and his chapter on the master-slave dialectic, considered by Taylor as the central passage of Hegel's *The Phenomenology of Mind* (Taylor 1975: 155). Taylor applies its basic thought of mutual recognition: My being recognized depends on me recognizing the one to recognize me as a person (Ibid.: 153).

According to Taylor, these intersubjective processes do not occur in a vacuum, but in a "moral space" or "moral frame." This space or frame consists of qualitative distinctions and strong values that shape standards independent from individual wishes or desires. According to Taylor, every moral frame is formed by respecting others, elements of a good life, and concepts of human dignity. Furthermore, it is characterized by something good that every person strives for. Its strong values explain and justify individual evaluations and motivations. Human agency is not possible outside of such a frame (Taylor 1989b: 3ff.). "Living within such strongly qualified horizons is constitutive of human agency, . . . stepping outside these limits would be tantamount to stepping outside what we would recognize as integral, that is, undamaged human personhood" (Ibid.: 27). This undamaged existence constitutes a person's identity. Accordingly, identity is constituted by a moral frame, a focus on the good, and the individual positioning within it. "Our identity is what allows us to define what is important to us and what is not" (Ibid.: 30).

Taylor sketches the moral frame as neither unhistorical nor unchangeable. As an example, he points out that today's moral thinking demands respect not only for men, whites, or citizens, but for every human being. That is neither coincidence nor the result of a conscious decision. Rather, in today's moral frame it is just considered as "utterly wrong and unfounded" to draw the boundary of human dignity anywhere else (Ibid.: 7). Additionally, moral frames can develop differently on a second, cultural level in terms of intensity, scale, and meaning. At the same time, they consist of "moral instincts" that lie beyond individual awareness (Ibid.: 8).

For Taylor, every individual identity is dialogic, constituted within a moral frame, distinct, and special. It is this distinction that both characterizes and enables individual identity. To live according to one's identity is the fulfillment of authenticity. However, Taylor warns about the monological fallacy that allocates authenticity only in a seemingly independent individual interior (Taylor 1994a: 31ff.). Instead, authenticity is constituted dialogically and within the predominant moral framework—just as is identity.

Taylor connects this successful formation of identity to his concept of liberty. Following Berlin, he differentiates between positive and negative liberty, with the latter meaning no external obstacles to agency (possibility) and the former meaning to be able to make decisions about oneself and one's life (fulfillment). Based on this distinction, Taylor's concept of liberty means the absence of external and internal obstacles for the realization of personal goals. This includes the possibility of a person being wrong about his or her goals and means. In order to be able to recognize personal goals, self-awareness and self-conception are necessary (Taylor 1985). In other words, the formation of a successful identity, which allows for conscious reflections on a given moral space, is essential for liberty. This goes back to Taylor's interpretation of Hegel, where the mutual acknowledgment of master and slave fails and turns into a life-and-death struggle (and, as a result, into a power relationship; Hegel 1977: §178ff.). According to Taylor, this happens because master and slave "are low on the scale of development" (Taylor 1975: 155). They have no consciousness of their generality and no access to generality. For recognition-seeking efforts to be successful, however, it is mandatory for the individual to see their connectedness to generality (Ibid.: 155ff.). This is where Taylor's moral frame gains its relevance. A successful, reflected, and individual identity is not only dialogical, but also needs to be able to consciously locate itself in the general moral frame.

Every identity needs to first gain its dialogical acknowledgment and general location. Therefore, there is always a possibility for it to fail. This is a crucial point in Taylor's argumentation regarding collective rights. Collective identity politics are based on the idea that a denial of recognition of a collective identity leads to repression because the refusal is internalized and becomes part of the individual identity (Taylor 1994a: 32ff.; also see Fanon 1986). With this shift, Taylor puts collective instead of individual identities in the focus of identity politics. This shift in focus is neither coincidental nor arbitrary, but immanent to his theory because, for Taylor, the individual identity is closely knitted to its respective culture.

For Taylor, an individual's culture plays an important role in his or her identity (Taylor 1993: 54f.) because the general moral frame can only concretize in the form of culture. Taylor underpins his understanding of culture with the "presumption . . . that all human cultures that have animated whole societies over some considerable stretch of time have something important to say to all human beings" (Taylor 1994a: 66). Respect and a corresponding right to respect a culture are, however, not synonymous with the assumption that all cultures are of the same value. For Taylor, such an affirmative judgment is not only problematic but, in fact, presupposes a "North Atlantic" standard against which every culture is measured (Ibid.: 71). "There must be something midway between the inauthentic and homogenizing demand for recognition of equal worth, on the one hand, and the self-immurement within ethnocentric standards, on the other. . . . What there is is the presumption of equal worth" (Ibid.: 72). This assumption serves as an open process of approximation to a culture whose value can only be determined within that process.

Although this assumption speaks to a differentiated account of culture, Taylor's remarks broaden a narrow idea of culture or society. According to Taylor, every political community demands sacrifices by its members, either by force, as is the case for dictatorships and totalitarian regimes, or voluntarily and by means of discipline. The latter, however, needs strong motives because general altruism, higher morals, or enlightened self-interest are not strong enough for this libertarian form of political community. The only motive to develop a sufficient binding mechanism is identification with a community facilitating solidary patriotism (Taylor 1989a: 165ff.). Thus, Taylor resorts to a classic communitarian argumentation: "I am not dedicated to defending the liberty of just anyone, but I feel the bond of solidarity with my compatriots in our common enterprise, the common expression of our respective dignity" (Ibid.: 166). The "common enterprise" of the political community simultaneously reflects and constitutes the personal self. Here, individual and collective identities are closely intertwined and mutually dependent: no individual identity constitution exists without political community, and no strong, self-defendant political community exists without identifying individuals.

With this link, Taylor justifies his advocating collective rights. Both individuals and cultures have the potential to develop a unique, distinguishable identity, a potential which is to be respected (Taylor 1994a: 41). A cultural, distinct identity is—as Taylor argues forcefully—formed, above all, by criteria like common language and history, a relevant cultural heritage, and continued existence over time. In their capacity as constituents of cultural identity, these criteria are immediately common goods[6] around which a collective life can be organized (Ibid.: 33). They form the communitarian common good, the substantial concept of a good life. From this the fact precipitates that they can be protected only as collective goods, in a collective way. Liberal, individual rights are insufficient for this.

> It might be argued that one could after all capture a goal like *survivance* for a proceduralist liberal society. One could consider the French language, for instance, as a collective resource that individuals might want to make use of. . . . But it also involves making sure that there is a community of people here in the future that will want to avail itself of the opportunity to use the French language. Policies aimed at survival actively seek to *create* members of the community, for instance, in their assuring that future generations continue to identify as French-speakers. There is no way that these policies could be seen as just providing a facility to already existing people. (Ibid.: 58f.; italics in the original)

Taylor believes that in order to give (present-day and future) individuals not only the choice for a certain language or culture but to also a chance to actively reproduce a certain minority's culture and language, and to secure its survival, special collective rights are necessary. That implies that the use of a minority language (as in Québec) may be forced by law. Although Taylor insists that by no means does he want to undermine basic liberal rights, he points out that there is a wide range of other rights for which it is not only possible but necessary "to weigh the importance of certain forms of uniform treatment against the importance of cultural survival, and opt sometimes in favor of the latter" (Ibid.: 61).

However, Taylor leaves the criteria for such weighing between liberal rights aiming for equality and cultural rights maintaining differences largely open. He thereby abandons his own justification of collective, culture-protecting rights at a crucial point, thus allowing room for political interpretation and conceptual blurriness. "In a strangely ambivalent way, Taylor's explicit argumentation often changes between essentialist and historicist, universalist and particularistic, realistic and relativistic positions" (Rosa 1998: 548).

In the light of this study's research question, Taylor's argumentation covers three primarily important issues. The first concerns the constellation of the individual and culture, the second focuses on Taylor's concept of culture, and the third calls for his normative yardstick.

The Individual and Culture

Kwame Appiah addresses the first issue by posing the question of individual autonomy. In his critique of Taylor, he claims it is problematic to elevate a culture's survival according to the status of a good that is worth protecting, because first, this severely limits the autonomy of (today's and future) individuals and, second, it links the choice for a language and culture to genealogical criteria: "The indefinite future generations in question should be the descendants of the current population" and not *any* people *anywhere* (Appiah 1994: 157).

The accusation of limiting individual autonomy could be met with the argument that, for Taylor, culture and autonomy do not stand in opposition. Instead, within the moral space only the latter enables the former.

> Autonomy and freedom remain "empty" concepts outside and beyond particularistic forms of life because they lack any field *in whose framework* self-determination can take place. Only a (prior) common culture or form of life opens up the range of options that a subject can experience and that allows for a meaningful and substantial *choice*. (Rosa 1998: 471; italics in the original; see also Mackenzie/Stoljar 2000a)

Based on this embedding of individuality and autonomy into a given culture, Appiah's second argument could be defused, too, because cultural imprints would have a central, constituting meaning for the exact people born into a respective culture, and not for anyone anywhere.

Nonetheless, one question remains: How can an individual be shaped by a given culture and at the same time develop an autonomy allowing for a reflexive or critical attitude toward that very culture? In other words: Does the relation of culture and individual autonomy mean that the latter can only be achieved within a certain cultural frame?

Taylor emphasizes that development and changing of positions are possible in the moral space. He differentiates "between the later, higher, more independent stance and the earlier, more 'primitive' form of immersion in community" (Taylor 1989b: 38). For Taylor, however, the later quest for independence is culturally determined. Using as an example the "Indian pattern," Taylor thinks he can show that the quest for independence is not a necessary step (Ibid.: 40). In any case, this step does not mean to leave but to remodel the frame. Individuality always remains within what Taylor calls the given, independent moral space. It is unclear though, what exactly this constellation means for individual autonomy, how it restricts or enables agency, and how individual autonomy is tied to a culture or even the culture of origin.

Taylor's Concept of Culture

This is followed by a second issue of criticism and the question of how a culture is bound to the general moral frame. In other words: Is the moral frame located on a super-cultural level or do moral spaces collide on the cultural level? At first glance, Taylor's emphasis on different cultural characteristics of moral spaces (Ibid.: 16) seems to contradict his assumption of the existence of a universal, instinctive moral basis (Ibid.: 4f.). However, he specifies an ontogenetical order: Moral instincts exist before a cultural specification. Yet in terms of their concrete scope, form and extent, the universal moral instincts are culturally determined on a second level (Ibid.: 25ff.). This suggests that cultural conflicts only occur on the second level and that a cultural synthesis on the general level of moral instincts is possible. Taylor, however, rejects the possibility of a universal moral. Cultural imprints seem to encompass the instinctive and more universal level when he assumes that "this 'instinct' receives a variable shape in culture" (Ibid.: 5). Accordingly, the universal moral instinct would never appear purely but always culturally shaped.

This understanding gives momentum to a critique of Taylor's concept of culture. Andreas Reckwitz suspects that, for Taylor, cultures are internally homogeneous and externally distinct from each other. Taylor, he goes on, works with a totalitarian concept of culture because he equates the limits of cultures with the limits of moral frames (Reckwitz 2000: 302ff.). According to Reckwitz, Taylor assumes a "distinction between cultural communities that each have a collective identity . . . and thereby develop their own 'collective goals'" (Reckwitz 2001: 182; italics removed). If "differences in meanings were not presupposed as phenomena *within* collectives and, ultimately, within the mental structure of actors, but as phenomena *between* collectives," the demand for collective rights and to protect particular cultures would seem reasonable (Reckwitz 2000: 504; italics in the original)—with its problematic consequence of reinforcing differences between seemingly internally homogeneous cultures, especially if one culture is assigned an exceptional legal position compared to another that does not share the preferred collective good. This, in turn, can lead to suppression of the former's cultural identity (Rosa 1998: 482), thus reproducing a never-ending circle of suppressed cultural identities that can only be met by forming ever-smaller culturally homogeneous blocks.[7]

The moral frame could potentially offer a way out of such a static and totalitarian concept of culture. Taylor, however, does not show how this could be achieved without retreating to some kind of naturally given universalism on the level of moral instincts.

Taylor's Normative Yardstick

A third issue of criticism is concerned with weighing between conflicting values and needs. This weighing also plays an important role in the possible perpetuation of ever-smaller homogenous cultural collectives. Although Taylor rejects universal criteria, a normative yardstick needs to be found for weighing the "demand for recognition" (Taylor 1994b: 25) between different cultures. Taylor does not offer criteria to decide for or against particular individual or collective rights. To help orientation, one could, however, consult the order he defines for hyper goods and regular goods:

> General and equal respect as well as the modern concept of liberty in the sense of self-determination are hyper goods; community, friendship or traditional identity are regular goods. Still other goods, which according to Taylor constitute less important goals, are sensuality and sexual satisfaction. (Reese-Schäfer 2000: 67; italics removed; see Taylor 1989b: 63)

To use this order in a general and normative way would, however, correspond to an externally imposed normative yardstick or moral—something Taylor criticizes in other theoretical approaches. Discussing an instinctive morality, free of personal leanings (Ibid.: 4f.), Taylor tries to find immanent yardsticks. "Taylor is looking for an explanation lying within the people or things themselves. He looks for substantial characteristics . . . , for the essential basis of our moral feelings" (Reese-Schäfer 2000: 59; see also Schweppenhäuser 2005: 147). If, however, moral frames are culturally determined without a universal point of reference, then the quest for a yardstick goes in circles: It needs to find criteria to effectively weigh between different cultural values whose very conflict lies in the fact that immanent standards are conflicting and external standards cannot be consulted.

The questions posed here will be referred to in this study in light of different potential solutions. At this point, the three issues of criticism help to highlight the issue's complexity and prevent against one-sided and simple answers.

Taylor's approach can be summarized as follows: Taylor underlines how individual and collective identities are constituted by language and culture. From this, he derives a right to recognition of these constituencies of identity. Thus, distinct and relevant cultures need legal protection because they make up the identity of the people living in them and because they represent a substantial, collective good that only within an enclosed community develops its binding force, which in turn is indispensable for democratic societies. For Taylor, culture and identity play a crucial role for the justification of collective rights—both from analytical and normative perspectives. From an analytical perspective, identity and culture are of fundamental importance to individuals and thus demand collective protection. From a normative perspective, Taylor is concerned with a yardstick for preserving and reproducing identity and culture.

WILL KYMLICKA'S LIBERAL GROUP-DIFFERENTIATED RIGHTS

The most influential liberal strategy to legitimize collective rights was developed by Kymlicka. Just as were Taylor's, Kymlicka's works were motivated by the dispute over Québec between francophone and anglophone Canadians. His objective is to make the liberal project more just (Kymlicka 2001a: 69) and—corresponding to the second line of argument addressed in table 1.1—to formulate a liberal justification of collective rights.

Kymlicka's theory of group-differentiated rights aims to overcome the dichotomous allocation of individual rights to liberal thinking and of collective rights to communitarian thinking. Other than collective rights, group-differentiated rights entitle both individuals and groups. This is, however, not true for every group, as Kymlicka argues: group-differentiated rights do not apply to unions, companies, or the group encompassing all of humankind. Rather, Kymlicka focuses on *cultural* groups (Kymlicka 1995b: 34f.). This is why his concept of culture is crucial for the theory of group-differentiated rights.

Kymlicka defines culture neither too broadly (in the sense of civilization) nor too narrowly (in the sense of customs). "I am using 'a culture' as synonymous with 'a nation' or 'a people'—that is, as an intergenerational community, more or less institutionally complete, occupying a given territory or homeland, sharing a distinct language and history" (Ibid.: 18). He does not think cultures to be homogeneous blocks without communication and mutual influences—on the contrary, for Kymlicka, cultures have multiple sources that might root in other cultures as well. Nevertheless, he deems every culture distinct and specific because each gives a unique meaning to those diverse mutual influences. These meanings are embedded in cultural institutions and language and are shared by the cultural community. This is why there are, despite cultural exchange, fundamental and observable differences between cultures (Ibid.: 102f.).

According to Kymlicka, even if a culture changes its character, it remains identical to itself through its distinct institutions, traditions, and language. As such, a culture can be in danger—not, as Kymlicka emphasizes, in its supposed purity, but in its existence.

For Kymlicka, the first important justification of group-differentiated rights lies in the fact that a distinct culture allows for the formation of individual identity and for subject constitution. Cultures constitute individual identities by giving specific meanings to experience, practices, norms, values, and actions. This is where Kymlicka allocates the value of "distinct" cultures. Because distinct cultures offer specific knowledge and meaningful ways to act, they also offer the basis for individual decisions. Such imprints bind the individual closely to its respective culture of origin (Ibid.: 83ff.).

> No doubt all of these factors play a role in explaining people's bond to their own culture. I suspect that the causes of this attachment lie deep in the human condition, tied up with the way humans as cultural creatures need to make sense of their world. . . . But whatever the explanation, this bond does seem to be a fact, and, like Rawls, I see no reason to regret it. I should emphasize, again, that I am only dealing with general trends. . . . But most people, most of the time, have a deep bond to their own culture. (Ibid.: 90)

Thus, Kymlicka connects the communitarian assumption of the importance of one's own culture for the formation of individual identity with a liberal orientation toward equality and freedom. He tries to avoid pressing the two schools of thoughts into a hierarchy: In his effort to define group-differentiated rights, he claims to bring to the foreground the removal of inequality between groups, and therefore ethnocultural justice, instead of hypostasizing the individual over the group, or vice versa. Neither should individual human rights contribute to ethnocultural inequality, nor should collective rights compete against individual human rights. This is why both need to be addressed at the same time and be taken equally seriously (Kymlicka 2001a: 81).

Therefore, a second central reasoning in Kymlicka's argumentation in favor of group-differentiated rights lies in the assumption of structural inequality between culturally distinct groups. This reasoning is based on Kymlicka's understanding of nation-states and on his criticism of liberal state theories. Kymlicka emphasizes that every nation-state promotes a certain culture. This is why states are, contrary to liberal assumptions, not neutral but, as a basic principle, characterized by the hegemony of a certain culture over other cultures (Kymlicka 1995b: 107ff.; 1997: 22ff.).

From these two premises, Kymlicka derives the need for group-differentiated rights: First, he argues, there exists structural injustice between cultural groups in one state. Second, the survival of cultural groups needs to be protected against the state's majority culture because only an individual's own respective culture is central for that individual's identity formation. Although it is surely possible to change from one culture to another, Kymlicka argues, the price for this change is too high unless it is based on a personal and free decision.

This indicates a first distinction between group-differentiated rights and collective rights. Kymlicka introduces different types of groups. With national minorities and ethnic groups, there are two main groups that demand group-differentiated rights. Ethnic groups arise from individual or family migration. Their basic characteristic is the voluntary decision to migrate. Ethnic groups do not demand secession but acknowledgment of their ethnic identity within the hegemonic institutions. They are distinct only in family life and in their voluntary association (Kymlicka 1995b: 10ff.). As Kymlicka points out, they need to be distinguished from national minorities:

I will use the term *national minorities* to refer, not to immigrants, but rather to historically settled, territorially concentrated and previously self-governing cultures whose territory has become incorporated into a larger state. The incorporation of such groups has typically been involuntary, due to colonization, conquest, or the transfer of territory between imperial powers, but in some cases reflects a voluntary federation. (Kymlicka 1997: 19; italics in the original, see also Kymlicka 2011b)

Looking at present-day transnational developments, Kymlicka further sub-categorizes the national minority group into indigenous groups, on the one hand, and sub-state/stateless or minority nations, on the other (Kymlicka 2007: 66ff.; 2001b; Banting/Kymlicka 2006).[8] According to Kymlicka, both groups have in common (contrary to ethnic groups) that they already had their own institutions, language, and history—in short: a "societal culture"—before they were incorporated into the new state. Since societal cultures constitute sense and subjectivity, they need to be protected by group-differentiated rights. This protection applies to national minorities only, not to ethnic groups (Kymlicka 1995b: 77ff.).

For Kymlicka, a pivotal criterion to differentiate national minorities and ethnic groups is the degree to which a change from one culture to another is voluntarily. This means Kymlicka opposes a genealogical understanding of national groups as suggested by his initial distinction of allochthonous and autochthonous groups. "It is important to note that national groups, as I am using that term, are not defined by race or descent" (Ibid.: 22). All cultural groups, he insists, are "racially and ethnically" mixed due to migrations and exogamic marriages (Ibid.: 23). Thus, voluntariness and not ancestry is the criterion for whether a group has a legitimate right to strong group-differentiated rights beyond the recognition of their ethnic identity. This is based on the assumption that national minorities have forcefully been integrated into a culturally distinct state system. The formation of ethnic minorities, on the other hand, has its roots in voluntary migration, which implies acceptance of the host country's societal culture.

To keep this ideal categorization practical in reality, Kymlicka has to make some serious concessions: African Americans, he argues, can be allocated in neither group because they neither migrated voluntarily nor do they have a distinct culture. The goal of the Civil Rights Movement was integration, not separation. Refugees and former national or religious minorities that were promised self-determination at an earlier point in time do not fit this categorization either (Ibid.: 24ff.). To maintain the two categories of national minorities and ethnic groups viable and connectable, all of the aforementioned groups have to be excluded from the analysis.

This means that Kymlicka's group categories come with some limiting preconditions, difficult distinctions, and exceptions. Nonetheless, he insists, they are valid for many existing groups. He furthermore claims that exceptions are only the result of "past injustices and inconsistencies," adding, "I believe that a fairer and more consistent immigration policy will work, over time, to prevent such hard cases" (Ibid.: 25f.).

To do justice to the liberal criterion of voluntariness in the concept of group-differentiated rights, Kymlicka establishes another fundamental limitation: "We need to distinguish two kinds of claims that an ethnic or national group might make. The first involves the claim of a group against its own members; the second involves the claim of a group against the larger society," with the former being "internal restrictions" designed to prevent internal dissent and the latter being "external protections" designed to fend off intrusions by the majority society. "Liberals can and should endorse certain external protections, where they promote fairness between groups, but should reject internal restrictions which limit the right of group members to question and revise traditional authorities" (Ibid.: 37). As with his other distinctions, Kymlicka points out briefly that some aspects go beyond this dichotomy in that external decisions do have influence on intragroup relations and that there can be close connections between external protection and internal restrictions (Ibid.: 36, 42). However, Kymlicka does not find his argumentation of differentiating internal restrictions (to be rejected) and external protection (to be supported) impaired by this. What is important, he concludes, is that the general category of group-differentiated rights can encompass both forms, so that a more precise distinction is necessary in order to not cut back the individual rights of group members (Ibid.: 41).

The distinction between internal restrictions and external protection shows another point of reference that shapes Kymlicka's liberal argumentation for group rights: the value of liberty, which is closely tied to the criterion of voluntariness. Kymlicka's understanding of a "good life" does not only include the idea of a life in accordance with inner and cultural values, but also the possibility to question these values. Kymlicka emphasizes that this does not mean that problems concerning certain values should be pointed out from "outside." This would be an approach of which Kymlicka accuses interventionist liberalists and "new communitarians" (Kymlicka 1994: 263). Because of the assumption of the preexistence of common values, "communitarianism can only be endorsed from the third-person perspective" (Kymlicka 1988: 197). In contrast to this, Kymlicka underlines the importance of culture for an individual's liberty and thinking, or what he calls an individual's "negative capability" (Kymlicka 1994: 271, following Unger 1986: 93). This capability is realized only by the information, choices, and experiences that "our culture" provides (Kymlicka 1995b: 81; 1988: 182f.).

This brings the concept of identity to the center of Kymlicka's argumentation. Identity is the hinge that closely connects an individual to his or her cultural group. By giving a meaning to human action and experience, culture constitutes the individual's identity, which, in turn, is a precondition for coherent action and reflected decisions. Following this understanding, Kymlicka separates the meanings of collective identity into two levels:

> Indeed, it is precisely because national identity does not rest on shared values ... that it provides a secure foundation for individual autonomy and self-identity. Cultural membership provides us with an intelligible context of choice, and a secure sense of identity and belonging, that we call upon in confronting questions about personal values and projects. (Kymlicka 1997: 43)

National identity differs from traditional or ethnic identity in that it is emptied of values and norms. Its binding force lies in its institutions, its language, and its culture (Ibid.: 43f.; see also Tamir 1993). It is expected to offer a meaningful basis for individual decisions for or against specific norms. With this idea, Kymlicka tries to counter a communitarian understanding of identity according to which values are not chosen but already exist in a context that only needs to be "discovered" by individuals.[9] This supra-individual, national level of identity constitution is supposed to give space for the choice between different values. Underneath this national level, Kymlicka allocates societal cultures that provide the cultural and normative frame of reference for individuals. This division, however, contrasts with his criticism of the assumption of a culturally neutral state.

This and further gaps in Kymlicka's approach earned him the accusation of having delivered a poorly developed theory and that his "interest in culture and cultures is only a normative-political interest, an interest in how specific collective rights of ethnic minorities can be legitimized" (Reckwitz 2001: 184). Although this reservation can be countered by Kymlicka's many theoretical considerations, these considerations themselves open up a field of uncertainties. Three main points of criticism can be discerned. They refer to Kymlicka's normative yardstick, his distinction of different types of groups, and to his ambivalent concepts of culture and identity.

Kymlicka's Normative Yardstick

The first point of criticism concerns the normative frame of reference or yardstick. If Kymlicka does actually develop an exclusively normative theory, a standard of criticism should be explicable. And, indeed, normative points of reference can be found in the quest for ethnocultural justice and an improved liberal state. Kymlicka emphasizes that he focuses mainly on the rights of *liberal* national minorities (Kymlicka 1997: 43f.). Another point of reference is the ideal of a successful identity constitution by the culture an individual belongs to. These remarks are framed with the concept of voluntariness, which is a central and reappearing idea in

Kymlicka's theory and which is supposed to explain the different treatments of national minorities and ethnic groups.

Using the example of settlement politics, Kymlicka explains injustice toward national minorities. A state, he argues, undermines a national minority's rights by settling people from the dominant culture into that minority's territory. A minority must have options to counter such settlement by either preventing it or by extensively conditioning and sanctioning it. Kymlicka claims that Western nations protect their borders the same way—which, instead of criticizing it, he defends as a legitimate instrument to protect their own cultures. To underline his point, he cites pictures that frame migrants as a threat: "The majority, like the minority, has no desire to be overrun and outnumbered by settlers from another culture" (Kymlicka 2001a: 75). In other words: Cultures should be able to keep themselves "pure," after all. Kymlicka describes his approach as follows: "I am discussing what justice requires for minorities in the *world as we know it*," and not, he continues, in a hypothetical world without borders that would treat national minorities differently (Ibid.; italics added).

This restricts the normative yardstick decisively. First, Kymlicka's argument relies on given power relations that are questioned only to a certain point (i.e., the ethnocultural injustice). Second, by distinguishing different types of groups, he introduces a further level of inequality.

Different Types of Groups

The categorization of group types leads to the second point of criticism. According to Kymlicka, national minorities have their own societal culture that needs to be protected—also and especially in a distinct state. Ethnic groups, however, have to submit to the majority society's culture because they voluntarily decided to leave their country of origin. In the case of national minorities, Kymlicka seems to assume two levels of identity constitution—a cultural and normative level and a national and value-free level. This begs the question if (and how) ethnic groups have a second level of identity formation as well. Entitlement to the culture of origin expires, according to Kymlicka, because of the voluntariness of the migration. He emphasizes that ethnic groups "do not constitute cultures. Their distinctiveness is manifested in their private lives, and does not affect their institutional integration" (Kymlicka 1991: 239). Ethnic distinction is, rather, "manifested primarily in their family lives and in voluntary associations" (Kymlicka 1995b).

At the same time, Kymlicka challenges the separation of an ethnic private sphere and the state. The "'strict separation of state and ethnicity' view . . . is not only mistaken, but actually incoherent. . . . The state unavoidably promotes certain cultural identities, and thereby disadvantages others" (Ibid.: 107f.). Only this disadvantage makes group-differentiated rights necessary—although not for ethnic groups. This supports the conclusion that ethnic groups have the right to only one identity-constituting level, while for national minorities, the second level of identity constitution is to be protected. The central criterion for this unequal treatment is voluntariness.

The problems with the criterion of voluntariness will be examined more closely in the section on Okin. It is important to point out here the false dichotomy of voluntary and involuntary migration. In migration studies, an interplay of push and pull factors, of internal motivation and external necessity to migrate is widely acknowledged. Even the binary separation into intrinsic and extrinsic motivation is debatable. Furthermore, transnational, simultaneous, and multi-tracked migration movements play an increasingly important role (Vertovec 2001; Thapan 2005).

A definition of voluntary migration could be approximated by asking whether a realistic alternative to migration exists, that is, if there is a viable choice. Still, this does not resolve the asymmetry in Kymlicka's migration theorem: Who migrates voluntarily has to assimilate to majority institutions; who migrates involuntarily, however, cannot claim national minorities rights either. Rather, the reasons for involuntary migration need to be tackled (by means of international redistribution, for example) so that migrants can "return" (Kymlicka 1995b: 99). This is linked to the nation-state's effort to protect its own culture against everything that seems to be alien—an effort that is mentioned, but not criticized, by Kymlicka.

Kymlicka's theory of group-differentiated rights implies impermeable and static cultural boundaries. It thus amounts to the distinction of autochthonous and allochthonous groups, after all.

Concepts of Culture and Identity

The distinction of autochthonous and allochthonous groups relates to the third issue of critique, the inconsistent definition of identity and culture in Kymlicka's theory. Certain cultures are to be protected while, at the same time, he wants to integrate into his approach a *postethnical* opening.

> Minority nationalists assert that as "nations within," they have the same rights of self-government as the majority, and form their own self-governing political community. It is consistent with that view to insist that all nations—minority and majority—should be postethnic or "civic" nations. This indeed is one way to understand the idea of *liberal* nationalism: liberal nationalism is the view that nations have rights of self-government, but that all nations, majority or minority, should be postethnic. (Kymlicka 1998: 77; italics in the original)

Kymlicka distances himself from a communitarian understanding of multiculturalism and its identity-preserving function. Instead, by using a liberal concept of multiculturalism, he points out that cultures and identities are dynamic and changeable (Kymlicka 2007: 98f.). Nonetheless, his argumentation for group-differentiated rights implies that culture and cultural identity have a solid core that demands for their protection and conservation.

Critics of collective rights highlight that cultures can be repressive. This makes it mandatory to counteract every form of suppression, independent of group affiliation (Griffin 2008: 269, see also Spinner-Halev 2001: 98; Okin 1999a: 20ff.; Stapleton 1995: xxxvi). Kymlicka argues, in return, that illiberal national minorities should be liberated only gently and, in a best-case scenario, from the inside (Kymlicka 1995b: 153ff.). The claim to protect clearly demarcated cultures coincides here with a reference to the dynamics of and possibilities to transform cultures—without Kymlicka taking a closer look at the antinomic character of both argumentations. By distinguishing internal restrictions and external protections, Kymlicka additionally implies the possibility to more or less clearly separate the inside and outside of a culture. His solution, again, is voluntariness. The individual right to leave a group should always be protected (Ibid.: 158).

Kymlicka's concept of culture oscillates not only regarding the questions of being open or closed off, dynamic or rigid. On the one hand, he argues, culture is not valuable in itself but because human beings, through their access to societal culture, dispose of meaningful options (Kymlicka 1997: 34). On the other hand, the argument for group-differentiated rights is based on the assumption that only the individual's *own* culture plays an important role for the formation of identity. This assumption, however, is not explained any further. Pointing at a culture's constituting character for identity and the ability to act is insufficient because one might object that a meaningful frame for agency and identity could be provided by "*some* culture" (Griffin 2008: 267; italics in the original).

Kymlicka's theory presents an undefined twofold character of a culture being open and closed off, of being dynamic and rigid. Unconnected as they are in his theory, these contradicting elements ultimately allow for argumentative arbitrariness.

In summary, two assumptions are crucial to Kymlicka's argumentation for group-differentiated rights. One is the presumption that structural inequality exists between different cultures within nation-states. The second assumes the respective cultures as so important for individual identity and the ability to decide, reflect, and act that they need to be protected. Freedom and voluntariness are the main normative yardsticks in the theory of group-differentiated rights. To guarantee liberty and to compensate cultures that were assimilated involuntarily, these cultures (and only these) should be entitled to group-differentiated rights—in the sense of external protection, not to produce further inequality between and within groups. Yet, Kymlicka's binary categorization cannot capture the complexity of existing processes and phenomena. It remains unclear if and how a culture can be open and postethnic, while at the same time it needs to be defended against an "outside." Kymlicka's theory of a liberal, nationalist minority addresses several important questions and contradictory constellations that need to be dealt with. However, eventually it falls short in dealing with collective human rights and their contradictions, both theoretically and empirically.

SUSAN MOLLER OKIN'S FEMINIST LIBERALISM

Okin's controversial theory is in a stark contrast to Taylor's communitarian concept and Kymlicka's liberal justification of collective rights. Her feminist rejection of collective rights extends the pattern of argumentation discussed so far. Okin critically examines both liberal and communitarian approaches without giving up the liberal framework.

In general, feminist theories argue somewhat outside the debate on liberalism and communitarianism because feminist perspectives can support and criticize both approaches. Feminist criticism characterizes the individual portrayed in liberal and universal rights as mostly male, white, and Western. Conversely, a feminist perspective also allows for arguments in favor of a universalism liberated of its androcentrism (see Peters/Wolper 1995). Demands for collective rights are supported for serving the different needs of women of different cultures—or they are rejected for defending potentially repressive cultural practices. Thus, feminist analyses have the task of criticizing both sides at the same time (Bell 1992; Shachar 2009; Benhabib/Cornell 1987).

Okin's firm rejection of collective rights led to comprehensive criticism, inside and outside feminist discourse. "Okin's discussions of gender and culture were among the most controversial parts of her work; in correspondence with me, she said they had been misrepresented more than anything she had ever written" (Jaggar 2009: 168).

Okin's society theory is outlined in some detail below because it is the basis of her discussion of collective rights, interpreted further on.

Within the debate on liberalism and communitarianism, Okin is described as a "liberal feminist" (Shachar 2009: 146), according to the first line of argument (1) described above. She argues, with a feminist perspective, in the tradition of Rawls. Okin criticizes Rawls for portraying the individual as the male head of the family, who under the veil of ignorance, opts to favor the principles of justice. Rawls justifies this with the need to guarantee intergenerational justice (Rawls 1971: 128ff.). According to Okin, however, Rawls thereby neglects the question of justice or injustice inside the family. In his hypothetical original position, it is of no importance whether the individual is the head of the family or not (Okin 1989: 92ff.). Generally, the problem presented by Rawls's and other liberal theories of justice lies in their disregard of the institutions of family and household. According to Okin, Rawls presupposes a fully developed, moral individual while the unpaid (and usually female) work of upbringing children (the moral individuals of the future) is assumed as given. Thus, the private sphere is ignored, although it is gendered and structured according to power constellations in most societies. This, writes Okin, neglects both gender inequalities as well as the fact that the family is the primary place of moral development. Children who grow up in unjust structures hardly become adults who (aim to) implement a fully just society. For example, gendered parenthood forms (early) childhood identification and individuation in gendered ways (Chodorow 1978; Okin 1989: 131f.). In patriarchic structured families, "the first and most formative example of adult interaction usually experienced by children is one of . . . domination and manipulation or of unequal altruism and one-sided self-sacrifice" (Okin 1989: 17).

Nonetheless, as Okin argues, liberal and communitarian theories of justice implicitly presuppose justice within the family. In line with the rejection of state intrusion into privacy, liberal approaches bypass family injustice (Ibid.: 74ff.). Communitarian theories simply assume common values, meanings, and traditions of justice, and marginalize analyses of women's and families' situations (Ibid. 41ff.). Communitarian assumptions of a supposedly natural family hierarchy and female subordination even explicitly affirm gender-specific injustice. Michael Sandel, for example, marks small social groups like the family as a sanctuary of intimacy, common identity, and shared values. On the one hand, argues Okin, this idealized and mythical perspective removes intra-family and gendered injustice from the discussion and, on the other hand, disguises the fact that "however much the members of families care about one another and share common ends, they are still discrete persons with their own particular aims and hopes, which may sometimes conflict" (Ibid.: 32).

The protection of the individual and of its individuation possibilities, she goes on, needs to be guaranteed in the private sphere as well. In this context it is important to remember that "the individual" has two genders with—because of the gendered social order—different needs and problems. Okin emphasizes that gender related differences are not naturally invariable but socially constructed and reproduced (Ibid.: 171ff.).

Okin develops her idea of "humanist justice" (Ibid.: 171) by drawing on Rawls's basic assumptions. According to Okin, Rawls recognizes the importance of the family as a "moral school," although he presupposes it to be justly structured.

> In the original position, knowing neither what our sex nor any other of our personal characteristics will be once the veil of ignorance is lifted [we will] arrive at and apply principles of justice having to do with the family and the division of labor between the sexes that can satisfy these vastly disparate points of view. . . . There are some traditionalist positions so extreme that they ought not be admitted for consideration, since they violate such fundamentals as equal basic liberty and self-respect. . . . I think we would arrive at a basic model that would absolutely minimize gender. . . . We would also, however, build in carefully protective institutions for those who wished to follow gender-structured modes of life. (Ibid.: 174f.)

Since this socialization will not be implemented in the short- and medium-term, it is important to institutionally counter women's and children's social vulnerability and gender inequalities in the meantime.

Hereby, Okin outlines the normative framework of a liberal, gender-equal society that she also refers to when considering collective rights. Her basic assumption is "that there is considerable likelihood of conflict between feminism and group rights for minority cultures, and that this conflict persists *even when the latter are claimed on liberal grounds, and are limited to some extent*" (Okin 1998a: 664; italics added, see also Okin 1999a). She criticizes the communitarian (3) and the liberal line of argument (2)—the latter prominently represented by Kymlicka—for ignoring the private sphere, family, and gender inequality within groups while the primary content of collective cultural practices concerns sexuality and reproduction and, thus, mostly women and girls. Additionally, Okin argues that the primary place for cultural socialization to occur is within the family. This explains why collective rights are designed to protect cultures that support and facilitate the control of women by men (Okin 1998a: 667).

Okin's theory shifts the focus of analysis into the foreground, an approach that is not seen with either Kymlicka or Taylor. Both of the latter consider the societal culture or the moral frame to be imperative for the constitutive construction of the individual's identity. According to them, only this culture, or moral frame, allows for a coherent self, self-consciousness, self-worth, and collective identity. Life without culture would be impossible or unbearable. Okin adds to this understanding a layer of power analysis that decisively shifts the perspective on culture.

> For surely it is *not* enough, for one to develop self-respect and self-esteem, that one belong to a viable culture. Surely it is *not* enough, for one to be able to "question one's inherited social roles" and to have the capacity to make choices about the life one wants to lead, that one's culture be protected. At least as important to the development of self-respect and self-esteem as one's culture is *one's place within that culture*. And at least as important to one's capacity to question one's social roles

is *whether one's culture instills in and enforces on one particular social roles.* (Ibid.; 679f.; italics in the original)

Okin makes power relations and inequalities visible by asking for an individual's position and role within a culture. It is not the distinction of a culture that should be focused on, but its internal social structure. While Taylor considers the good of collectivity and participation in a common whole essential for meaningful cultures (Taylor 1989a: 165f.)—"discriminations of right or wrong, better or worse, higher or lower, which are not rendered valid by our own desires, inclinations, or choices" (Taylor 1989b: 4)—Okin criticizes the assumption of common values (Okin 1989: 42ff.) and highlights gender-specific meanings of cultural argumentations. At the same time, she understands cultural structuring as a social, and, thereby, contingent and changeable, space.

In this context, Okin questions the binary division of distinct cultures. To accomplish this, she introduces the figure of an individual who is familiar with more than one culture and is thus able to criticize her or his culture of origin from a certain distance (Okin 1998c: 339). However, at another point during her argumentation, she points out the limitative and deterministic danger of this argument. The figure described, she says, is neither sufficient nor necessary to criticize culture. Additionally, the argument is based on a dichotomy between cultures from an internal versus external perspective (Okin 1998b: 46).

Kymlicka's differentiation between external protection and internal restrictions is based on this differentiation, too. He picks up Okin's note that sexual discrimination is, first, almost universal, and second, committed covertly in the private sphere: "I accept Okin's claim that we need a more subtle account of internal restrictions which helps us identify limitations on the freedom of women within ethnocultural groups" (Kymlicka 1999: 32; see Okin 1999a: 20ff.). He considers protection, by means of collective rights, from external pressure compatible with this argument (Kymlicka 1999: 32). Okin, in contrast, challenges the dichotomy between the inside and the outside of a culture. She gives the example of local, non-Western women's movements, which can experience considerable strengthening by cooperating with international and Western organizations (Okin 1998b: 46ff.).

The dichotomous inside-outside separation is problematic also in light of the voluntariness criterion to which Kymlicka assigns decisive importance. The voluntariness criterion is connected to an exit option. This option is based on the assumption that collective rights deserve to be protected as long as every individual has the option to leave a certain cultural collective.

Okin fundamentally challenges both assumptions, the concept of voluntariness and the exit option. In her discussion of repressive structures within (Western) families, she delineates the interrelation of the exit option, power, and agency. When a person's capability of leaving a group (in this case, a marriage or a family) is limited, then that person really does not exert influence within that group, since it is only a realistic threat to leave the group that gives that person power. On the other hand, whoever can leave a group easily has a potentially smaller motivation to promote improvement for the less powerful within the group (Okin 1989: 137; see Hirschman 1970: 43ff.).

In reference to collective rights, Okin describes how the exit option is much less available to women and girls than to men in cultural and religious collectives. Female behavior is much more controlled, women are bound tighter to the private sphere, they have less access to education—which itself reproduces narrow gender roles—they have fewer rights regarding marriage, divorce, child custody, and pregnancies, and they are held responsible for preserving the culture and traditions. It is this "depth of acquired cultural attachments, which can render the exit option not merely undesirable but unthinkable" (Okin 2002: 222). As a result, those who need the exit option most have the fewest possibilities of employing it.

Okin accentuates the danger of cultural or religious imprints to restrict individual knowledge of freedom and equality possibilities (Okin 1998c: 312). It is, therefore, necessary and possible to extend experience and knowledge beyond one's own culture. "One need not rely on the Marxist theory of false consciousness to recognize that persons subjected to unjust conditions often adapt their preferences so as to conceal the injustice of their situation from themselves" (Okin 1999b: 126). However, Okin argues, not only external influence allows for criticism of cultural practices. Cultures are heterogeneous in themselves. Norms, practices, and interpretations are disputed within cultures, and there is deviance even in the most repressive countries (Okin 1998c: 326ff.).

To Okin, repression means, among other things, limitation of identity. Successful identity, in contrast, is characterized by the possibility to reflect, by self-consciousness, and by the knowledge of (liberal) rights. There are women who "cannot comprehend themselves as legal personalities . . . because their religious and cultural surroundings prevent the development of an identity that allows them to comprehend themselves as an individual equipped with rights in the first place" (Ibid.: 338). Okin considers aspects and influences that do not contribute to this model of enlightened identity as not identity constituting. She rejects, for example, the assumption that clitoridectomy[10] is identity constituting and considers the phenomenon that "many people think their belief to be identity constituting" (Ibid.: 340) as simply "wrong conviction" (Ibid.: 332). In other words, according to Okin, practices and religion are not considered identity constituting when they are repressive and do not contribute to the individual's ability to reflect and act. This leads to a narrowly defined normative identity concept. This narrow concept provides the basis for

Okin's disputed argument that it would be better in some situations if a culture would perish or completely change instead of being sustained by collective rights (Okin 1999a: 22f.). The basic assumption is that if repressive practices are not identity constituting, they do not need legal protection.

Okin's argumentation against collective rights can be critically discussed in light of the three fields of culture, identity, and the normative yardstick.

Culture

In the first field, Okin's suggestion that cultures may well be changed profoundly or left to perish meets resistance. According to critics, it is a sign of Okin's lack of respect for non-Western cultures and identities (Parekh 1999: 72). The idea of "destroying our culture and starting with a clean slate just does not make sense" (Raz 1999: 97; also see Honig 1999: 40; An-Na'im 1999b: 61). Homi Bhabha points out that Okin adopts a problematic concept of culture from her subject of critique. A static and homogenizing concept of culture is inherent to utilizations of culture that aim at legitimizing repressive practices. By simply adopting this concept, Okin reproduces an inadequate concept of culture instead of critically challenging it (Bhabha 1999: 81).

In contrast to Okin, critics suggest separating gender-specific repression from culture or religion. "Culture is something rather more complicated than patriarchal permission for powerful men. . . . There are brutal men (and women) everywhere. Is it their [cultural/religious] identity that makes them brutal . . . or is it their brutality?" (Honig 1999: 36, latter ellipsis in the original)

This, however, misinterprets the core of Okin's understanding of culture. Okin describes (one's own) culture not as indispensable for the constitution of individual identity, but as a space marked by power relations.[11] This perspective allows for disclosing (gender-)specific inequalities that are legitimized and justified by referring to culture. This focus makes Okin's concept of culture look entirely pejorative, but it also opens up possible alternative readings. Either, the assumption of a culture's heterogeneity and changeability means that cultures can also be structured emancipatory, or Okin envisions a society not defined by culture. The question of alternative forms of socialization remains largely unanswered, though.

Identity

The second field of critique relates to this through the question of whether or not Okin neglects cultural factors of identity constitution. At times, she suggests that repressive cultural elements are not relevant for the formation of identity. By doing this, she develops a normative concept of identity that disregards the far-reaching and identity-constituting effects of repressive socialization and that contrasts an entirely affirmative concept of identity with a pejorative understanding of culture.

Okin's discussion of the exit option and of the voluntariness criterion, however, also allows for an identity concept that includes cultural and family imprints—even if they are repressive. It is this internalization of cultural values that makes it so difficult to leave a culture. At this point, culture and individual identity are not dichotomously opposed, but they are concepts that may include both emancipatory and repressive elements that may be subject to change. The question remains if Okin conceptually separates identity formation and internalization mechanisms in order to save a normative concept of identity.

Okin's Normative Yardstick

Related to this is the third field of criticism: the question of the normative yardstick. According to what criteria can repressive elements of identity or culture be separated from emancipatory ones? The normative basic assumption Okin makes is one of a liberal-democratic society in which gender-specific (and other) inequalities are no longer hidden and reproduced in the private sphere. Whether it be the family or the cultural group that constitutes this private sphere is secondary to Okin. If, however, the boundary between emancipation and repression is marked only by liberalism, not only Eurocentric interpretations (for a critical perspective, see Honig 1999: 36ff.; Al-Hibri 1999; Gilman 1999: 55ff.), but also limitations of liberal freedoms are possible: "The danger of tying freedom to rationality, and rationality to particular outcomes, is that this leads us to describe as unfree even those who have chosen thoughtfully and carefully but badly" (Kukathas 2009: 199).

In summary, Okin's criticism of collective rights is based on her definition of the terms culture and identity. She neither wants to neglect liberal majority cultures repressing minorities nor "abolish culture" (Okin 1999b: 117f.). Rather, cultures, in light of their power relations and gender-specific effects, should not receive protection by collective rights. Okin challenges the assumption of an ineluctability of a cultural frame for individual identity by asking for the form and content of processes of cultural socialization and subject constitution.

CONCLUSION

The portrayed theories provide the basis for a discussion of justifications, possibilities, and limits of collective human rights. Kymlicka, Taylor, and Okin revolve around the questions of how norms and values enter individual identity, from which culture these values originate, and why or if and how they deserve special protection. Taylor and Kymlicka think identification with one's own group of reference indispensable for a "welfare state" (Kymlicka 1995b: 77) or a "republic" (Taylor 1989a: 170) to work. They translate this necessary identification as "patriotism"[12] (Ibid.: 166) and as "liberal nationalism" (Kymlicka 1997: 13). For Taylor, liberty is manifested in the decision to make sacrifices in solidarity with one's own people and to participate in its constitution (Taylor 1989a: 170ff.). Kymlicka does not oppose this with the (for him only seemingly liberal) argument of the national community's neutrality. Liberalism, he argues, does not mean the absence of culture, but everyone's possibility to integrate himself or herself into the common civil society of a state (Kymlicka 1995a). His liberal concept of group-differentiated rights maintains at the same time the possibility of individual decisions for or against common values (Kymlicka 1988: 189). In contrast, Okin addresses group internal differences in light of their voluntariness and freedom. She points out the deep individual imprint, left by power-based cultural collectives, that makes choosing between values and cultures difficult. It does not constitute a reason for the protection of the collective, but from an emancipatory perspective, it champions the need to be criticized and opened.

Although outlining Okin's, Kymlicka's, and Taylor's arguments does not cover the whole field of debate around communitarianism and liberalism, their theoretical premises and the resulting points of critique are crucial to the discussion of collective human rights. Their positions have, if in variations, been adopted many times. Culture and identity as well as the assumptions on subject constitution and voluntariness prove to be central points of reference. These concepts are referred to as normative yardsticks in arguments for as well as against collective human rights. All the theories discussed have limits that illustrate the need for more precise definitions of culture, identity, and subject constitution.

NOTES

1. Kymlicka, for example, points out that the accusation of atomism and neglecting the context, brought up against liberals, can be rebutted with arguments immanent to liberal argumentation; see Kymlicka (1988: 181).

2. There are theoretical approaches beyond the focus on human rights that go beyond the opposition of communitarianism and liberalism. See, for example, Etzioni's responsive communitarianism in Etzioni (1993, 1996) or approaches to a communitarian liberalism in Walzer (2009) and Selznick (1992). For further classification models of liberalism and communitarianism, see Taylor (1989a: 160); Forst (1994a: 182ff.); Rawls (1985).

3. But "one does not have to necessarily accept this self-perception"; see Reese-Schäfer (2000: 69).

4. For Taylor, culture and language are closely related. While he talks about language rights here, he is generally concerned with cultures as political communities.

5. Appiah (1994: 154) specifies and extends Taylor's concept of the constitution of individual identity by dialogue, pointing to societal institutions such as religion, society, school, state, and family.

6. Taylor develops his concept of mediately and immediately common goods with reference to the political community. They are a central factor for identity building and unfold as common goods only through joint experience and collective meaning. Taylor (1989a: 168ff.) contrasts this with convergent goods that are achieved collectively but realized on an individual level.

7. This is opposed to Taylor's demand for cultures to preserve their distinction but at the same time be open to other cultures; see Taylor (1994a: 63) and Bedorf (2010: 43).

8. Definitions of both categories are difficult and highly disputed. Nonetheless, the incorporation of indigenous groups into modern nation-states has usually been more violent. The indigenous groups were confronted with resentment and accusations of being uncivilized and backward in their development; see Kymlicka (2007: 266f.). Furthermore, they were excluded from the process of state formation, whereas stateless nations were losers but still active participants in the conflicts; see Kymlicka (2001b: 122). These (and further) classifications are legally necessary for Kymlicka because neither are different minority groups satisfied with the lowest common denominator of their interests nor could the sum of all interests be enforced as one universal form of minority rights; see Kymlicka (2001a: 83).

9. Kymlicka (1988: 191ff.) criticizes this setting provided by Sandel (1982: 58) and MacIntyre (1984: 204f.), among others.

10. Clitoridectomy is a form of female genital mutilation/circumcision. For an in-depth discussion of the controversial term and of the role of the praxis for identity constitution, see Mende (2011a: 59ff. and 154ff).

11. See also Tamir (1999: 51); Post (1999: 68); Sassen (1999: 78); Raz (1999: 97f.); Nussbaum (1999: 133f.); An-Na'im (1999b: 63f).

12. Also see this statement, "the essential condition of a free (nondespotic) regime is that the citizens have this kind of patriotic identification," in Taylor (1989a: 170).

Part II

Rethinking the Key Themes

Society, Culture, Identity

Charles Taylor, Will Kymlicka, and Susan Okin, the three authors chosen here to exemplify demands for or against collective human rights, refer to culture and identity in different but respectively decisive ways. Closely tied to this are concepts of the individual and society. In light of these concepts, the three theories can shortly be summarized as follows:

Taylor measures a culture's relevance against its contribution to humankind. If its contribution is important, the respective culture is central to the constitution of individual identity and thus deserves protection. The moral space is, according to Taylor, an all-encompassing frame inside which individuals and identities constitute themselves according to cultural particularities. An individual with its (individual and collective) identity can reflect on this space, position himself or herself within it and, if necessary, even change it. However, the individual cannot leave this space.

Kymlicka outlines a concept of culture that, on the one hand, allows for cultural hybridity and dynamics, but, on the other, assumes cultures to be distinctive and to be protected in that distinction. He assumes every state to host multiple cultures and to usually try to establish one of them in particular, to the detriment of the others. Culture, he argues, is decisive for the formation of individual identity as well as for an individual's decision-making ability and capacity to act. It offers a sphere of knowledge in which consciousness and (if necessary, critical) reflectivity can develop. The meaning of one's own culture is so important and formative for the individual's identity that a culture can only be switched at a high cost.

Okin highlights the internal plurality and heterogeneity of cultures. She primarily discusses gendered cultural positioning, as marked by structures of power and inequality. Cultural practices are performed by, and the necessity of cultural reproduction is placed upon, women first and foremost. Therefore, the existence of culture is not the only relevant factor in developing someone's identity and individuality; another factor is an individual's position within a culture formed by gender roles and power inequalities. Thus, Okin focuses mostly on the repressive dimensions of culture. She argues that an alternative emancipatory concept lies in a successful, fully developed individual identity. This allows for awareness and the ability to reflect, as opposed to cultural internalization—which she sees as limiting.

The approaches are characterized by two traits whose examination can decisively consolidate the discussion on collective human rights. First, contradicting dimensions are juxtaposed without further consideration of their contradictions. This is most visible in Kymlicka's concept of a society or culture that is simultaneously both static and dynamic, hybrid and distinct in the same moment. Second, certain ideas of successful identity (Okin), cultural meanings (Taylor), or measurements of specific weight between individuals and society or culture (Kymlicka) are presented and set as normative yardsticks.

This is why part II will examine the relationships between the individual, society, culture, and identity, with special attention to the analytical and the normative level, which prove to be inseparable. This shows how implicit and explicit presumptions about those relations determine the patterns of argumentations for or against collective human rights.

TWO

Society and Culture

Culture and identity are embedded in an encompassing constellation that stretches between the poles of individual and society—or, in other schools of thought: between agent and structure (Wendt 1987). The normative weighing of these poles distinguishes the traditional communitarian and liberal lines of argument. "When individual human rights are involved, the individual is the *measure of all things*.... Conversely, where collective human rights are concerned, it is the overall picture that counts. The crux of the issue is the deprivation of rights, not of this or that individual, but of the whole group communally" (Dinstein 1976: 103; italics added).

The normative question is accompanied by an analytical one, often framed ontologically as a question of how to determine both poles: "I have no algorithm to settle which should be first: the individual or the community" (McDonald 1991: 237). "In a sense, the debate can be seen as a kind of sociological chicken and egg question akin to whether individual or society comes first" (Poletta/Jasper 2001: 299). Such an order is supposed to show a solution for dealing with collective human rights. The question of whether the individual or a group/community should be the metric for criticism and for human rights is one of the central criteria points for distinguishing between the four ideal lines of reasoning described in chapter 1. "In short: conceptions of human beings, and thereby motivational hypotheses as basic assumptions of the relation of individuals and society, delimit the claims in the controversies on liberalism (or, according to Etzioni, 'individualism'; to Taylor, 'atomism') versus communitarianism" (Ritsert 2001: 71; italics removed).

With reference to Theodor W. Adorno, it can be shown that the two poles, individual and society, are intrinsically linked to a degree where it is impossible to say what came first. Thus, instead of asking the question of what came first, I will discuss an approach that reflects an always-reciprocal constitution and construction of the individual and society. In a second step, I will position and define culture within this relation.

INDIVIDUAL AND SOCIETY

There are three insufficient approaches used to explain the relationship between the individual and society. In the first, the individual is seen as the raison d'être or the starting point of being, as something given and monadically precluded from the outside world. Society, then, would only be the sum of its pieces. The second approach considers society to be the only relevant category of analysis, and the individual as secondary. A third approach builds on the assumption of a reciprocal relationship between the individual and society in which the individual influences society and society influences the individual.

Adorno criticizes all three perspectives in that they assume the existence of the individual and society a priori, even before a possible reciprocal relationship forms. But, rather, there is no individual existence per se, which can be discovered beyond, or even be freed of, its formation by society. "As soon as we attempt to do so and, by turning our cognition inwards, strive for once to attain complete self-reflection, we lose ourselves in a bottomless void, . . . we clutch, shuddering, at nothing but an insubstantial ghost" (Schopenhauer 1995: 358, cited in Adorno 1978: 153). Rather, the relation of the individual and society is, according to Adorno, shaped by internal and external mediations: Individuals and society are entrenched in an intermediated relation in which the respective opposite pole can not only be found on the other side of the relation, but also *within* that very pole itself.[1] Individuals and society constitute each other and, simultaneously, acquire each other's independence and autonomy. This constellation will now be explicated in detail by looking at its respective parts.

The individual does not contain a core that is untouched by society. Nor does it contain an internal vacuum around which the formations by society wrap. This would correspond to the idea of an externally determining relation (i.e., the third approach mentioned above). The concept of internal mediation, in contrast, allows for the individual to be understood as through and through constituted and constructed—but not determined—by society.

> Not only is the self entwined in society; it owes society its existence in the most literal sense. All its content comes from society, or at any rate from its relation to the object. It grows richer the more freely it develops and reflects this relation, while it is limited, impoverished and reduced by the separation and hardening that it lays claim to as an origin. (Ibid.: 154)

Individuality, consciousness, reflexivity, autonomy, and the ability to think and act are achievements facilitated by society. At the same time, they can point beyond the given. This basic constellation can have many forms, and is historically contingent. Individualization is characterized by its distinction from the natural world and the objective world, and by the formation of self-consciousness. A separating (and appropriating) behavior toward nature that also allows for needs planning is facilitated on a larger scale only in and by society. Self-consciousness has to relate to at least one other self-consciousness. This means that it needs intersubjectivity—which also exists within society only. This neither determines the individual nor restricts him or her to one society in particular. Yet, he or she can criticize and transcend society only in and through societal constitution.

Individuality, can, however, also be limited and hampered by society. Societal antagonisms as well as emancipatory and repressive societal factors reappear internally on the individual side of the relation. Thus, the individual's constitution through society can, on the one hand, support autonomy by facilitating the ability to act and to reflect. On the other hand, it can also be repressive and thereby limit autonomy and the formation of individuality.

This internal mediation also exists on the societal end of the relation. Adorno emphasizes that the term *society* "implies that there exists between people a functional connection, which varies considerably . . . and which leaves no-one out, a connectedness in which all the members of the society are entwined and which takes on a certain kind of autonomy in relation to them" (Adorno 2002: 29f.). Society is, on the one hand, a whole that leaves nothing and no one untouched—because anything seemingly outside of society is in fact affected by society. On the other hand, society is not independent. "It always contains both these moments at the same time; it is realized only through individuals but, as the relationship between them, it cannot be reduced to them. On the other hand, it should not be seen as a pure, over-arching concept existing for itself" (Ibid.: 38).

Society, in the sense of an organized whole, includes the institutionalization of humans living together. Institutions may have a coercive character, yet they are basal and necessary for communal life and are therefore productive, too. In this ambivalence, or "dialectic of society" (Adorno 1956a: 28), neither the removal nor the hypostasis of societal institutions is compatible with the idea of an emancipatory society. Both would lead to coercion and "the dissolution of all protecting humane guarantees" (Ibid.).

The constitution of society by its opposite, the individual, becomes clear in the Hegelian idea of the interdependence between the general (object) and the special (subject). Something only constitutes itself *as* something when it is determined and recognized as an object—a process for which a determining and recognizing subject is necessary (Adorno

1982). More concretely, societal processes depend on individuals. Exchange, economic and social (re-)production, agency, and acts of violence and power are exercised by individuals. Society is "a mediated and mediating relationship between individuals" (Adorno 2002: 38). Subjectivity is indispensable for the reproduction of society. At the same time, the latter cannot be reduced to the former. Just as the individual is constituted but not determined by society, society is likewise characterized by both its constitution of individuals and its (relative) independence from individuals. Additionally, society is heterogeneous in the way it faces the individual. This heterogeneity not only includes repressive elements, but is also the basis for the constitution of individuals.

In sum, the mediated relationship between the individual and society is marked by their co-dependent mediation. Each one of them, as a precondition, contains its opposite; one is constitutively necessary for the other. Beside these internally mediated relations that exist on both sides of the constellation, an external contrast exists between the two poles; it is constitutive for the relationship as a whole. The indispensability of this opposition becomes visible in an idea of emancipation that aims at the dissolution of the opposition and, thereby, at identity and equation of both poles. If, however, individual and society became one and the same, individuality could not exist, just as changing a society would be impossible. This would mean subjection to nature, immediateness, and immaturity. The dichotomous separation of both poles, on the other hand, as represented by the non-mediated and one-sided concepts of the individual and society introduced above, would be as repressive as an identity of both poles. An individual reduced to him or herself would be nothing but a mere object; society would be only a static block.

Both forms—the dichotomous opposition of the individual and society as well as the identifying dissolution of this opposition—are not only repressive from a normative perspective, but are also deficient from an analytical perspective. The mediated relationship of the individual and society does take very different forms in space and time. Qualitative differences, for example, become manifest in the formation of power relations and inequalities. However, the basic structure of the mediated relationship is uncircumventable. The supposition of an individual outside society or of a society completely independent from individuals is unsustainable both logically and empirically "because the concept of the mediation between the two opposed categories—individuals on one side and society on the other—is implicit in both" (Ibid.: 38).

This philosophical foundation of a mediated subject-object constellation allows for conclusions important to the discussion of collective human rights. First, the question of an ontological "first" becomes irrelevant if a strictly antinomic relation between the individual and society is assumed. The question is replaced by a perspective that apprehends the historical dimension of a "first" that has developed and is not simply given. Second, the only vaguely discussed idea of reciprocity is concretized. It is true that Will Kymlicka, Susan Okin, and Charles Taylor operate with a societal/cultural constitution of the individual that extends beyond dichotomous ideas. However, the analysis of internal, and external, mediated relationships allows a substantial concretization and extension of this assumption.

> All participants of the controversy know, of course, that "the self" does not hover completely isolated in social space. A self always forms in social relationships with significant others and within the general conditions of its historic situation. However, it does not dissolve in these relationships and dependences but can, facing them, maintain "autonomy" of thinking and the free will. The relation of *being determined* and the individual's *self-determination* poses a problem for all participants. (Ritsert 2001: 78; italics in the original)

The concept of mediation between the individual and society allows discussions on collective human rights to bypass dichotomous approaches on both the normative and the analytical level. A simultaneity of reciprocal constitution and the relative independence of both sides becomes conceivable, without resulting in arbitrariness. This facilitates an analytical openness based on which normative dimensions will be elaborated that do not a priori determine the field of discussion toward one side or another.

CULTURE

Empirically, culture is one of the central points of reference in the debate on collective human rights. It is referred to in both human rights documents and demands for human rights. At the same time, the term is very open for interpretation. Analytically and conceptually, culture can play a decisive role in extending and enriching the concept of the relationship between the individual and society. "Culture is destiny" (Zakaria/Lee 1994). "Culture is *not* destiny" (Donnelly 2006: 612; italics in the original). Therefore, it is important to clearly define the analytical and normative assumptions that the empirical usage of the concept of culture establishes or presupposes. In other words: "The world is obviously right—culture does matter. However, the real question is: '*How* does culture matter?'" (Sen 2007: 103; italics in the original)

The term *culture* has been defined in very different ways, not only in its long history, but also in more recent discussions. Formulated pointedly, these definitions can ideally be subsumed under a monolithic and a dynamic understanding of culture. The monolithic understanding, developed by anthropologists in the early twentieth century, conceptualizes culture as internally homogeneous, ethnically based, and externally distinct. Opposed to this stand deconstructivist, poststructuralist, and postmodern concepts developed in the late twentieth century that, depending on their respective focus, understand cultures as flexible, open, diffuse, hybrid, praxeological, heterogeneous, polyphonic, discursive, and/or contradictive.[2]

Monolithic and dynamic concepts of culture, however, can neither be separated dichotomously nor put into a chronological order. Fractures occur, for example, in the development of ethnic political movements or in current demands for collective human rights. "It appears that people—and not only those with power—*want* culture, and they often want it in precisely the bounded, reified, essentialized and timeless fashion that most of us now reject" (Brumann 1999: S11; italics in the original; also see Brightman 1995; Sahlins 1999).

Beyond this idealized contrast between dynamic and monolithic cultural concepts lie approaches that criticize both aforementioned concepts for their tendency toward reifying culture as an object (of research). They emphasize that culture is constituted and constructed by subjective, interactive, and societal processes (Hobsbawm/Ranger 1992; Anderson 1983; and see Stavenhagen 1995: 66f.). Moreover, they accuse both liberalism and communitarianism of making culture seem to have existed forever instead of asking for the conditions of its constitution (Cowan/Dembour/Wilson 2001a: 18).

Further efforts to find a definition of culture that holds up to the standards of social sciences are marked by the question of how the relation between humans and culture is constituted: "From a process-oriented point of view, the individual produces culture, from a system-oriented point of view, the individual is a product of culture, and reproduces it through her or his own activities" (Eide 1995).

Another central question concerns the scope of the respective concept. Does culture encompass "all those practices . . . that have relative autonomy from the economic, social, and political realms" (Said 1994: xxi)? Does culture have a specific "momentum of its own" (Neidhardt 1986: 14)? Or is it more appropriate to assume that questions of "why and how cultures persist, change, adapt or disappear . . . are intimately related to economic, political and territorial processes" (Stavenhagen 1995: 67)?

Preliminarily, it can be summarized that the current use of the term culture is highly diversified: It is used to distinguish practices, knowledge, norms, and values; it is one of the subjects of conflicts in international relations; it serves as a political tool; it is rejected as both a concept and a phenomenon; and it can stand for a society, a world view, particular normative ideas, specific functions, or artistic artefacts.

This diversity reappears in the discussion on collective human rights. Chapter 1 showed how different concepts of culture lead to different effects. While Okin conceptualizes culture narrowly as restrictive and oppressive, Taylor and Kymlicka see it as an indispensable societal and moral frame, and at times even as a yardstick for decisions between collective and individual rights.

Culture is the normative yardstick for collective human rights in both the liberal (2) and the communitarian (3) support of collective rights. "Human beings have a right to culture—not just any culture, but their own" (Margalit/Halbertal 1994: 491). A typical example of the line of argumentation (2) is the following argument by Dwight G. Newman.

"Working with an ongoing background of the humanistic thesis—the assumption that it is individual well-being that is of ultimate concern [means] that groups must serve their members' interests in a general sense for the group's interests to have moral weight" (Newman 2006/2007: 282). At the same time, Newman assumes that culture is something of genuine individual interest. Hence, he concludes, individual autonomy may be restricted if cultural achievements enrich life in return. Newman illustrates his model with an example: In 1976, Australian anthropologist Charles Mountford published secret knowledge of the Pitjandjara, an Australian aboriginal group (Mountford 1976). That knowledge was reserved to certain segments of the aboriginal community. A lawsuit contesting the distribution of the book within the areas concerned was fought—and won. In his discussion of the case, Newman emphasizes that the judgment is correct not only legally, but also with regard to its far-reaching moral implications.

> One could take the view that all segments of the Aboriginal population have an absolute right to access any information published as part of their free speech interests. . . . However, if the ongoing survival of Australian Aboriginal culture is of value to all segments of the Australian Aboriginal community, then . . . it might well be that even those not having access to the knowledge are better off with the restriction retained in place, offering a sort of harmonization of the individual and collective interests. (Newman 2006/2007: 286)

Drawing on this argument, different models that all use culture as a yardstick can be demonstrated. First, culture can be hypostasized as an end in itself. Second, culture can be rated as so important for human and individual life that restrictions of individual autonomy are justified. Both interpretations consider culture as basal and indispensable for subject constitution. This means equating the function of culture with that of society, as outlined in the previous subchapter. Culture describes the indispensable connection between the individual and society. By making these generalizations, however, the concept of culture loses its analytical and normative specificity and, as a consequence, its relevance to demands for collective human rights. If the concepts of culture and society are interchangeable, or if, in other words, culture becomes a "condensed concept of culture-and-society" (Kroeber/Parsons 1958: 583), then culture does not require any special legal protection because, as an indispensable societal frame and as one part of the relation between the individual and society, it cannot be destroyed.

However, different forms of society or culture can lead to different ideas, norms, and morals. The mediated relationship between the individual and society is heterogeneous and contingent historically, spatially, and typologically. This constitutes the link to a narrower conception of culture.

> Culture is not simply a matter of colorful dances and rituals, nor is it even a framework or context for individual choice. Rather, it is the product of the association of individuals over time, which in turn shapes individual commitments and gives meaning to individual lives—lives for which individual choice or autonomy may be quite valueless. (Kukathas 1992: 122)

In a narrower conception, culture functions as a cross-generational criterion of distinction that allows an individual to distinguish between what belongs to him or her and what does not. Culture, in this understanding, is "the distinctive ensemble of more or less stable and general ways in which a community and its members act, an integer of customs, values and traditions, usually bound together by a common language and often by common group memories" (Schmitz 1991, cited in Dallmayr 2010: 5, also see Stavenhagen 1995: 66). The socializing and subject-constituting character of culture is seen in its ability to differentiate: "culture as difference" (Antweiler 2007: 19).

With reference to Andreas Reckwitz, both approaches—the open concept of "culture-and-society" and the narrow concept of "culture as difference"—can be criticized as totalitarian. The open concept includes everything created by human beings and every form of socialization. Thus, it includes "everything that is not nature" (Reckwitz 2000: 76). It is "non-nature" (Ibid.: 78). While Reckwitz finds fault in this concept's lack of analytical and systematic sharpness, this study focuses on the problem that culture *as society* doubles as a concept without adding any insight or analytical benefits.

Reckwitz criticizes the narrower concept of culture—and here he addresses Taylor first and foremost—for conceptualizing cultures as distinct and homogeneous entities, and for equating seemingly solid cultural borders with seemingly solid demarcations of groups, communities, ethnicities, or collectives, and their identities and morals (Ibid.: 182ff.).

In the context of collective human rights, these criticisms can be countered with two objections that will be the foundation for the concept of culture developed in the following. The two objections concern the scope of culture, as well as the question of whether or not culture is static and homogenous.

First, the focus of demands for collective human rights lies on a sub-social or sub-state concept of culture. Demands focus on cultural minorities within a majority of society that is distinct to them. Cultural rights are deemed necessary because different cultures, one of which will establish itself as dominant, exist within one society or state (see Stavenhagen 1995: 71; Kymlicka 1997: 22ff., 2002). A (minority) culture is (similar to a collective identity) positioned between the individual and the society.

These assumptions lead to the following conclusion: The intermediated relation of the individual and society contains a third, intermediary level, one that lies between the level of the individual and the level of society. This intermediary level can be described as culture. Thus, the basal constellation between the individual and society, as introduced above, can be extended to consist of three poles: the individual, culture, and society.

Adorno (1956b: 55) positions the concept of groups on such an intermediary level: "The tension between the individual and society, and the diverging of the general and the specific implies that the individual does not immediately subject itself to societal totality; intermediaries are necessary for this." A group's functions, mechanisms, and modes of action are just as dynamic and historically contingent as the mediated constellation of individual and society. "[The group] is no primeval eternal category, but itself a product of society" (Ibid.: 65).

Alexandra Xanthaki attempts to include these different levels into her discussion of collective and indigenous rights. She develops a circular model in which the individual, placed in the center, is surrounded by concentric circles whose influence grows with their proximity to the center. Additionally, wider circles influence closer ones. Family, therefore, constitutes a small and close circle, followed (and influenced) first by a wider circle representing the cultural community, then by one representing the state, the continent, and, finally, the whole world (Xanthaki 2007: 23ff.).

This model, however, lacks possibilities of interaction and movement between the levels or circles. "Although this concentric circle approach to identity is perhaps analytically convenient, it cannot begin to capture the complexity of identity formation. . . . One is, and is not, many things at the same time" (Goodale 2006: 641). In the circular model, the individual is presented as a fixed center that is created but does not create itself. The individual is "exposed to the specific culture of his family, the culture of his village. . . . Their lives and choices represent a mixture of characteristics of the above communities" (Xanthaki 2007: 23). In addition, it remains unclear why and how culture has certain functions within a society and how this reflects on society.

> Societal totality . . . is presented like a map in relation with the countries shown on it; its structure is supposed to only be dependent on the subsumed group, while the question of the latter's dependence on society's structure and mechanisms does not arise. The examination of the

individual and society's relation, in which the most different groups have different mediating functions, is reduced to the study of the dependence of individuals and groups. (Adorno 1956b: 60)

In the constellation of the individual and society, internally and externally mediated relationships occur between a culture (or a group) and the individual just as between a culture/group and society. On this basis, culture cannot be conceptualized as a separate sphere nor can it be equated with society or with individual identity.

This has significant implications for a discussion of collective human rights. If society as a supra-level is a decisive level of socialization, the assumption of cultural groups' imperative nature for individual identities cannot be upheld—especially not in the understanding of a cultureless individual who is thrown into a vacuum by virtue of being cut off from his or her culture. Moreover, if culture is not the only frame constituting individual identity, cultures can be changed, criticized, and rejected by individuals. Culture can, but does not have to be, a marker of difference between cultural groups. It can allow for open boundaries, permeability, and common grounds. In this way, Taylor's definitions of moral and cultural frames could be related and refined. For a more concrete account, the constellations of individual, culture, and society, as well as their consequences for collective human rights need to be explored in empirical case studies. This would not only allow us to comprehend degrees of internalization and identification, but also to analyze power relations within cultures and societies.

My second objection to the criticism of a totalitarian cultural concept within the framework of collective human rights concerns the accusation of being static. Collective human rights are not necessarily based on static concepts of culture. Rather, they can integrate the possibility of cultural dynamics and changeability. Kymlicka, for example, assumes that there is cultural hybridity and changeability, in spite of his assumption of a stable cultural core. The problem is that these contradictive qualities remain disconnected and juxtaposed. On the other hand, this leaves room for a concept of culture whose strength lies in the connectedness between contradictive constellations.

A productive concept of culture is able to endure its own, internal contradictions. In anticipation of the ensuing discussion of internal contradictions in the concept of identity, the following axiom applies to a more comprehensive concept of culture: "There is no culture or cultural identity without this difference with itself" (Derrida 1992: 9f.; italics removed). This basic assumption allows for the simultaneity of constant change and a given order within culture.

This simultaneity can be understood by looking at Mikhail Bakhtin's older distinction of organic[3] hybridity and intentional, conscious, dialogical hybridity. According to this framework, culture is, on the level of organic hybridity, always exposed to influences and changes beyond the will of the actors involved. At the same time, a stable cultural order, a naturalized core identity, exists that constitutes the basis for consciously fought cultural conflicts that can lead to intentional hybridizations (Werbner 2001: 135ff.; Bakhtin 1994).

Reckwitz develops a similar understanding in his knowledge-oriented concept of culture. Culture, he says, is, first of all,

> a network of patterns of meaning . . . of cultural codes that fabricate a system of crucial differentiations and classifications. . . . They offer meaningful differences and thus allow for the identification of objects by means of routinized attributions of meaning. The patterns of meaning produce . . . a cultural "order of things" that, at the same time, depends on a symbolic outside. (Reckwitz 2006: 36)[4]

According to Reckwitz, those patterns of meaning are internalized as social and collective practices that regulate behavior and agency. Together with discourses on representation, they define heterogeneous subject forms from which individual identities are "derived" by means of binary mechanisms of delimitation. The respective culture, upheld by practices, is changeable and dynamic due to a "structure of repetition" that is "a permanent possibility to shift, a subtle change of its form" (Ibid.: 37). Changes are possible through modified repetitions, unintentional failure, nuances, and lapses, unpredictability, and deviating interpretations (Ibid.: 49).[5]

Reckwitz's praxeological model of culture, however, proves to be only one side—the unintended, organic one—of the hybridity Bakhtin had in mind. For Reckwitz, cultural stability and cultural dynamics exist simultaneously, but he portrays culture as a routine, commonplace, collective, internalized habit and, thereby, starkly contrasts it against consciousness and individual reflection. This perspective has a long tradition: "The sum of the *matters of course* in a social system is what we call its culture" (Hofstätter 1959: 92; italics added). Okin, too, at times applies a one-sided concept of culture as an unquestioned and unreflected routine, by outlining culture as mostly repressive restriction that stands in opposition to individual reflection.

A conscious reflection on culture, however, comes to the foreground in times of conflict: "Culture, under normal conditions, is a latent background factor. Only if it becomes disputed within its own scope of application does its visibility increase" (Neidhardt 1986: 17). According to Bakhtin, conflicts are ubiquitous in the form of constant encounters with different cultures. If one takes seriously the second part of cultural hybridity as proposed by Bakhtin, encompassing consciousness and intention, then reflection becomes a key category: "A key issue is that of reflexivity within, as well as in the encounter between, cultures" (Werbner 2001: 149). Yet, reflexivity is neither an anthropological nor a cultural given; on the contrary, the ability of individual reflection is possible only within a society, as shown above.

If, however, the ability to reflect solely appears on the meta-level of society, and if culture only refers to routinized and internalized—in other words: unreflected—actions, then culture as a subject of collective human rights would be insubstantial. First, the protection of a domain that constitutively excludes reflection would be, from a normative perspective, at least questionable. Second, the argument of collective rights would result in a performative self-contradiction: How can something that evades conscious influence and changes only through unintended actions and repeated deviation be legally (that is: consciously) protected and reproduced? Collective rights deliberately interfere with culture. They are supposed to consciously counter a process that, unintended and unattended, could lead to the dissolution of certain cultures.

Thus, the debate on collective rights depends on a concept of culture that allows for the simultaneous existence of dynamics and statics and that does not exclude intention and reflection. Only this basis allows for the disclosure of both reflection-supporting and reflection-restricting dimensions of culture.

From a discussion of both a broader and a narrower conception of culture as well as of the scope of culture and the simultaneous existence of statics and dynamics, the following implications may be discerned, to form a more comprehensive concept of culture.

From a normative perspective, culture cannot be set as a standard, a yardstick, or a legal entitlement. Rather, a culture's respective constellations are crucial with regard to individuals, the state, and society, as well as its boundaries, inherent power relations, the relation between statics and dynamics, and emancipatory and repressive aspects—all of which need to be examined on a case level.

From an analytical perspective, an examination of culture depends on an understanding of its nonidentical parts.

> In this field it makes even less sense than usual to imagine the results of analytical distinctions to be mutually exclusive opposites. . . . This is true even more for the culture of larger collective entities: The issues here are complex correlations of different, often disparate elements, variable mixing ratios, mere juxtaposition, and highly indirect interrelations. (Neidhardt 1986: 12)

The following antinomic constellation of the nonidentical allows for more specific accounts than the idea of an "undefined more-or-less, as-well-as, neither-nor, better-than" (Ibid.: 13). It allows to include and explicate underlying preconditions and inherent contradictions.

Three key aspects demonstrate the nonidentical in the concept of culture. First, cultures are not identical to themselves. They are neither homogeneous nor monolithic. Second, cultures are not identical to the meta-level of society. There are different reciprocal relationships between the two levels. And third, cultures are not identical to the individuals living within them. There is room for a critical distance—for questioning, for change, and to reproduce or reject a culture. There are differences between collective and individual interests as well as between collective and individual autonomy.

Moreover, if such nonidentical cultures represent a possible intermediary level between the individual and society, then the possibility for a vast number of intermediary levels emerges. An intermediary level, then, is not just represented by a certain culture, but it can take the form of groups, cultures, collective identities, and more. On this basis, both the homogenous model of culture and the fear of cultural dissolution can be bypassed. Simultaneously, culture can be taken seriously as a level of socialization and identity constitution.

NOTES

1. This is based on defining relations that correspond to the logical constellation of a strict antinomy; see Müller (2011) and Ritsert (2004).

2. See, for example, Bhabha (1994); Mouffe (1995); Hall/du Gay (1996). For an overview of the term's history and for detailed categorizations, see Reckwitz (2002); Bachmann-Medick (2016), Mende (2011a: 39ff., 2011b: 530f.).

3. The use of the term *organic* in this context is not to be confused with the national socialist idea of culture as a common organism. The latter concept of culture "excludes the always dynamic and process-like relations of subject and object, of individual and society, and of humans and nature"; see Mende (2011b: 543).

4. This definition corresponds directly with Taylor's and Kymlicka's assumption that culture offers valuations and meanings and thereby the possibility to differentiate between good and bad.

5. The idea of criticism and change through deviating repetition is famously outlined by Butler (1993, 1990), too.

THREE

Identity

The term *identity* plays a crucial role in the debates on collective rights. It is, however, so diversified and over-determined that it can be used almost arbitrarily. In this chapter I will first examine the concept of identity and the possible dimensions of its meaning. Following, I will discuss the question of which analytical and normative functions can be related to collective human rights that refer to identity.

A short overview of the concept's dissemination in the twentieth century will illustrate its heterogeneous and contradictory usage. The concept of individual identity is used to describe a coherent subject of enlightenment as well as a sociological crossing of interaction and intersubjectivity (Hall 1992a: 274f.).[1] The idea of collective identity as a subject of political and social struggles spread in the course of the Civil Rights Movement in the United States, which served as an example for the demands of other marginalized groups. These struggles mostly concerned inclusion and integration, a group's participation within the social majority despite a different color of skin (or despite other mechanisms of exclusion such as sexual orientation). Instead of "despite," the movements increasingly demanded inclusion and recognition "because of" their otherness. Identities characterized as "different" were not to be hidden or assimilated any longer. Identities whose otherness was marked by the social majority's attributes now became the starting point for new self-concepts and for collective self-identification (see, for example, Hall 1996b).

This development proceeded differently in different societies and did not unfold in a linear manner. Contrary to the emancipatory ideas of the Civil Rights Movement, the repercussions of the Southeastern and Eastern European turmoil of the 1990s are seen as repressive resurrections of ethnic self-identifications, in which culturally defined collective identities were essentialized as homogeneous entities strictly separated and to remain separated (see Addis 1997: 115).

At the same time, poststructuralist and postmodern discourses evolved to no longer understand identity as innate, intrinsic, or deterministic. Divided interests instead of skin color or origin were to be the glue of a common but nonetheless flexible identity. Social movements and dynamic coalitions were brought to the fore. Identities were outlined as freely selectable and arbitrary mosaics. They were seen as disrupted and broken off, as contingent nets without an essence or center, with intersecting, overly determined paths.[2]

As a result, identity is used today to describe collective as well as individual phenomena. It is accompanied by an almost infinite range of attributes, such as nationality, ethnicity, gender, religion, and politics. Not only individuals, cultures, or groups can have identities, but also companies or states.[3]

However, neither the idea of fragmented identities nor the demands for homogenous cultural distinction are inventions of the twentieth century. As early as in the sixteenth century, Montaigne wrote: "We are composed of nothing but colorfully chequered patches, connected so loosely and slackly that each of them may flutter away any moment, just as it pleases; it is because of this that there are just as many differences between us and ourselves as between us and the others" (Montaigne 2008: ch. 1).

Concepts of dynamic and multiple identities can be found throughout the centuries and up to today, with one example being Rimbaud, who stated, in 1871, "I is another" (Rimbaud 1972: 250; see Welsch 2005: 327).

Therefore, the widespread narrative according to which the concept of identity gained momentum in the twentieth century as a tool to handle disintegrating effects of a modernizing world with ever more options to choose from applies only partly. "It is nothing new to be self-conscious about identity. . . . To suggest otherwise risks assigning most of human experience to a historical anteroom, waiting for modernity to turn the lights on" (Jenkins 2008: 36).[4]

Despite various peak phases and trends, the development and usage of the concept of identity is neither linear nor consistent. Contradicting concepts of identity do not simply replace each other, but exist simultaneously. The academic verdict on the concept of identity is, therefore, mostly unanimous. If not used as a mere tool, the focus lies on attesting its polyphony: "The concept itself remains something of an enigma" (Fearon 1999: 1). Its usage has become so diverse that it can mean everything and nothing (Gleason 1983: 914; Brubaker/Cooper 2000: 1). It is both over- and under-determined (Niethammer 2000: 38ff.). It has been degenerated to an insubstantial "plastic word" (Pörksen 1995) and dissolved in "definitional anarchy" (Abdelal et al. 2006: 695).

In light of these judgments, the development of a perspective dismissing the concept of identity altogether is hardly surprising. Among the most influential advocates of this position are Rogers Brubaker and Frederick Cooper. They suggest waiving identity as a category of analysis "for it is not clear why what is routinely characterized as multiple, fragmented, and fluid should be conceptualized as 'identity' at all" (Brubaker/Cooper 2000: 6). At the same time, there is no going back to the assumption that reifies identity as essence (Ibid.; see also Malešević 2006; Avanza/Laferté 2005). Instead of searching for better definitions of identity, or simply replacing identity with another concept, which would contain the very same weaknesses and contradictions, it would be best to "unbundle the thick tangle of meanings that have accumulated around the term 'identity,' and to parcel out the work to a number of less congested terms" (Brubaker/Cooper 2000: 14).

This approach, however, is confronted with a fundamental challenge. Brubaker and Cooper are "attempting to impose theoretical order on a human world in which indeterminacy, ambiguity and paradox are part of the normal pattern of everyday life" (Jenkins 2008: 9). The contradicting dimensions of meaning named (and rejected) by Brubaker and Cooper are as common as they are influential: A rigid and reified conception of identity might explain how identity functions as a strong motivator, as social glue or social coercion, as a political instrument, or as an attribute that is hard to escape. A concept that understands identity as fractured and diverse, in contrast, allows us to fundamentally criticize the aforementioned coercions, as well as ethnically motivated conflicts and racism. Theoretical approaches including only one of the contradicting poles of static and dynamic identity are correspondingly limited in their capacity to explain and scrutinize. Not only would the necessity remain to find a way to deal with different and, at times, contradicting social realities, but one would also have to reduce and divide a concept full of preconditions to a degree "where I have actually missed the subject and where I am left with nothing but the trivialities into which I have divided the subject, while what I am really interested in about the subject, what really is what I want to understand . . . has already been taken away" (Adorno 2010: 195).

If, however, these reservations lead to the conclusion that the concept of identity simply contains *all* dimensions of meaning attributed to it, then the criticisms of its inflationary use resulting in meaninglessness and insignificance are right.

In the following section, to avoid concluding with any of these one-sided or meaningless perspectives, I will develop an approach that takes the concept seriously both in and through its contradictions. I will show that the contradicting dimensions of meaning contained in the concept of identity belong together, and that they can only be fully understood if analyzed within their contradicting constellation. For a better understanding of identity, the concept will be neither divided nor reduced but "complicated" in order to capture its complexity. In the following section, I will therefore discuss two approaches that characterize identity by its contradictoriness. Because Charles Taylor, Will Kymlicka, and Susan Okin consult identity both on a normative and analytical level, these two levels will be focused on.

IDENTITY AND NONIDENTITY

A productively contradicting concept of identity is developed by Jacques Derrida, in his approach of deconstruction, and by Theodor W. Adorno, in his concept of dialectics. Deconstruction and dialectics refer to a lot more than only the handling of the concept of identity. However, the focus here will be on the question of how the two philosophers refer to the contradictoriness within the concept of identity in order to transform one-dimensional approaches into an appropriate constellation.

For Derrida and Adorno, the identical and the nonidentical are mediated in an antinomy, meaning that two opposing but equally valid propositions are inextricably linked. Because of this valuing of two contradicting propositions equally, antinomies are usually interpreted to be arbitrary. Derrida and Adorno, however, emphasize that only the antinomy allows us to meaningfully deal with the concept of identity.

Derrida relates every form of identity to culture: "There is no self-relation, no relation to oneself, no identification with oneself, without culture" (Derrida 1992: 10). He further stresses that "what is proper to a culture is to not be identical to itself. Not to not have an identity, but not to be able to identify itself . . . to be able to take the form of a subject only in the non-identity to itself or, if you prefer, only in the difference with itself" (Ibid.: 9; italics removed). All cultures and identities differ *from themselves*, that is, they are not identical to themselves. Only in this way can they constitute themselves as identical. This is based on the assumption that every culture (as a basis of identity) is always a culture of the other. Derrida gives various explanations for this assumption.

First, culture is not the same as nature. Rather, "for it is nature's way out of itself in itself, nature's difference *with itself*" (Ibid.: 27; italics in the original), culture is artificial in that it needs to be created. Therefore, it can only be acquired. Culture, as an artificial artefact, never fully (identically) belongs to anyone.

Second, there is always a variety of cultures and multiple readings of culture, and there is always an effort to enforce one culture over others and to homogenize. The idea of a uniform culture and a respectively accompanying identity is the result of enculturation, that is, the prevalence of one particular culture over other cultures. Culture is the result of enculturation by an other (Derrida 1992: 10ff., 1998).[5]

Third, the theorem of a constitutive outside[6] allows us to appreciate that the constitution of one's own identity depends on the construction of the other as different, delimited, and external: the construction of another *as* an "other."

In summary, for Derrida, culture and identity are always derived from the other. Their origin lies in the nonidentical, which is a precondition of their constitution. At the same time, however, every identity has to *pretend* to be unique, to be identical to itself and to be the true embodiment of the universal. Following Valéry, Derrida describes it as a common paradox that every particular cultural identity has to imagine itself as universal.

> Whether it takes a national form or not, a refined, hospitable or aggressively xenophobic form or not, the self-affirmation of an identity always claims to be responding to the call or assignation of the universal. There are no exceptions to this law. No cultural identity presents itself as the opaque body of an untranslatable idiom, but always, on the contrary, as the irreplaceable inscription of the universal in the singular, the unique testimony to the human essence and to what is proper to man. (Derrida 1992: 72f.)

This, he argues, is necessary for the existence of identity because a self-conception as nonidentical or infinite would dissolve it. For Derrida, the possibility of cultural identity lies in the ability to endure the impossible—the antinomy—of the nonidentical in oneself.

After giving these initial definitions, Derrida jumps to the normative level. The initially descriptive analysis becomes a normative demand, a "*duty*" (Ibid.: 76; italics in the original). Derrida develops the concept of a European identity that he wants to lead to neither Eurocentrism nor to anti-Eurocentrism. It should neither be constituted by regionalism, that is, fragmentation into many small identities, nor by homogenization, that is, the establishment of a single dominant culture. Derrida elevates the antinomy of the identical and the nonidentical to a norm that consists of the endurance of these contradicting demands: "*It is necessary*: it is necessary to make ourselves the guardians of an idea of Europe . . . that consists precisely in not closing itself off in its own identity" (Ibid.: 29; italics in the original).

Oliver Marchart describes Derrida's approach as deconstruction in two steps: At first, a dichotomy is dissolved and reformulated as an antinomy. Then—and this is where the "power-criticizing strength" of deconstruction lies (Marchart 2010: 272)—it is revalued. Derrida connects emancipatory potential in the antinomic identity. He rejects other versions of identity (fragmentation into the nonidentical or a centralized, homogenized identity) as repressive.

In Adorno's theory, the concept of the nonidentical plays an eminent role on various levels (see Ritsert 1997). He emphasizes that identifying thinking in static terms excludes many meanings, dimensions, implications, and other things unnamed, which he summarizes under the term "non-identical" (Adorno 2008: 29ff., Adorno 2004). Social phenomena are too complex to be fully determined by just one term. There is always something that goes beyond both the designation and the designated. "What is, is more than it is" (Adorno 2004: 161).

Adorno (like Derrida) refers to Hegel's assumptions here. For Hegel, the mediation of the identical and the nonidentical is found in the mediation of inside and outside. Determining an inside calls for a boundary defining, forming, and identifying it as an inside (as identical). To impose this boundary means making a statement on the excluded (the nonidentical) and the inside's relation to it (Hegel 2010: 98ff.; see Ritsert 2011: 21). Connected to this is the idea of a constitutive outside introduced above: Identity constitutes itself by what it excludes.[7]

Adorno grasps this constellation even more stringently. In a dialectical that is an intermediated constellation, the identical and the nonidentical are not only externally but also internally mediated by each other. The blueprint for this can be found, again, with Hegel: "On one side, the externality of otherness is within the something's own inwardness; on the other side, it remains as otherness distinguished from it; it is still externality as such, but in the something" (Hegel 2010: 103). The nonidentical does not remain externally opposed to the "more" of identity, but finds its way into its inwardness—without completely assimilating to and dissolving in it. "This 'more' is not imposed upon it but remains immanent to it. . . . The innermost core of the object proves to be simultaneously extraneous to it, the phenomenon of its seclusion, the reflex of an identifying, stabilizing procedure" (Adorno 2004: 161). Identity and the nonidentical are intrinsically mediated with each other. The nonidentical is contained in the identical, and simultaneously opposed to it. Yet, emphasizing the nonidentical does not aim to exclude identity, identifications, and definitions. Rather, the nonidentical can be achieved only "through identification" (Ritsert 1997: 40). Identifying thinking that at the same time leaves room for the nonidentical is necessary.

In a decisive step, Adorno continues: "Contradiction is nonidentity under the rule of a law that affects the nonidentical as well" (Adorno 2004: 6). Otherness is found not only in identity, but also in the nonidentical. The nonidentical contains its opposition—the identical—just as the identical contains the nonidentical. To this, Adorno relates the important note that emancipation and repression are found on either side of the antinomic constellation. Identity *and* the nonidentical can be both liberating and repressive.

> The contradiction of freedom and determinism . . . is a contradiction in the subjects' way to experience themselves, as now free, now unfree. Under the aspect of freedom, they are unidentical with themselves be-

> cause the subject is not a subject yet. . . . Freedom and intelligible character are akin to identity and nonidentity, but we cannot clearly and distinctly enter them on one side or the other. The subjects are free, after the Kantian model, in so far as they are aware of and identical with themselves; and then again, they are unfree in such identity in so far as they are subjected to, and will perpetuate, its compulsion. They are unfree as diffuse, nonidentical nature; and yet, as that nature they are free because their overpowering impulse—the subject's nonidentity with itself is nothing else—will also rid them of identity's coercive character. Personality is the caricature of freedom. The basis of the aporia is that truth beyond compulsory identity would not be the downright otherness of that compulsion; rather, it would be conveyed by the compulsion. (Ibid.: 299)

In other words, personal identity, as coherent consciousness of oneself, is the basis of (conscious, targeted) agency. This means, on the one hand, freedom from, for example, mere reflex[8] and immediacy. A coherent self and consciousness allow for experience, education, and reflection. On the other hand, identity in its hardening and constricting characteristics means a lack of freedom. It is repressive when rigidly cutting off desire, choices, distance, reflection, and difference (to itself, to others, or to a group).

These possibilities of deviation are included in the nonidentical. It means freedom from forced identity. On the other hand, a pure nonidentical would be mere nature, incapable of consciousness and (self-)reflection—a subjection to drive and instinct. This is the repressive dimension of the nonidentical.

It is central to understand that both are mediated by their opposing poles; the identical by the nonidentical, and vice versa. Autonomy, agency, and reflection (on the individual level) as well as the openness toward "the other" as demanded by Derrida (on a collective level) need both identity and nonidentity. The nonidentical—the "other"—is never radically different or dichotomously separated from the identical. Rather, it is situated within an intermediate relationship, in which neither side exists without the other. There is no identity without the nonidentical or the other—just as there would be no concept of the other without a concept of identity.

Although Derrida's and Adorno's approaches share several similarities, they nonetheless diverge in multiple ways, two of which I will outline because they mirror the close interconnection between the analytical and normative levels of this analysis.

First, the approaches diverge in terms of their levels of reference. Derrida has Europe's cultural identity, that is, a collective level, in mind when defining the concept of identity. Yet, he emphasizes at one point that his theses of identity constitution are valid on all levels, on the individual level as well as on the collective (Derrida 1992: 10). Although developing at first a general, epistemological concept of identity, Adorno's normative yardstick of reflection and liberty unfolds on the individual level.

Another disparity between the two approaches lies in their moral philosophical position. Derrida emphasizes that a general solution for the antinomy problem is not only impossible but would even be harmful, for it would undermine what is special about every specific constellation and thus lead to technocratic power (Ibid.: 72). Nonetheless, his argument includes two steps—first showing the antinomy and then elevating it to a normative duty. Derrida characterizes this duty of antinomy as the opposite of a general, deterministic, and arbitrary solution. Adorno, on the other hand, integrates these two steps. His argument, the dialectical antinomy, already allows for criticism; it does not have to be added subsequently. The analytical and normative level are tightly interwoven and linked. Moreover, Adorno points out that no concept, including the concept of dialectics, is safe from abuse, arbitrariness, or technocratic use (Adorno 1978: 244ff.). This means that emancipation is by no means automatically included into the dialectical antinomy. Mediated constellations of identity and the nonidentical can be both repressive and liberating. The existence of an antinomic constellation alone is no guarantee for emancipation.

In summary, the figure of a dialectical or antinomic mediation is central to a substantial discussion of the concept of identity. Identity and the nonidentical are contrastingly opposed, while indispensably referring to each other and simultaneously constituted only through each other—without integrating in the process. This constellation allows for the analysis of a concept as heterogeneous as the concept of identity to succeed in disclosing emancipatory and repressive dimensions. This would hardly be possible with a concept of identity divided out into its aspects and cleared of all contradictions and varieties of meaning.

The relation between identity and the nonidentical constitutes a key antinomy that is basal, though not yet sufficient for an examination of heterogeneous conceptions of identity. At least three more levels play important roles in identity concepts and discussions on collective human rights. They are built on this key antinomy and they, too, will show an interconnectedness of analytical and normative aspects.

STATIC AND DYNAMIC IDENTITY

A crucial contradiction inherent to concepts of identity lies in the clash of static and dynamic facets. For Brubaker and Cooper, this is a pivotal reason to abandon identity as a category of analysis. Identity, on the one hand, is seen as something that can, should, or has to be chosen, changed, formed, and performed (Bal 2009: 11). (Post-)Modern society seems to be a supermarket offering a huge variety of possible identities. Accordingly, the term identity is used in the plural (Nancy 2013). Because identification represents a process never completed, the actor-focused verb "to identify oneself" is seen as the only appropriate way to talk about identity (Hall 1996a: 1ff.). Categories, attributions, experiences, and influences are different currents that cross and mix, thereby producing ever-changing identities. These are "constructed by a diversity of discourses, among which there is no necessary relation but a constant movement of overdetermination and displacement" (Mouffe 1995: 33). Identities are understood as multiple, hybrid, meandering, and changing, depending on the situation. "Identity is limited, preliminary, fragile—and inevitably so" (Straub 1998: 82; see also Gilroy 1993; Bhabha 1994; Hall 1996a; Martín Alcoff 2003).

The idea of fluent identities is limited by social and societal structures (Young 1997), which are always already given and which cannot be changed solely by individual willpower or excluded from an individual's identity. One can choose between certain options (of identity), "but we do not determine the options among which we choose" (Appiah 1994: 155). Identity is shaped by institutions, society, religion, the state, education, prevalent norms and rules, practices, and concepts (Ibid.: 154). These factors can form identity in the long term and tie it to a stable framework. Gendered, ethnical, and economic power structures decisively take part in shaping this framework. Although poverty and nationality, for example, are not sufficient to constitute individual identity, they determine which options are available in the supermarket of identities after all.

Apart from external mechanisms and attributions, the static dimension of identity also contains a voluntary, conscious act of holding onto a core identity that is seen as stable and unchangeable—or at least strategically essential. For psychological, political, social, economic, or legal reasons, identity is reified as something that needs to be achieved or held onto (Spivak 1988; Hall 1997: 184).

At the same time, societal givens have a contingent, historical, changeable, and human-made character. Accordingly, the seemingly static structures do not rule out dynamic processes of reflection, choice, and negotiation (Young 1994). Both sides penetrate and permeate each other. They cannot be separated in a binary way.

This "double movement" (Mouffe 1995: 34) of static and dynamic factors can be conceptualized only if the two factors are not dichotomously torn apart—but are examined within their mediated constellation. Then it becomes clear, too, that simply replacing the term "identity" with "identities," "identification," or the verb "to identify" is of limited reach. A one-sided perspective on the dynamic dimensions of identity leaves the analysis just as fragmentary as a focus on only the static dimension would.

From a normative perspective, repressive and emancipatory elements can be found in both dynamic and static dimensions of identity. Freedom, agency, and individual self-determination are linked to dynamic aspects of identity. Simultaneously, every loosely fluttering identity mosaic, consisting of breaks and fragments, has its limits. "Only a positioning within that coordinate system of the physical, corporal, social, moral, and temporal space allows for autonomous agency and for that space to obtain the sensible and meaningful contents that can, in turn, reproduce, stabilize, and maintain personal identity" (Straub 1998: 86). Stability, continuity, and consistency are indispensable for the formation of identity. In light of the entanglement with the nonidentical or the "other," Derrida and Adorno emphasize that these static factors of identity are partially an illusion, although a necessary one. In order to constitute itself as an independent, stable (collective or individual) subject, the subject needs to imagine itself as autonomous and distinct from the other, the nonidentical, and the dynamical. At the same time, stability always contains hardening, stasis, and coercion.

Mediation of static and dynamic factors is, in conclusion, indispensable on both the analytic and the normative level. Neither of the two sides can be hypostasized or detached from the other, because this would neglect crucial dimensions of identity-formation processes—be they repressive or emancipatory.

INTERNALLY AND EXTERNALLY ATTRIBUTED IDENTITY

The constellation of internal ("one's own") and external ("alien") attributions is a decisive part of any identity concept. The set-up of this constellation is related to the question of whether political sciences should focus on purely empirical, so-called hard, facts, or on a group's (or individual's) self-conception.

Approaches following the latter reject external attributions as stereotypes that play no significant role in the formation of identity. Other authors, on the other hand, highlight that "it is the power of categorisation—the subjugation of the internal moment of identification by the external—that characterises the modern human world" (Jenkins 2008: 201). For Richard Jenkins, external attributions are key for modern identity constitution. Nonetheless (or because of this) he develops a dialectical model of internal and external factors. Both, he argues, take part in the formation of identity. Jenkins emphasizes that they are to be understood as neither dichotomous nor sequential, but are mutually dependent in simultaneous processes. Identity, then, is a social, never concluding process of constant interaction with others (Ibid.: 17, 47).

This external constellation in which mediated internal and external factors become part of identity constitution can be extended substantially by including relations of internal mediation. The poles do not just complement each other in an additive way. Rather, the mutually dependent constitution of internal and external factors permeates both poles. Internal attributes are not rooted in an isolated, nonsocietal self, but shaped by the interaction with and their recognition by the external world. Conversely, external categorizations, discourses, and attributions do not immediately determine the formation of identity. They can be challenged, distracted, deviated; they can conflict or blend with each other or with internal factors.

In his master-slave parable, Hegel develops the image of a through and through relational self whose constitution depends on the recognition and attribution by (relevant) others (Hegel 1977: § 178ff.). The idea derived from this, of a dialogical self, has lasting influence on identity theories, as represented by Taylor.

> We define our identity always in dialogue with, sometimes in struggle against, the things our significant others want to see in us. Even after we outgrow some of these others—our parents, for instance—and they disappear from our lives, the conversation with them continues within us as long as we live.... Thus my discovering my own identity doesn't mean that I work it out in isolation, but that I negotiate it through dialogue, partly overt, partly internal, with others.... My own identity crucially depends on my dialogical relations with others. (Taylor 1994a: 33f.; see also Calhoun 1994: 20; Gilroy 1993: 53; Habermas 1974: 99)

The development of internal factors that constitute identity is related to its intersubjective, external recognition. Iris Marion Young elaborates on this thought by pointing out social positioning that does not determine identity, but allows for and simultaneously limits agency (Young 1997: 265f.). This brings to the fore the repressive potential of external attribution and its interplay with internal attribution.

Repressive moments manifest when external attributions do not overlap, or do so only very little, with internal identifications. At best, they can be identified and rejected as stereotypes. However, a critical distance from attributions that are categorizing and not self-assigned is not always possible. Influential external attributes such as gender, ethnicity, or nationality shape self-perception and internal attributions in a way that is hard to avoid. "Individuals make their own identity, but not under conditions of their own choosing" (Martín Alcoff 2003: 3). Even the "production of one's own identity" depends on forms of agency that are not equally available to everybody.

There are numerous examples in history of how marginalized groups internalized the dominant (usually white, male, and heterosexual) perspective and considered themselves inferior (Fanon 1986). In order to escape these repressive effects, the Black Power Movement consciously took over, revaluated, and positively re-coded external (pejorative) attributions, using them as starting points to reconstruct a confident self-identity. This apparent detour is closely tied to mechanisms of racism, due to which it is not "enough to require being treated with equal dignity *despite* being Black, for that will require a concession that being Black counts naturally or to some degree against one's dignity. And so one will end up asking to be respected as a Black" (Appiah 1994: 161; italics added, also see Hall 1996b: 443).[9]

In order to challenge dichotomizing power relations, revaluating pejorative external attributions to affirmative internal ones can be a decisive step. Apart from its liberating and emancipatory effects, however, this can also be accompanied by repressive elements. Revaluated, internal, and self-chosen identities may well be coercive as well.

> Demanding respect for people as blacks and as gays requires that there are some scripts that go with being an African-American or having same-sex-desires. There will be proper ways of being black and gay, there will be expectations to be met, demands will be made. It is at this point that someone who takes autonomy seriously will ask whether we have not replaced one kind of tyranny with another. . . . I would like not to have to choose. I would like other options. (Appiah 1994: 162f.)

External as well as internal attributions—for both individuals and groups—can have repressive effects. Looking only at a dialogically constituted identity bears the danger of overlooking repressive factors. At the same time—and the dialogical approach makes this very clear—neither external nor internal factors are solely repressive. Rather, they can both be productive and emancipatory, encouraging identity constitution and enabling agency.

In conclusion, internal and external attributions are mediated and mutually constituting. They are not two separate bundles (in the form of mere stereotypes or an isolated inside) that overlap at a certain point, thereby producing identity. Processes of identity formation are, rather, shaped by external and internal attributions that are already mediated and shaped by each other and that can challenge, translate, and form each other. Both poles can hold emancipatory and repressive elements.

COLLECTIVE AND INDIVIDUAL IDENTITY

At first sight, the constellation of collective and individual identity seems to be closely related to the constellation of externally and internally attributed identity. Accordingly, some authors, referring to the distinction between internal (subjective) and external (intersubjective) identities, suggest a sharp analytical distinction between collective and individual identity:

> Individuals and groups remain analytically distinct objects, each requiring its own conceptualization. The essential difference lies in the *collective* meaning inherent in social identities. Whereas individual identities are subjective, collective identities are "intersubjective"—comprised of shared interpretations of group traits or attributes. (Abdelal et al. 2006: 701; italics in the original)

At this point, the constellation of internal and external dimensions of identity is indeed relevant—differently, though, than implied by Rawi Abdelal et al. Rather, the two dimensions shape both collective and individual identity. A categorization that understands individual identities as merely subjective, that is, internal, and collective identities as merely intersubjective, that is, external, shows only parts of the whole constellation—or shows it distortedly, because external factors (which include the intersubjective and societal level) are also part of individual identities. External categories like gender and nationality as well as attributes acquired during intersubjective exchange are constitutive of self-formation. Conversely, collective identities are also shaped by internal and subjective interpretations and interests. Therefore, the constellation of internally and externally attributed identity and the constellation of individual and collective identity cannot be parallelized.[10]

Instead of dichotomously separating individual and collective identity (as done by Abdelal et al.), other approaches highlight the reciprocity between collective and individual identity. "Collective identities are in constant interplay with personal identities, but they are never simply the aggregate of individuals' identities" (Poletta/Jasper 2001: 298). Jenkins emphasizes that the concepts of collective and individual identity are "routinely entangled with each other," that they "can be understood as similar in important respects," that they reciprocally imply, produce, and reproduce each other, and that "the theorisation of identification must therefore accommodate the individual and the collective in equal measure" (Jenkins 2008: 37f.).

Thus, the focus lies on a reciprocal relationship between individual and collective identity. Its character should, however, be differentiated in more detail. A basic distinction of the two relies on the fact that individual identity is tied to a specific physical body. There is no group-level equivalent to this, and no tangible collective body. One may object, however, that body and individual identity are not automatically connected and that the symbolic meaning of the body is comparable to the symbolic social body of the collective (Assmann 1995: 132). Still, this parallelization has its limits. For example, the circle of members within a collective identity cannot be determined as precisely and static as an individual identity can be associated with a particular body (Straub 1998: 98).

By differentiating two approaches, Jürgen Straub (following Assmann) defines the concept of collective identity more precisely: The "standardizing perspective" is completely separated from a group's self-conception and, therefore, not a useful perspective. It rather mirrors an inadequate correspondence between external and internal attributions. In the "reconstructive perspective," on the other hand, only internal, self-chosen identifications, or identifications based on "tacit knowledge," play a role: "*Collective* or *we-identity* means the picture a group develops of itself and that its members identify with. Collective identity is a question of identification by the individuals involved. It does not exist 'per se'" (Assmann 1995: 132; italics in the original; Straub 1998: 98ff.).

Yet, the differentiation between a standardizing and a reconstructive perspective bears a problem that results from mixing the two conceptual pairs internal-external and individual-collective. It is true that an externally attributed collective identity that does not correspond to internal attributions whatsoever can be criticized on a normative level. Nonetheless, it may play an important role on the analytical level. This does not mean that every external attribution is identity constituting. Neither is the concept of an ontological collective identity (which indeed is not a useful concept) in any way a counterpart to an internally attributed collective identity. What does follow, however, is that there exist external attributions that contribute to the constitution of collective identities and that cannot (or can hardly) be avoided. The example given above of an appropriation and revaluation of an initially externally attributed (pejorative) and later self-chosen, positive, collective identity shows the possible constellations and transitions of the two forms.

From a normative perspective it becomes clear, again, that repressive and emancipatory elements can appear on all sides. Collective identities, "as group membership from which there is in principle no escape" (Dench 2003, cited in Bauman 2003: 89), can be so encompassing and profound that they hardly leave any room for deviation (and the non-identical). Consciously embraced collective (counter) identities, on the other hand, can serve as a basis for social, political, or economic struggles. Simultaneously, there is a danger for collective (counter) identities to remain, under reversed signs, in the binary constellation of the existing power relations.

> People are assigned to an "ethnic minority" without being asked for their consent. They may be glad of the assignment, or grow to enjoy it and even come to fight for its perpetuation. . . . The point is, though, that whether this does or does not happen has no tangible influence on the fact of enclosure, which is administered by the "powerful collectivities" in charge, and perpetuated by the circumstance of their administration. (Bauman 2003: 89f.)

Collective identities can harden into internal group constraints. They can form and enrich the possibility of individual experience, reflection, and criticism, but they can also reduce, homogenize, and inhibit deviation and autonomy.

In the same way as collective identity, the emancipatory potential of the individual identity depends on substantial, normative, and societal frames. A liberal, democratic understanding of individual identity probably offers more room for agency than a narrow framework. Detached from social conditions, however, concepts of an independent individual identity do not make sense. Here, the analysis of the socialized individual and the constitutive role of identity and its mediation with the nonidentical apply. Consciousness, coherence, and continuity are a crucial basis for agency and thinking that always take place within a social (or collective) context. The development of individual identity is a never-ending process, marked by cognitive, linguistic, moral, and motivational development processes. However, it is discontinuous and ruptured as well as influenced by unconscious factors, too (Habermas 1975: 42ff.).

Above, the nonidentical was defined as the uncircumventable and correcting antinomic opposite of the general concept of identity, constituting identity and at the same time saving it from being hypostasized and reified. Now the question arises of whether individual and collective identity might be mediated in the same uncircumventable way. This question is of the utmost importance from both a theoretical and a political perspective, because none of the other dimensions of identity is as controversial as the concept, scope, and meaning of collective identity. It lies at the heart of the debates on collective human rights.

IS COLLECTIVE IDENTITY A CONSTITUENT OF INDIVIDUAL IDENTITY?

It is of little surprise that the concept of collective identity is used analytically and normatively in many different ways. At one end of the spectrum, collective identity is being linked to a "tendency towards fundamentalism and violence . . . beyond positive law" (Niethammer 2000: 625). This tendency also escapes opposite intentions because it is part of "the construction of the concept and the social mechanics of its practice" (Ibid.: 626). According to this view, collective identity is referred to when the law does not apply, or when the law ought to be transcended. Because of this, collective identity cannot be remodeled by legal relationships. Additionally, every collective identity needs something excluded that is not only something diffusely different, but represents a collective itself that can be attributed pejoratively—a clearly identifiable enemy (Ibid.: 11ff.). Generally, collective identity makes it impossible to see one's own and the other's nonidentical aspects (Ibid.: 627). It one-sidedly dissolves the antinomic tension between identity and the nonidentical.

On the other end of the spectrum, collective identity is seen as a desirable good that needs to be achieved, found, fulfilled, fought for, or recognized. These approaches appear not only in identity politics, but also in international human rights documents (for a critical examination, see Niethammer 2000: 9ff.; Danielsen/Engle 1995). Collective identity is imagined as an ideal for two reasons. On the one hand, it is seen as a basis of social movements and demands for recognition, participation, or independence. The definition, on the other hand, of collectives and minorities in international and national law tends to pressure collectives to self-identify as collectives if they want to be entitled to those rights.

The spectrum also includes positions that make an effort to unite the two contradictive approaches.[11] Jürgen Habermas assumes a mediated relationship between collective and individual identity: A particular, that is, a "rational" form of collective identity is an uncircumventable condition for the formation of individual identity, Habermas argues. Since, however, collective identity in a modern society is no longer marked by unified traditions and knowledge, the question needs to be reformulated: "Can complex societies form a rational identity" (Habermas 1974: 91)? This demands for a new understanding of identity.

> The new identity of a society which extends beyond state boundaries can neither be related to a specific territory nor rest upon any specific organization. The distinguishing characteristic of this new identity can also no longer be that of association or membership. Collective identity, and this is the thesis I intend to advance, can today only be grounded in the consciousness of universal and equal chances to participate in the kind of communication processes by which identity formation becomes a continuous learning process. Here the individual is no longer confronted by collective identity as a traditional authority, as a fixed objectivity on the basis of which self-identity can be built. Rather, individuals are the participants in the shaping of the collective will underlying the design of a common identity. (Ibid.: 99)

Similar to the constellations of the opposite pairs introduced above, Habermas develops a relation in which individual and collective identity constitute and become part of each other. Decades later, Habermas emphasizes this concept by pointing out that not only a citizen's individual identity, but also the context of his or her collective identity should be legally protected (Habermas 1994: 113). Collective and individual rights are not mutually exclusive, he concludes, as long as the former does not take the form of a "preservation of species by administrative means," but serves the recognition of the individual member (Ibid.: 130).

Habermas's approach allows the discussion of three crucial problems that come with the definition of a mutually constitutive relation between collective and individual identity. These are the analytical scope, the normative content, and the normative exclusions of concepts of collective identity.

The Analytical Scope of Collective Identity

A first problem concerns the scope of the concept of collective identity. The assumption that individuals and their individual identities do not exist inside a vacuum, or within an isolated container, is fairly uncontested. They are mediated by society. The role of collective identity is less clear, though. If it is equated with society, one of the two concepts becomes conceptually superfluous and redundant. If understood as a sub-level of society, its function as an intermediary between the individual and society needs a more detailed examination. This also raises the question of what role collective identity plays in constituting the individual and his or her identity (which are also constituted by society).

Habermas describes the development of individual identity as developmental steps that are marked by fractures and crises. According to psychoanalytic and cognitive developmental psychology, there are neither "clear indicators for a subjective separation between subject and object" (Habermas 1979: 100) during infancy, nor does the differentiation between the collective and society play a role at this point in life. After two intermediate steps, Habermas sees the full development of a reflexive and independent individual identity in the conscious understanding and, if necessary, criticism of existing norms, "so that theories can be traced back to the cognitive accomplishments of investigating subjects and norm-systems to the will-formation of subjects living together" (Ibid.: 102). Thereby, individual identity becomes "more abstract and, at the same time, more individual to the degree that the young child appropriates extra-familial role systems up to and including the political order, which is interpreted and justified by a complex tradition" (Ibid.: 109). In this model, collectives are presented as intermediate stages of identity formation that are traversed from smaller systems of reference (family) to bigger systems of reference (modern constitutional state). If values of the collective group are recognized as being merely particular, they can be questioned and rejected in favor of a general, universal moral (Habermas 1974). This assumption decisively limits the meaning of collective identity: If collectives are no longer of any importance for individual identity once it is developed, it is unclear why they need legal protection.

The Normative Content of Collective Identity

From a moral philosophical perspective, the concept of collective identity poses a second problem. In political sciences as well as in politics, collective identity is either rejected as repressive or defended as emancipatory. This spectrum reflects the constellation of conflict between communitarian and liberal positions. Habermas's approach is in line with the liberal argumentation for group rights (2) (see table 1.1). It consists of the recognition of collective rights—if, and as long as, they serve the individual. The controversial starting point culminates in the questions of whether and to what extent a collective is constitutive for the individual, whether it has value independent of this, and whether it needs to be protected by special rights. It needs to be examined in light of the analytical and normative content of the concepts that collective identity is respectively based on.

Habermas strives for an emancipatory understanding of collective identity that strengthens individual identity. Although he points out that the development of individual identity does not proceed without fractures (Habermas 1975: 47f.) and that it might fail (Ibid.: 42), his model shows, in some aspects, (uni-)linearity: the missing subject-object distinction turns to the slow, naïve adaption of existing norms, which in practice, turns to a more and more reflexive, universal, and abstract individual identity—from a static to a more dynamic and reflexive identity. Regarding both the collective and individual identity, Habermas claims, "In both dimensions identity projections apparently become more and more general and abstract, until finally the projection mechanism as such becomes conscious, and identity formation takes on a reflective form, in the knowledge that to a certain extent individuals and societies themselves establish their identities" (Habermas 1979: 116).

The model "from static to dynamic," however, needs to be restricted because dynamic and societal conditions can be found even in moments that appear static and undetached.[12] In a linear conception, the repressive potential in both the static *and* the dynamic aspects tends to be neglected.[13]

By outlining an open, universal, discursive collective identity, Habermas tries to develop an emancipatory model of collective identity that strengthens and supports individual identity. He leaves the sub-state level of collective identity in favor of a more general and comprehensive level. Habermas discusses the problem of internal homogeneity and (pejorative) distinction from the "other," which plays an important role on the sub-state level of collective identity, as follows: "The whole of mankind is an abstraction, it is not just another group which on a global scale could form its identity, similarly as did tribes or states, until such a time as mankind were again to coalesce into a particular entity, let us say, in defence against other populations in outer space" (Habermas 1974: 94). Habermas's suggestion of an abstract, cosmopolitan collective identity that encompasses all human beings consists of three points: (1) detaching collective identity from specific, traditional world views; (2) emphasizing the flexible, dynamic, and internally attributed aspects of identity; and, (3) connecting collective identity with universal morals. Globalized humankind, he argues, can develop a meaningful collective identity if global society can provide humans with moral orientation and normative integration. Currently, however, the world is globalized by market laws instead of by the moral sphere (Ibid.: 97). An emancipatory global society could develop a reflexive, discursive, and open collective identity only when based on universal morals, which are the basic norms of communicative reason or communicative rationality (Ibid.: 99). In more recent studies, Habermas expounds on the problems posed by the concept of a world government. Nonetheless, he adheres to the possibility of a collective identity, beyond smaller groups of reference and nation-states, that is no longer defined by association or membership—but instead is constituted democratically and universally (Habermas 2010).

In his discussion of Taylor's multiculturalism, Habermas returns to the question of distinct collectives and cultures within a democratic state, thereby shifting his focus. According to Habermas, members of a state must have the opportunity to opt for or against a sub-state culture. A modern society has to be able to endure deviation, reflection, and conflicting truths. This makes it necessary for the state to protect certain foundations of collective identities (Habermas 1994: 113ff.). At this point, Habermas emphasizes that the "identity of the political community ... is founded on the constitutional principles anchored in the political culture and not on the basic ethical orientations of the cultural form of life predominant in that country" (Ibid.: 139). In order to safeguard the democratic state and the rule of law, protection of its political culture is necessary.

Bringing together his thoughts on moral-bound identity and on cultural identity, Habermas distinguishes two levels of collective identity. The first is the lifeworld-related and particular sub-state or cultural level. The second represents the political level that is comprised of universalistic morals and the democratic state. Immigrants may be expected to assimilate to this second level, as Habermas argues, in order to protect the state and the "identity of the political community." Immigrants should not be forced, however, to acculturate or assimilate to cultures on a sub-state level. Upholding or changing a sub-state level culture should be the subject of joint decisions and processes (Ibid.: 135ff.).

In a certain way, it can be claimed that Habermas pursues Okin's criticism of the separation of the public and the private spheres. The criterion of distinction between the two spheres (and between interference and non-interference) is no longer the privacy of practices, which would leave repressive family and intra-collective actions untouched. In another way, however, the problem is reproduced in Habermas's model. If the criterion of distinction between the two levels remains a cultural one, then a general and open level is distinguished from a particular and secluded level whose "internal" affairs are not to be interfered with from "outside." Rather, the distinction of a universal and a particular level of collective identity needs to critically examine dichotomous inside-outside distinctions, static and dynamic dimensions, and the relation of particular and general interests—while simultaneously operating beyond culturally fixed patterns of justification and looking at emancipatory and repressive implications on all sides.

The Normative Exclusions in Collective Identity

Habermas discusses both levels of collective identity (the general, state and the particular, sub-state level) in an orientation toward reflection, democracy, and freedom. This normative reading of collective identity leads to a final, third problem.

There are two possible objections to Habermas's model. First, he assumes a meta-level, on which differences can be solved discursively. This assumption can be criticized as universalism or as Eurocentrism masquerading as universalism (see Hall 2000: 223f.). Second, Habermas ties the protection of collective identity to narrow normative criteria. Similarly, Kymlicka argues in his model of group-differentiated rights that these rights are provided only for liberal and not for illiberal groups. It is, however, this liberal condition that is rejected in communitarian and collective rights arguments. According to these arguments, Eurocentrism constitutes the basis of individual rights and at least partly determines the necessity of collective rights in the first place. This Eurocentrism is reproduced if collective rights are tied to liberal criteria. In contrast, minority collectives and cultures have to be recognized even if they differ from liberalism.[14]

This argumentation would lead to a purely analytical concept of collective identity, liberated from normative implications. If collective identity is committed to neither liberal and open nor homogeneous and secluded content, it can be used as a category of analysis that allows for the examination of mediated constellations of statics and dynamics, of general and particular aspects, and of inside and outside. If, however, collective identity is used or referred to as a law, a human right, a justification, or a legitimization, then the line demarcating the normative level is crossed. The difficulty lies in the fact that a dichotomous separation of a purely analytical use and a normative use is hardly possible.

The discussion of these three problems in concepts of collective identity—its analytical scope, normative content, and normative exclusions—allows for reconsiderations of the question posed herein: Is collective identity, in the logic of mediation, constitutive and uncircumventable for individual identity? The questions of how the repressive elements of collective identity can be dealt with and to what extent collective identity demands for a collective and hostile "other" are related to this.

If nonidentical elements are always part of an identity, and if intermediate relations substitute dichotomies, then it is possible to imagine a collective identity that is conscious of its nonidentical aspects—one that does not depend on repression, homogenization, and dichotomous distinction from the "other." In that case, however, the concept of collective identity has to include the possibility to waive that very identity. In other words, collective identity might be a constituency of individual identity. It is, however, only one of many possible constituting mechanisms. Collective identity can be both repressive and emancipatory, just like the other dimensions of identity. However, its emancipatory opening has to theoretically and practically allow for its own dissolution and replacement by other mechanisms of socialization and identity formation.

In sum, the constellation of individual and collective identity can be a part of identity formation, but—contrary to the other opposite pairs—it does not form an uncircumventable and constitutive relationship.

CONCLUSION

The outlined approach allows a discussion of the various substantial aspects of different concepts of identity and it offers a basis to examine analytical and normative references to identity in the debate on collective human rights. It comes with a triple demand: For an adequate understanding of identity, first, it is crucial to examine its aspects within their respective constellation. The eight elements of the concept of identity— identical/nonidentical, static/dynamic, internal/external, and, with a shift, collective/individual—are antinomic pairs. They are neither dichotomously juxtaposed nor can they simply be summed up. Rather, they interact on different levels. The analytical strength of the concept of identity lies in its inherent contradictive and mediated relationships.

Second, in the antinomic logic of mediation, contradictions do not need to be united in a synthesis. Therefore, the term identity as a general term can be confusing, especially because it reappears in the mediated constellation as the counterpart of the nonidentical. In the following, identity does not stand for a harmonious synthesis or a one-sided hypostasis of one of its elements, but for a dynamic constellation that includes the mediation of identity and the nonidentical as well as the discussed opposite pairs.

Third, a normative reference to identity as a yardstick for criticism or for human rights turns out to be rather difficult. This is because both repressive and emancipatory dimensions can be found on all sides of the mediated constellation. No side (like, for example, dynamic or internal identity) can be severed from its opposite and be emancipatory. On the contrary, severing and hypostasizing one single element has considerable repressive potential. The emancipatory possibilities of identity lie in its mediated constellation, as shown by the work of Derrida and Adorno. Yet, this constellation can appear with different emphases and weight. It can take on emancipatory and repressive forms. It is therefore not possible to refer to *the* antinomic concept of identity as a normative yardstick.

Rather, the focus lies within the question of which relations of stability and dynamics, identity and the nonidentical, internal and external attributions, and the individual and collective identity are more likely to support or suppress emancipation. This question can hardly be answered in general and with a static formula, but needs to be examined empirically and context-related.

It makes sense to use the concept of identity for analytical purposes, but only if relationships of mediation and contradiction are considered. The (antinomic) concept of identity can hardly be used as a normative yardstick, though, because its constellations are too manifold and too nonidentical. However, the concept enables a discussion that considers repressive and emancipatory elements on all sides.

NOTES

1. For an overview of the term's history, see Straub (1998: 76ff.); Gleason (1983: 911); Brubaker/Cooper (2000: 2); Cerulo (1997: 386); Jenkins (2008: 31); Langbaum (1977: 25); Nunner-Winkler (2002: 64f.); Calhoun (1994: 13) and Niethammer (2000). These studies highlight especially Erik Erikson's psychoanalysis (1968) and Erving Goffman's and Anselm Strauss's symbolic interactionism (1963 and 1959, respectively) as important influences for the modern concept of identity.

2. See paradigmatic approaches as diverse as those of Spivak (1999); Mohanty (1997); Melucci (1995); Mouffe (1995); Laclau/Mouffe (2001); Foucault (1984: 95); Bell (1980: 243); or Welsch (2005).

3. For an overview of the rapid spread of the term, see, for example, Gleason (1983: 912ff.); Brubaker/Cooper (2000: 2ff.); Cerulo (1997); and Mackenzie (1978).

4. See Niethammer (2000: 56) and Straub (1998: 78).

5. Kymlicka (1997: 22ff.) uses very similar arguments in reference to cultural majorities and minorities in a state.

6. Derrida develops the idea of the constitutive outside, which can already be found with Hegel (see below), inter alia in Derrida (1976). See also Laclau/Mouffe (2001); Butler (1993); and the discussion in Marchart (2010: 193f.).

7. In poststructuralist and postcolonial theories, the constitution of identity by constructing and excluding "otherness" plays a decisive role, too. See, for example, Bhabha (1994); Said (1978).

8. Note the crucial distinction between, on the one hand, a reflex that is immediate and intuitive, and on the other hand, reflection or reflexivity that refers to conscious, deliberate, thoughtful agency and thinking. For an elaborate distinction based on Hegel, see Müller (2011: 80ff.).

9. Also see Frantz Fanon's discussion on this: "Shame. Shame and self-contempt. Nausea. When people like me, they tell me it is in spite of my color. When they dislike me, they point out that it is not because of my color. Either way, I am locked into the infernal circle" (1986: 88).

10. This is also the basis of Straub's criticism of the fact that "the understanding of the meaning of collectives for the constitution and qualitative definition of personal identity is mixed with the discussion on *collective* identity" (1998: 96; italics in the original).

11. Gayatri Spivak's concept of strategic essentialism, for example, provides for collectives to temporarily unite, without hiding internal differences in the long term, in order to achieve political goals. Spivak thinks her concept to be misunderstood if the essentialism of a collective overshadows its time limit, financial situation, context dependence, and historicity; see Spivak (1988) and Spivak/Danius/Jonsson (1993). For

approaches that consider strategic essentialism—including cultural generalizations or exotic attributions—somewhat helpful, see Kahane (2003), Conklin (1997), Nagle (2009).

12. Jessica Benjamin, for example, rejects the idea of an initial unity between the infant and mother, which is explicative of the linear process of detachment. Instead, she proposes an intersubjective approach to humans as social beings that have desire for the other *as* the other. By this interpretation, relationship dependence and independence exist simultaneously; see Benjamin (1988: 15ff.).

13. At another point, though, Habermas (1974: 101) points out that the idea of the aspired discursive collective identity cannot be either only retrospective or only prospective because the former would be too static and the latter too arbitrary. Similarly, Derrida (1992: 19) suggests that both merely repetitive memories and anything completely new have to be mistrusted.

14. See, for example, McDonald (1991) and Sandel (1982), but also Kukathas (1992), a liberal supporter of group rights.

Part III

Indigenous Human Rights

Parts I and II offer a conceptual-analytical basis for discussing the opportunities and limits of collective human rights. They highlight the theoretical complexity that makes it difficult to find generally valid, universal answers. Therefore, I will empirically examine in part III how demands for collective human rights are articulated, justified, and implemented and what roles the analytical and normative dimensions play in this context.

Demands for indigenous rights are, in various ways, suitable for an empirical analysis of the demands for collective human rights. First, according to proponents of indigenous human rights, they represent a crucial new step in the development of international human rights and a main reason for the prominence and the popularity of collective human rights (Svensson 1992: 365; Messer 1997). Demands for indigenous rights have contributed decisively to a correction of the existing definition of human rights and a restoration of the UN as a human rights agency (Xanthaki 2007: 285). Conversely, human rights contribute to the development of indigenous strategies against state suppression and to the evolution of a new, global indigenous identity (Niezen 2003: xvi). Indigenous rights and international human rights are connected in a symbiotic relationship (Thornberry 2002: 1; Brownlie 1992).

Second, indigenous demands assume a decisive role for all sides of the collective rights controversy: Arguments supporting collective rights see indigenes as an ideal example of marginalized groups that have legitimate claim to collective rights (Anaya 1997; Holder/Corntassel 2002; McDonald 1991). Moderate positions see a solution to the conflict between individual and collective rights in indigenous rights, because they constitute a mediation of both types of rights (Holder/Corntassel 2002; Svensson 1992). And, in the case of indigenous groups, even convinced advocates of individual human rights opt for a collective rights exception (Donnelly 2006: 615).

Third, the underprivileged status of indigenous groups is seen as an indicator for the urgency of indigenous collective rights. It is "widely recognised that indigenous peoples are amongst the most marginalised and vulnerable around the world and their human rights situation is in need of urgent attention" (Xanthaki 2007: 1; see also Anaya 1997: 228; Niezen 2003: 5). They are fighting "one of the longest and most important kinds of struggles over recognition in the world" (Tully 2008a: 223).

Fourth, the debates on indigenous rights contain all the contradictions and problems characterizing the debate on collective rights. Culture, identity, and indigeneity are particularly encouraging controversies. "The public assertion of a separate identity can provoke rejection and counter-reaction" (Thornberry 2002: 14).

All in all, controversies over indigenous rights very clearly demonstrate the potential strengths and weaknesses of extending international human rights to include collective rights. Part III examines and discusses the content, the scope, the history, and the effects and implications of (demands for) indigenous rights. An introduction to the historical and present field of indigenous human rights is followed by an empirical analysis of documents submitted to the United Nations Permanent Forum on Indigenous Issues (UNPFII), a UN agency pivotal for indigenous struggles. This analysis will provide insight into key concepts and their functions, as well as into patterns of justification for and against collective human rights in general and indigenous human rights in particular.

FOUR
Indigenous Rights in History and the Present

This chapter retraces how the "most marginalised and vulnerable" groups (Xanthaki 2007: 1) could become a strong and highly visible international movement. Since the following historical overview cannot account for all aspects of this development, the focus will be on the international institutionalization of the movement. Additionally, the term indigeneity and the central document of international human rights for indigenes, the United Nations Declaration on the Rights of Indigenous Peoples (UNDRIP), will be introduced and examined.

THE INTERNATIONAL INDIGENOUS MOVEMENT

As a result of century-long expropriation, colonization, and discrimination, indigenous groups are currently exposed to multiple disadvantages that vary regionally. Vis-à-vis, within their respective major societies, most indigenous groups are disproportionately poor, unemployed, and illiterate. One third of the world's poorest inhabitants of rural areas are indigenous, and child mortality is higher among indigenes than among non-indigenes. Access to land, property, health care, and educational institutions is often limited. Average labor wages as well as life expectancy are lower for indigenes than for other people. They are more likely to become victims of (forced) prostitution and are affected often more directly and more immediately by expropriation of culturally specific goods and intellectual property, large construction projects, and environmental catastrophes.[1]

The "discovery" and subsequent conquest of the Americas and Australia led to an extensive colonization of indigenous groups during the sixteenth through nineteenth centuries. This development was (to varying degrees depending on location) accompanied by slavery, forced assimilation, land conflicts, expropriations, destructions of local structures, wars, targeted killings, and abuse, "resulting in human suffering and turmoil on a massive scale" (Anaya 1996: 3; see also Batstone 1991; Jennings 1976; Trigger 1992).

Legal contracts with or concerning indigenous groups are historically evident since the beginning of the expropriations. "Agreements supply a missing link in the history of European expansion, for which the other doctrines—papal donation, discovery, conquest, terra nullius, etc.—do not fully account" (Thornberry 2002: 78). Since the end of the fifteenth century, selected theorists such as Las Casas, Vitoria, and Pufendorf, as well as some international treaties, were of the opinion that land belonging to politically organized groups cannot be treated as terra nullius, that is, as uninhabited land. Practice, however, deviated significantly from this point of view. A break in the treatment of indigenous groups occurred toward the end of the nineteenth century when the respective international treaties were formally nullified or overridden by national laws (Lindley 1926; Marks 1991). Different approaches to land expropriation were developed, one of which was the doctrine of terra nullius (Alexandrowicz 1967; Thornberry 2002: 75). It was applied mostly to conflicts between European powers, along with the discovery doctrine (Lindley 1926: 18). Another method was to contractually guarantee protection for indigenous groups in return for their land.

"In this perspective the contemporary emergence of indigenous rights is not so much the progressive development of new law, but rather the restoration of rights previously existing and acknowledged" (Marks 1991: 4f.)—although not without ruptures and contradictions. This correlates with indigenous groups' efforts to enforce their interests not against but within Western law (Sieder/Witchell 2001). The three unsuccessful trials of the *Cayuga Indians*, the *Island of Palmas*, and *Eastern Greenland* in the early twentieth century are, however, symbolic of the persistent powerlessness of indigenous groups within that system (Thornberry 2002: 82ff.).

In the twentieth century, the International Labour Organization (ILO) was one of the first international and non-indigenous organizations to address the situation of indigenes. In 1921, two years after its foundation, it started to conduct studies on indigenous labor and living conditions. In 1957, the ILO passed Convention No. 107, the Convention concerning the Protection and Integration of Indigenous and Other Tribal and Semi-Tribal Populations in Independent Countries, along with the accompanying recommendation No. 104. Convention No. 107 was the first modern, internationally binding document to focus on the needs of indigenes. It was ratified by twenty-seven states and is still valid today in those countries that did not ratify any subsequent conventions (Xanthaki 2007:

49ff.). The radical and controversial stipulations of Convention No. 107 are aimed at overcoming the marginalization of indigenes by improving their participation in the larger, predominant society. It deemed indigenous customs to be obstacles to a successful integration (Ibid.: 51). This perspective has led to criticism, especially because Convention No. 107 lacks regulations for indigenous self-government and "refers to—but does not stress—the importance of collective ownership. This compromise has caused major criticism . . . partly because of its reluctance to go all the distance with collective rights" (Ibid.: 61; see also Rodríguez-Piñero 2005). In retrospect, Convention No. 107 nonetheless played an important role in the development of indigenous rights (Xanthaki 2007: 66).

Institutionalizations of indigenous rights took place within the indigenous movement, too. In 1924, Australian Aborigines founded the Australian Aboriginal Progressive Association, parallel to the (fruitless) efforts of the Council of the Iroquois Confederacy to make its conflict with Canada a subject of discussion in the League of Nations. Indigenous organizations became more visible in the 1960s in Australia, Canada, and the United States, and in the 1970s in Central and South America (Thornberry 2002: 21; Anaya 1996: 46; Wiessner 2008: 1152ff.).[2] Following the initiative of anthropologists and human rights activists, the International Work Group for Indigenous Affairs (IWGIA) was founded in 1968 as a non-governmental organization (NGO). In 1974, the World Council of Indigenous Peoples and the International Indian Treaty Council became the first transnational indigenous NGOs with consultative status at the United Nations Economic and Social Council (ECOSOC) (Igoe 2006: 412; Wilmer 1993). The following year, the doctrine of terra nullius was questioned for the first time by a modern, Western court in the course of the *West Sahara* trial (Thornberry 2002: 84).

An important step in the constitution of the international indigenous movement was the participation of indigenous representatives in an anthropological conference in the Barbados in 1977. Previous meetings, which had taken place as recently as 1971, did not include indigenous representation. The declaration of the 1977 conference demanded for the inclusion of indigenous groups into the UN system. As a result, 150 indigenous representatives participated that same year in the UN Conference on Discrimination against Indigenous Populations in the Americas, where they emphasized the necessity of collective indigenous rights (Meentzen 2007: 36).

Five years earlier, the United Nations Sub-Commission on Prevention of Discrimination and Protection of Minorities had commissioned a report on the situations of indigenous groups that was compiled between 1972 and 1986 by Special Rapporteur José Martínez Cobo (Martínez Cobo 1986). The report not only initiated follow-up studies and more considerations of indigenous concerns, but also became a "standard reference for discussion on the subject of indigenous peoples within the United Nations system" (Anaya 1996: 51). In the course of this development, the Working Group on Indigenous Populations (WGIP), constituting of five experts for five regions, was founded in 1982. Its annual meetings were attended by indigenous groups (independent of their formal status of recognition), government representatives, NGOs, and experts. Their task was to develop and monitor international standards for indigenous rights. The working group was located on the lowest level of the UN hierarchy. While this status reduced visibility, it greatly facilitated attendance by all interested indigenous representatives (Pritchard 1998).

The Cobo Report and the WGIP were important foundations for further developments, and they stimulated visibility for the international indigenous movement. As part of this development, the ILO updated its guidelines and with the participation of the United States and thirty-eight other states, passed Convention No. 169 in 1989: The Convention concerning Indigenous and Tribal Peoples in Independent Countries or, shorter, The Indigenous and Tribal Peoples Convention. As of January 2016, it has been ratified by twenty-two states.[3] Criticisms of Convention No. 107 were weighed carefully during this time, and indigenous institutions were finally being favored over integration. The principle of self-determination was brought to the fore of global consciousness. Indigenous groups were recognized as peoples for the first time, although they still lacked international legal status. Many indigenous activists and theorists see Convention No. 169 as decisive for the development of international rights for indigenes (see, for example, Anaya 1996: 49f.). Others decry the fact that the convention was designed without the immediate participation of indigenous representatives (see Xanthaki 2007: 68ff.).

Between 1985 and 1993, the WGIP worked on a draft for the Declaration on the Rights of Indigenous Peoples, which, after being accepted by the aforementioned sub-commission, was referred to a drafting commission founded for this very purpose. However, it took many more years before the declaration was finally passed by the UN General Assembly.

At the 1993 World Conference on Human Rights in Vienna, the first suggestions regarding a permanent forum for indigenous concerns were made, which were elaborated on in subsequent workshops. In 2000, the United Nations Permanent Forum on Indigenous Issues (UNPFII) was founded. It indirectly replaced the WGIP as a permanent body of the ECOSOC. Since 2002, the UNPFII has held annual meetings where about one thousand government representatives, indigenous representatives, and NGOs exchange ideas and contribute to the mandate of the Forum. The Forum's function is to provide expertise, information, and recommendations that will shed light on indigenous issues. In total, seven world regions are represented by elected Forum members: 1) Africa, 2) Asia, 3) Central America, South America, and the Caribbean, 4) the Arctic, 5) Eastern Europe, Russian Federation, Central Asia, and Transcaucasia, 6) North America, and 7) the Pacific. Eight of the sixteen Forum experts are chosen by governments and eight are chosen by indigenous organizations (through the ECOSOC). The eight experts who are present on behalf of indigenous groups represent each of the seven world regions. There is one extra seat that is rotated among the first three regions for the mandated two-year period.

In 2001, the UN Commission on Human Rights (UNCHR)[4] appointed a Special Rapporteur on the Rights of Indigenous Peoples, who works in close cooperation with the UNPFII. Founded in 2007, the Expert Mechanism on the Rights of Indigenous Peoples (EMRIP) became the institutional successor of the WGIP. Currently, there are three UN bodies concerned with indigenous needs and demands. They are supported by the Second International Decade of the World's Indigenous People (2005–2014), which directly followed the first (1995–2004).

In the early 1990s, African groups appeared as new actors on the stage of the international indigenous movement, which until that point had been dominated by American, Australian, and New Zealander groups. A trigger for this can be seen in the speech of the Maasai activist Moringe ole Parkipuny who, at the 1989 WGIP conference, addressed violations of human rights concerning groups with distinct cultures; particularly the hunter-gatherers and pastoralists in East Africa (Parkipuny 1989). Subsequently, more African activists emphasized parallels between the problems of underprivileged groups in Africa and of indigenous groups on other continents (Hodgson 2009: 4). In 1994, a Maasai NGO joined with Barabaig and Hadzabe NGOs to form a network called the Pastoralists Indigenous NGOs Forum (PINGO) that started to regularly attend UNPFII sessions and became a lobbyist group for other indigenous groups in East and South Africa (Igoe 2006: 400). In this way, African and Asian groups strove for recognition within the movement for indigenous rights. In doing so, they faced several difficulties. "The late entry of Africans into the indigenous peoples' movement posed a structural disadvantage, as they had to engage the longstanding practices, discourses, and assumptions of the U.N. Working Group" (Hodgson 2009: 8). Moreover, the African advances prompted mixed reactions in the international indigenous movement because they led to a far-reaching revaluation of the concept of indigeneity (as discussed below).

The climax of indigenous interests extended into international law is represented by UNDRIP, which was adopted by the UN General Assembly in 2007 by 144 votes in favor and 4 against, with 11 abstentions.[5] This adoption was the result of years of intense negotiations, revisions, and rejections (the last rejection in 2006 in a campaign led by Namibia). The UNDRIP is not a legally binding document, but many activists see it as an important moral and political victory, as a necessary basis for national implementations and further developments, and as a decisive breakthrough for the institutionalization of collective human rights (Anaya/

Wiessner 2009; Allen/Xanthaki 2011; Charters/Stavenhagen 2009; Pelican 2009: 52). Others, however, see it rather as a compromise—especially in comparison with the original 1982 draft of the WGIP—that was reached only by giving up many positions, that does not contain any powerful mechanisms, and whose actual role for the indigenous movement cannot yet be estimated (Watson/Venne 2012; see also Hodgson 2009: 22; Holder/Corntassel 2002). Both sides are united in their criticism of the "implementation gap between laws and practical reality" (Stavenhagen 2009: 367). They argue that the developments described above do not mean that the "movement has secured benefits sufficient to the needs and challenges faced by indigenous peoples. International recognition [counts] not as an end in itself but as a means to empower indigenous communities" (Morgan 2011: 140).

INDIGENEITY AND INDIGENES

The central reference point for demands for indigenous rights is the concept of indigeneity. Yet, its definition, scope, and content are controversial. The conflicts surrounding the category of indigeneity represent crucial arguments for and against collective and indigenous human rights.

An estimated 370 million indigenes live in the world, spread across 90 countries. They speak around 4000 of 7000 languages, 90 percent of which are thought to be endangered (DESA/UNPFII 2009: 1ff.; Thornberry 2002: 15ff.). The same process that made the international indigenous movement more visible also led to a rise in the number of groups that described themselves, or were described by others, as indigenous. Not only did indigenous groups increasingly advocate rights, but also more and more groups have emerged, striving for the status of being an indigenous group in order to claim indigenous rights.[6] This does not, however, justify a dichotomy between authentic versus strategic or agenda-pushing demands. Rather, this is a testament to the mutually constitutive relationship between movements, demands for rights, and granted rights. The juridification of certain spaces or issues is not only a result of a demand for rights, but a frame and a definition of these demands, thus producing its legal subjects.

The designation "indigenous" was preceded by many other labels, some of which still exist. Apart from terms such as tribal people, autochthons, natives, aboriginals, Indians, hunter-gatherers, and nomadic or pastoral peoples, also pejorative terms (like "primitives") circulated. Over time, these labels were pushed back or revaluated (Thornberry 2002: 12f.; Kuper 2003: 389). During colonialism and before its affirmative appropriation, the term "indigenous" described the people born in colonized countries. With demands for recognition of self-descriptions, designations such as "First Nation," "First People," "The People," or "El Pueblo" were established. This magnifies the terms' political brisance: The designation of "indigeneity" is usually defined by a priority clause (the question of who was there first), which in turn shapes the development, conflict, and ultimately the transnational discussion of indigenous human rights.

With the foundation of the WGIP at the very least, the need for a binding definition of indigeneity became obvious. The 1982 constituting session opted, for the time being, against a definition (UN Doc. E/CN 4/ Sub 2/1982/33: para. 42). The second session discussed a working definition that Special Rapporteur Martínez Cobo had given in his report (see Pritchard 1998: 42f.). This definition shaped discussions as a "vague gate keeper" (Thornberry 2002: 33) for many years and is still relevant today:

> Indigenous communities, peoples and nations are those which, having a historical continuity with pre-invasion and pre-colonial societies that developed on their territories, consider themselves distinct from other sectors of the societies now prevailing on those territories, or parts of them. They form at present non-dominant sectors of society and are determined to preserve, develop and transmit to future generations their ancestral territories, and their ethnic identity, as the basis of their continued existence as peoples, in accordance with their own cultural patterns, social institutions and legal system. . . . On an individual basis, an indigenous person is one who belongs to these indigenous populations through self-identification as indigenous (group consciousness) and is recognized and accepted by these populations as one of its members (acceptance by the group). This preserves for these communities the sovereign right and power to decide who belongs to them, without external interference. (Martínez Cobo 1986: para. 379ff.)[7]

When determining indigenous status based on historical continuity, the possession of a distinct self-assigned identity, and the priority argument, mechanisms of inclusion and exclusion, stand out. The chairwoman of the WGIP approved these mechanisms in 1996 (Daes 1996).

These criteria, however, have faced some problems, especially since the 1990s: First, a binding and externally attributing definition regarding self-definition has been criticized (see Pritchard 1998: 43f.; Kingsbury 1998). Second, the priority criterion was challenged by (among other things) the entry of African and Asian groups into the indigenous movement (see Waldron 2002; Hodgson 2002; Barnard/Kenrick 2001). African and some Asian groups faced the problem that the priority criterion applies to *all* non-Europeans in their countries—also to the repressive majority (see African Commission's Working Group on Indigenous Populations/Communities 2009: 33). Because of this, repression, marginalization, and exclusion based on differing cultural lifestyles were brought to the fore in order to be able to identify as part of the international indigenous movement. The IWGIA contributed to this conceptual shift, against the resistance of other influential indigenous activists (Hodgson 2009: 5ff.).

However, eliminating the priority criterion is controversial to this day. Special Rapporteur S. James Anaya, for example, emphasizes that African and Asian indigenous groups "are *indigenous* because their ancestral roots are embedded in the lands on which they live, or would like to live, much more deeply than the roots of more powerful sectors of society" (Anaya 2009a: 1; italics in the original). Special Rapporteur Martínez Cobo, on the other hand, pleads for a clear distinction between indigenous groups, on the one hand, and ethnic minorities or colonized groups (under which he subsumes African and Asian groups), on the other, because the differences between indigenous groups and minorities are so far-reaching that international law should neither treat indigenes as minorities nor vice versa—even if recent developments showed certain overlapping structures (Martínez 1999: para. 69ff.).[8]

Despite this resentment, the integration of selected Asian and African groups into the indigenous movement prevailed. This brought criteria like cultural distinction, historical continuity, political marginalization, and collective self-definition to the fore of indigeneity. Based on this, an open catalogue of criteria is supposed to facilitate dynamics, encourage development, and leave room for negotiations regarding international law. Yet this catalogue is not only upheld against states and majorities, but also against groups that designate themselves as oppressed and distinct minorities and are seen as a threat in the competition for international attention. "The question of who is indigenous . . . is a complex amalgam of power, logic and right, in which international law itself plays a constructive (or deconstructive) role through recognition processes and incentives for groups to access international norms through configuration or re-configuration as indigenous" (Thornberry 2002: 60).[9] This double protection against majorities and other minorities refers to a central concept—the concept of peoples: "Aboriginal peoples would no longer be erroneously assimilated to some sort of minority or unrealistic province-like status [if regarded] in this distinctive and historically accurate way, as 'peoples'" (Tully 2008a: 238).

The designation as *a people* is as desired as it is disputed. One example for this is the choice of names of UN bodies and UN declarations on indigenous issues. The WGIP talks of indigenous *populations*, the UNPFII is searching for indigenous *issues*, and the (much older) NGO IWGIA is concerned with indigenous *affairs*. The special rapporteur, the expert commission, the UN world conferences, and the declaration of 2007, on the other hand, speak of peoples.

The letter s that transfers "people" into "peoples" represents all the issues that are at stake regarding demands for collective rights and collective self-determination (see Thornberry 2002: 41f.). To Special Rapporteur Anaya, indigenous groups are " *peoples* in that they comprise distinct communities with a continuity of existence and identity that links them to the communities, tribes, or nations of their ancestral past" (Anaya

2009a: 1; italics in the original).[10] The aspect of consanguinity, which is part of the recourse to ancestors as well as the distinction from other groups, is supposed to prove that an indigenous group is a people.

The significance of the category "people" for indigenous groups, however, is also doubted. "If indigenous peoples are peoples, why qualify them by calling them indigenous? If they are not peoples, why call them peoples, all the while endeavoring to distinguish them from minorities" (Schulte-Tenckhoff 2012: 76)? States fear, in light of the international right of peoples to self-determination, that recognizing "indigenous peoples" might lead to far-reaching demands for self-determination and secession (see Thornberry 2002: 41ff.; Xanthaki 2007: 71f.). The ILO Convention No. 169—one of the first international documents using the term "people" for indigenous groups—was adopted only with the addendum that the term "*peoples* in this Convention shall not be construed as having any implications as regards the rights which may attach to the term under international law" (Article 1.3; italics in the original).

Conceptual critics, on the other hand, link the concept of peoples to the "very general European belief that true citizenship is a matter of ties of blood and soil" (Kuper 2003: 395).[11] Moreover, the concept produces a distinction between allochthonous and autochthonous groups that leads to further inequalities.

> The precarious status of San peoples in southern Africa, for example, shows first that it is not always possible to identify who is indigenous and who is not, secondly that those peoples best placed to claim the privileges due to indigenes are not necessarily those most in need of assistance, and thirdly that a focus on indigenousness may well reinforce the very structures of discrimination that disadvantage these peoples in the first place. (Suzman 2003: 399)

In summary, the controversies over the terms "indigeneity" and "peoples" cover a wide spectrum. On one side, the terms are criticized fundamentally for being deterministic and excluding, and for producing new hierarchies by, for example, marginalizing other disadvantaged parts of the population. On the other side, indigeneity is hypostasized as a clearly distinguishable objective factor that suffers from "total preservation syndrome" (Brownlie 1992: 74).

In the middle of the spectrum, the following approach has developed:

> Although "indigenous peoples" is not a valid concept in anthropological [or political science or legal (J. M.)] analysis, it nonetheless has reality and meaning for those who identify themselves as indigenous. This applies to [all those groups] whose situation cannot be ignored merely because their claims to indigeneity may be arguable. (Pelican 2009: 54)

The mechanisms and discourses coming with the term *indigenous peoples* can be politically and strategically powerful. Being identified as indigenous can give access to national and international law and resources. At the same time, the concept produces inclusion and exclusion. It differentiates between minorities and indigenous groups, and between autochthonously and allochthonously marginalized groups, thus (re-)producing inequalities.

THE UNDRIP

The central reference point of demands for indigenous rights is (apart from ILO Convention No. 169) the United Nations Declaration on the Rights of Indigenous Peoples. It is the basis of judicial decisions and a benchmark for numerous evaluations, programs, and recommendations (Anaya 2009b: 105). To become legally binding, it has to be translated and implemented into national law. Another way to look at the UNDRIP's juridification lies in the subsequent development of binding UN agreements. Anaya even argues that the UNDRIP should be seen as customary international law, because it was adopted by the majority of states and contains many norms that were formulated before in other, legally binding documents (Anaya 2009b: 79f.; Anaya/Wiessner 2009: 101f.). This diagnosis, however, is everything but uncontroversial (Morgan 2011: 146).

In terms of content, the UNDRIP is currently the furthest reaching international document on indigenous rights. It is the result of years of tough negotiations and compromises. It shapes the character of indigenous demands and at the same time, is the subject of controversial discussions and interpretation. In the next section, I will outline its key points as a basis for assessing the results of the ensuing empirical analysis.

Indigeneity as Collective Identity and Cultural Practice

The interconnected concepts of identity, indigeneity, and culture are relevant for the majority of rights formulated in the UNDRIP. Article 2 contains the right of indigenes to freedom from discrimination, especially "based on their indigenous origin or identity." Article 8 broaches the issue of the destruction of "their integrity as distinct peoples, or of their cultural values or ethnic identities." States are supposed to develop mechanisms to prevent or compensate for these destructions. According to Article 11.1, indigenes have "the right to practice and revitalize their cultural traditions and customs," including those from the past, whose destruction is to be compensated for, as stated in Article 11.2. Articles 12 through 16 and Article 31 specify this right in terms of future generations, education, the media and language, and cultural heritage and knowledge. Finally, Article 33.1 formulates a right to identity: "Indigenous peoples have the right to determine their own identity or membership in accordance with their own customs and traditions."

Instead of giving a static definition of indigeneity, the UNDRIP emphasizes the right to self-identification—similar to ILO Convention No. 169. This approach is based on the working definition (cited above) from the Cobo-Report (DESA/UNPFII 2009: 6f.). The term identity, which is used in the UNDRIP in relation to both individuals and groups or peoples, can hardly be defined bindingly, as was shown in chapter 3. The same is true for the term culture, which is closely tied to identity in the UNDRIP. Thus, indigeneity, culture, and identity can be read and interpreted in various ways. While notes on specific customs, parenting, and language issues are formulated in detail, the right to self-identification, for example, leads to considerable legal but also conceptual problems: If, as discussed in chapter 3, identity is constituted by external and internal factors, and is defined differently on the individual level as opposed to the collective level, then the right to a purely internal (i.e., subjective and intra-collective) determination of identity clearly has limits.

In light of a concept of culture in which conscious and unintended processes are mediated, the UNDRIP's reference to past, present, and future cultural elements as subjects of protection and preservation (Article 11.1) also bears difficulties: It touches, among other things, the freedom of choice and autonomy of future generations.

Indigenous Autonomy and Self-Determination

Indigenous self-determination is regarded as the "key to the implementation of solutions for their problems," as the "heart" and the "cornerstone" of the UNDRIP, and as the essential precondition for all other indigenous rights (see Xanthaki 2007: 131; Wiessner 2008). It constitutes, on the other hand, the "most debated point of contention" as well (Pulitano 2012: 16). Demands for political, social, or cultural self-determination, self-government, sovereignty, and/or autonomy (to different degrees depending on the case) are all summarized by the concept of self-determination. This term is one of the main reasons why states maintain hesitant or dismissive attitudes toward the UNDRIP; it is feared for its potential to promote demands for secession and to disintegrate a state's territory. Article 3 of the UNDRIP states: "Indigenous peoples have the right to self-determination. By virtue of that right they freely determine their political status and freely pursue their economic, social and cultural development." Articles 4 and 5 specify the right to self-determination as "autonomy or self-government in matters relating to their internal and local affairs" (Article 4) and as "right to maintain and strengthen their distinct political, legal, economic, social and cultural institutions" (Article 5). Furthermore, indigenous groups should be able to define their institutions, determine who is a member of their group (Article 33.2), maintain their legal systems (Article 34), and determine the individual's responsibility toward the community (Article 35). In addition, Article 46.1 excludes interpretations "which would dismember or impair, totally or in part, the territorial integrity or political unity of sovereign and independent States."

This constitutes an approach to self-determination that takes into account national fears of secession and that, at the same time, is broad enough to give leeway to different indigenous demands (Wiessner 2008: 1166). This simultaneity is facilitated mostly by the concept of internal self-determination (see Anaya 2009c: 60f.). The concept of internal self-determination aims at developing distinct mechanisms within a state and thus preventing secession, with one example being a group's right to deal with internal issues according to its own traditions and in its own courts or institutions of arbitration. Internal self-determination is "the right of these peoples to negotiate freely their political status and representation in the States in which they live" (Daes 1993: 9) — without thereby developing a third sovereignty or a power comparable to that of the state (Wiessner 2008: 1169). "This process does not require the assimilation of individuals, as citizens like all others, but the recognition and incorporation of distinct peoples in the fabric of the State, on agreed terms" (Daes 1993: 9, see also Anaya 2009c: 62). The UNDRIP safeguards this incorporation within the fabric of the state with the right to a nationality (Article 6), rights "established under applicable international and domestic labor law" (Article 17), and the right to "participate fully, if they so choose, in the political, economic, social and cultural life of the State" (Article 5).

However, from a conceptual point of view, there is no unambiguous distinction between internal and external self-determination. According to Sarah Pritchard, internal self-determination means that an issue is addressed without external interference and that relevant external decisions require indigenous approval. External self-determination, on the other hand, contains the possibility for indigenous groups to establish their own networks within the international community, to negotiate, and to manage international funds (Pritchard 2001: 335f.). Other approaches define external self-determination as freedom from external interference and internal self-determination as self-government (Eide 1986). James Tully, on the other hand, criticizes the concept of internal self-determination, in the sense of solving internal issues internally, as an extension of the colonial system of *indirect rule*—which can be overcome only by indigenous peoples having their own constitution instead of being bound to the respective constitution of the state they live in (Tully 2008b: 284ff.). In general, the conceptual amalgamation of the two levels indicates that internal and external self-determination represent "a uniform law in different legal relations" (Pritchard 2001: 344).

Lands, Territories, and Resources

A third crucial and controversial subject regarding demands for indigenous rights is the possession and disposal of lands, territories, and resources. The UNDRIP directly and indirectly addresses this issues in various articles. The key article, however, is Article 26:

1. Indigenous peoples have the right to the lands, territories and resources which they have traditionally owned, occupied or otherwise used or acquired.
2. Indigenous peoples have the right to own, use, develop and control the lands, territories and resources that they possess by reason of traditional ownership or other traditional occupation or use, as well as those which they have otherwise acquired.
3. States shall give legal recognition and protection to these lands, territories and resources. Such recognition shall be conducted with due respect to the customs, traditions and land tenure systems of the indigenous peoples concerned. (UNDRIP, Article 26)

Additionally, Article 27 states that trials and decisions regarding indigenous lands are to be fair, independent, transparent, and to allow indigenous participation. Article 32 confirms that the use of land, territories, and resources shall be self-determined and/or based on the indigenous free, prior, and informed consent (FPIC). Expropriated lands, territories, and resources have to be compensated for appropriately (Article 28) and indigenes are not to be removed from their land forcefully and without FPIC (Article 10). Article 8.2b-c reformulates these indigenous rights as active duties of the state, which has to provide effective mechanisms to prevent expropriation and forced relocation. Additionally, indigenes have the right to an intact environment (Article 29) and to cross borders (Article 36). They have the right to not have military bases and operations on their territories—except if this is in the public interest or conceded to by the indigenes affected (Article 30).

These rights are supported significantly by Article 37, which demands for the recognition of and adherence to older treaties and agreements. In North America for example, these agreements are an important part of the historical relationship between indigenes and non-indigenes, and they are mostly concerned with rights of use and property of lands, territories, and resources. These agreements are crucial to demands for self-determination, too: Historical negotiations, relations, and treaties are seen as examples of how indigenes acted and were treated, and should act and be treated again, as sovereign nations (Martínez 1999).

Another source of legitimation for indigenous land rights is the "distinctive spiritual relationship with their traditionally owned or otherwise occupied and used lands, territories, waters and coastal seas and other resources" (UNDRIP, Article 25). This provision is intended to allow indigenous groups to address historical expropriations, even if they have no (written) contracts with colonial powers or if their territories were expropriated based on the terra nullius doctrine. However, the concept of spiritual relationships goes beyond such pragmatic considerations. Lands, territories, and resources are closely tied to cultural identity, assuming that "forcing them to hand over such land is tantamount to allowing them to be exterminated. In a word it is ethnocide" (Martínez Cobo 1986, Annex 4: 32).

The issue of lands, territories, and resources was and is being discussed controversially—in the drafting process of the UNDRIP as well as in its application and implementation. Particularly challenged is the collective rights component within the demand for collective land ownership and the distinction between material and spiritual concepts of land use (see Martínez Cobo 1986; Daes 2001). Using "distinctive spiritual relationships" as a yardstick to differentiate between indigenous groups and other disadvantaged groups (re-)produces exclusion and inequality related to land use and land property (Errico 2009: 69; Pritchard 2001: 46). The question of who is designated the power of decision-making is relevant, too, as this statement made at the WGIP conference in Geneva shows:

> States act as if they could grant us land rights only by means of compromise. To us, however, they do not have the power to decide on land, earth, or the weather. Yet, they do dispose of the brutality and of the military and economic power to keep us away from the basic things in life. (cited in Gesellschaft für bedrohte Völker n.d.: para. 3.5.1)

This question poses a fundamental conflict of interest that even the UNDRIP cannot easily resolve. Comprehensive land demands would not only necessitate new maps and borders but also broad displacements and relocations of current populations.

The 1997 decision of the Canadian Supreme Court in *Delgamuukw vs. British Columbia* is a landmark in international law. The decision seeks to deal with contradicting national and indigenous interests. The court acknowledged old treaties and a formerly existing indigenous sovereignty as legitimation for current land claims, thereby reaffirming corresponding UNDRIP articles. The indigenous claims can, however, be restricted (and this, too, is in accordance with the provisions of the UNDRIP) if there are good reasons and if indigenes were consulted prior to and compensated after the decision. A precise definition of what constitutes a "good reason," however, again leaves plenty of room for interpretation. A second important court decision is concerned with resource conflicts in which, aside from indigenous groups and states, transnational corporations are increasingly involved. The Supreme Court of the Philippines ruled that, based on the constitutional rights of the state, indigenous claims to national resources are valid only on the surface of the earth (Errico 2009: 69).

These rulings, which will not stand alone in the near future, show that the UNDRIP provides not only a yardstick and framework, but also that its implementation depends on judicial and executive interpretations and applications.

Collective Rights

In all three areas discussed so far—cultural identity, self-determination, and lands, territories, and resources—collective rights play an important role. For the indigenous movement, collective rights are seen as the "only way for their survival and development" (Xanthaki 2007: 13; similarly: Pritchard 2001: 200) and as "one of the most important purposes" of the UNDRIP (statement of an indigenous representative, made in 1989, cited in Xanthaki 2007: 13). Although the extent and importance of the collective rights dimension is discussed in various ways, the canon of the international indigenous movement almost unanimously adheres to the demand to add collective rights to indigenous human rights.

International law recognizes a collective component, as long as peoples are granted self-determination. This corresponds to a ruling by the Human Rights Committee in *Kitok vs. Sweden*, in 1988 (UN Doc. A/43/40 1988), according to which an individual cannot file a complaint based on a violation of the right to self-determination as granted by Article 27 ICCPR because it is not an individual right (see Pritchard 2001: 204). Meanwhile, the status of indigenous groups as a people and the definition of a people remain disputed.

Culture, indigeneity, and identity are seen in many demands as collective goods that provide the basis for collective rights for self-determined indigenous peoples. "Culture, ordinarily, is an outgrowth of a collectivity, and, to that extent, affirmation of a cultural practice is an affirmation of the associated group" (Anaya 1996: 101).

Lands, territories, and resources are often understood as inalienable and undividable. Land ownership is possible in many indigenous communities only collectively. Correspondingly, individual entitlement to land is seen as a danger to the commons (Xanthaki 2007: 31; Speed 2006).

In all three subject areas, the collective dimension can conflict with individual rights; for example, if individuals are not interested in reproducing cultural practices or learning an indigenous language, or if they want to sell their share of the land (e.g., in order to pursue a different way of life with the proceeds), or if they want to self-determine their affiliation to a cultural community. This last possibility was tried in the landmark decisions *Canada (AG) vs. Lavell* (1974) and *Santa Clara Pueblo vs. Martinez* (1978) (see Valencia-Weber/Zuni 1995; Eisenberg 2003). Both trials were concerned with exclusion from indigenous communities on gender grounds. Lavell and Martinez are indigenous women who married exogamously and were—with their children—subsequently excluded from their respective indigenous groups and from all rights and land titles that came with it, even after they divorced their husbands. The fact that these rules of exclusion did not apply to exogamous married men was crucial to the trials. Santa Clara Pueblo was, at the time, already largely self-governed and the membership rule was an indigenous one. The court did not challenge the practice in order to respect an indigenous self-definition. Although the membership rule in the Canadian trial was based on national law, the court did not change it. However, the trial of *Sandra Lovelace vs. Canada* (1977–1981) successfully challenged the respective law.

The three trials were the subject of intense controversies not only at their time. The indigenous practices were criticized for their gendered and sexist inequality. Feminist criticisms of the membership rules, in turn, were accused of lacking an understanding of indigenous thinking, which supposedly holds different ideas of gender relations than Western feminism.[12] The idea of gender equality conflicted with indigenous (collective) self-government, self-definition, and self-determination.

The trials show two things: first, a comprehensive concept of self-determination contains the danger of individuals being insufficiently protected from intra-group arbitrariness and inequalities; second, a narrow version of internal self-determination is tied to existing state structures, which can be repressive as well.

Likewise, being bound to collective land ownership may impose gendered, financial, and job-related limitations on individuals.

> A solution will have to surrender the (reactionary) assumption that in order to retain their identity, all members of the tribe must adopt traditional kinds of occupation which are land-consuming. . . . Why is it assumed that the only way Indians can retain their identity and tradition is by adhering to the same kinds of occupations their forefathers, or foremothers, pursued? . . . These assumptions are particularly damaging for women. (Tamir 1999: 51)

The UNDRIP does consider potential conflicts between collective and individual rights. For example, it states that indigenous rights have to be compatible with the UN Charter (UNDRIP, Article 46.1), the Universal Declaration of Human Rights (UNDRIP, articles 1, 34, 46.2), with international standards of human rights and basic freedoms, and with the "principles of justice, democracy, respect for human rights, equality, non-discrimination, good governance and good faith" (UNDRIP, Article 46.3). Gender aspects are addressed in Article 44 that stresses the rights of individuals: "All the rights and freedoms recognized herein are equally guaranteed to male and female indigenous individuals" (UNDRIP, Article 44). Article 22.2 specifies: "States shall take measures, in conjunction with indigenous peoples, to ensure that indigenous women and children enjoy the full protection and guarantees against all forms of violence and discrimination" (UNDRIP, Article 22.2).

All these premises do not necessarily have to, but potentially might conflict with demands to conserve indigenous traditions, culture, identity, lands, and self-determination. This is where the general debate on collective rights continues.

NOTES

1. All information is taken from IFAD nd and DESA/UNPFII 2009 that offer comprehensive and country-specific statistics. For more data, see Hall/Patrinos (2012) and Stephens et al. (2005).

2. In the early 1960s, for example, indigenous peoples in the United States organized themselves in the National Indian Youth Council and the American Indian Movement (see Anaya [1996: 61]), the latter of which became famous during its occupation of the historic site of Wounded Knee in 1973. For local developments of indigenous movements, see Oliveira (2009: 1f.); van Cott (1995); Yashar (2005); Gray (1997) for South America; Igoe (2006); Hodgson (2009, 2002) for Africa; Maynard (2007); McGinness (1991) for Australia; and Tyson (2010); Nathan/Kelkar/Walter (2004); Kingsbury (1998); Roy Burman/Verghese (1998) for Asia.

3. These are (with their respective year of ratification): Argentina (2000), Bolivia (1991), Brazil (2002), the Central African Republic (2010), Chile (2008), Colombia (1991), Costa Rica (1993), Denmark (1996), Dominican Republic (2002), Ecuador (1998), Fiji (1998), Guatemala (1996), Honduras (1995), Mexico (1990), Nepal (2007), the Netherlands (1998), Nicaragua (2010), Norway (1990), Paraguay (1993), Peru (1994), Spain (2007), and Venezuela (2002).

4. The UN Commission on Human Rights was replaced in 2006 by the United Nations Human Rights Council that took over most of the UNCHR's tasks.

5. Australia, New Zealand, Canada, and the United States, the four countries that voted against the declaration, changed their stance in subsequent years and now officially support the UNDRIP. The abstentions came from Azerbaijan, Bangladesh, Bhutan, Burundi, Georgia, Kenya, Colombia, Nigeria, the Russian Federation, Samoa, and Ukraine.

6. See Niezen (2003); Canessa (2007, 2006); Guenther (2006).

7. Additionally, the definition names specific criteria: "This historical continuity may consist of the continuation, for an extended period reaching into the present of one or more of the following factors: a) Occupation of ancestral lands, or at least of part of them; b) Common ancestry with the original occupants of these lands; c) Culture in general, or in specific manifestations (such as religion, living under a tribal system, membership of an indigenous community, dress, means of livelihood, lifestyle, etc.); d) Language (whether used as the only language, as mother-tongue, as the habitual means of communication at home or in the family, or as the main, preferred, habitual, general or normal language); e) Residence on certain parts of the country, or in certain regions of the world; f) Other relevant factors."

8. For a similar assessment, see Schulte-Tenckhoff (2012), and for a critical one, Kymlicka (2011a).

9. For indigenous groups' privileges vis-à-vis so-called allochthonous groups as a means of referring to indigeneity and tradition, see Ranger (1992).

10. Anaya makes use here of a common definition of the term "people" that was first given by a UN study. It emphasizes the relation to the land and the existence of a distinct identity; see Cristescu (1981: para. 279).

11. For an opposing view, see Kenrick/Lewis (2004); Barnard (2004).

12. See the discussions in Archambault (2011); Bell (1992); Fredericks (2010); Nagengast (1997); Spinner-Halev (2001); Richards (2005), as well as the more general contributions in Cohen/Howard/Nussbaum (1999).

FIVE
Indigenous Demands in the United Nations

Is it really true that "whether we like it or not, identity and culture, and their representation, are self-declared priority issues for most indigenous people" (Guenther 2006: 18)? So far, this book has shown that concepts of culture and identity decisively shape the discussion on collective human rights. In their (constitutive) blurriness, these concepts also leave plenty of room for interpretation, effects, and implications. Evidently, culture and identity, as extended by the category of indigeneity, play an important role in the development and justification of international indigenous rights. Using the example of indigenous rights, in this chapter I will empirically examine the potentials and limits of collective human rights. In this context, heterogeneous and overlapping arguments and their implications become especially clear.

The focus of analysis will be on indigenous organizations because non-state organizations and actors within the civil society are of increasing importance for the development of transnational norms and discourses (Morgan 2011: 139ff.; Alston 2005; Andreopoulos/Arat/Juviler 2006). Additionally the analysis must focus on demands for indigenous rights at a global level. On an international scale, the efforts and accompanying difficulties of bringing together diverse interests under the concept of indigeneity become more visible than they would be in a local-based case study.

In this chapter, I will focus, first, on the issues and conflicts in discussions on indigenous rights. Second, I will analyze how, in what contexts, and with what (normative) premises and effects culture, identity, and collective rights are referred to. Third, I will address the question of which mechanisms of inclusion and exclusion are tied to respective argumentative patterns.

The most important international body concerned with indigenous issues, the United Nations Permanent Forum on Indigenous Issues (UNPFII), is the institutional framework for this empirical examination. The UNPFII is an advisory body to the Economic and Social Council (ECOSOC). Alongside the Special Rapporteur and the Expert Mechanism, it is the central UN agency mandated to deal with indigenous issues. The annual UNPFII sessions held in New York with more than a thousand participants are an important space for NGOs and indigenous as well as government representatives to meet, talk, and network. The sessions proceed similarly every year. Recurring agenda items (some of them have fixed numbers) are the opening session (01), the discussion of the special theme (03),[1] the comprehensive dialogue with United Nations agencies and funds, and the dialogue with the Special Rapporteur. In 2009, the agenda was changed significantly: Up until then, agenda item 04 consisted of six sub-items whose subject was the implementation of the respective recommendations made by the Forum.[2] In 2009, the question of the implementation of the UNDRIP was introduced as agenda item 04a instead. This change of procedure acknowledged and upgraded the status of the UNDRIP as an international basis for indigenous rights (together with ILO Convention No. 169). At this point of the agenda, indigenous, governmental, and NGO representatives, as well as UN institutions, have the annual opportunity to present their reports, complaints, objections, or declarations.

Agenda item 04a of every UNPFII session includes the topic of indigenous human rights in its broadest sense. It offers a chance to comprehend the complexity of indigenous human rights issues and to examine how culture and identity are referred to, as well as how patterns of justification are constituted and what matters indigenous groups are concerned with.

I chose agenda item 04a for the empirical analysis for the following reasons. First, the item connects the UNPFII and the UNDRIP, thereby uniting the cornerstones of international indigenous rights and indigenous demands for rights, which are the result of years of indigenous struggles and international discussions. Furthermore, the framing (Finnemore/Sikkink 1998: 897) and institutionalization of norms within the UNDRIP shape the discourse and discussions on indigenous rights.

A second reason for the relevance of item 04a lies in the broadness of its content. It is unparalleled by other agenda items of UNPFII sessions, due to their focus on selected key themes.

Third, the annual recurrence of the item since 2009 allows for a diachronic examination that can show potential changes over time.

Fourth, an agenda item on the implementation of indigenous human rights promises insights into correspondences and gaps between human rights terminology and reality.

During the course of each UNPFII session, all documents are published in the online documentation system DoCip and linked to the UNPFII website.[3] Most of the documents are in English, French, or Spanish. The orally presented statements thereby become "open, published artefacts" (Scott 1990: 14ff.). They are stable, representative, transparent, and verifiable (see Scott 1990: 6; Flick 2007: 325f.).

The material examined in this study consists of the documents produced under agenda item 04a of the UNPFII sessions that are available in the DoCip archive. A full survey of the documents from the two crucial 2009 and 2012 sessions (at which agenda item 04a was a key player) represents a sufficient spectrum for a theoretical saturation.[4]

The selected documents do "not represent a simple display of facts or reality. Rather, they were always compiled by someone (or by an institution) for a particular (practical) purpose" (Flick 2007: 324). This construction of realities by patterns of justification and argumentation will now be analyzed both structuring and interpretively. The aim is to examine the different dimensions of indigenous rights as well as their conflicts and their (inherent) contradictions.[5]

The material from agenda item 04a consists of scanned original documents that bear a handwritten note of categorization, made by the UN administration.[6] All texts were professionally written and edited; they do not represent spontaneous reactions. They follow the dictated style of conciseness and purpose, a fact that became clear during the participant observation. The authors can be categorized in three large groups:

1. *Governments* present reports and statements in which they report on measures of UNDRIP implementation. They act as either permanent UN representatives or as delegates. In the following, I will count government institutions and ministries as part of this group.
2. *Indigenous organizations* account for the group that delivers by far the most interventions and statements. This group is made up of large indigenous umbrella organizations, indigenous NGOs, indigenous entities of administration (parliaments etc.), and other non-institutionalized representatives of particular indigenous groups.
3. *UN agencies* amount to the third largest group of authors. In the documents, they present (accountability) reports and interventions. The group consists of UN agencies, UN specialized agencies, UN bodies, UN committees, and UN funds.

Some scattered authors belong to neither of the three groups. They represent non-indigenous NGOs, churches, and international organizations. Their presence at the forum is, however, very limited and they usually act only in cooperation with representatives of one of the three large groups.

In an abductive categorization process, I reconstructed a total of six subject areas that constitute the central points of reference of indigenous and other stakeholders' documents:

1. Culture, identity, and indigeneity
2. Lands, territories, and resources
3. Participation and self-determination
4. Individual human rights
5. Collective rights
6. Internal group differences

I will examine all six areas regarding their content and their justification. They contain partially contradicting functions, contexts, intentions, and interpretations. The possibility mentioned above that references identity and culture can support or marginalize differing argumentations. This will thereby be empirically explicated and outlined by looking at the respective effects and implications. I will also examine how explicit and implicit presuppositions not only exclude other concepts, but, in extreme cases, undermine the very argument they are used in as well. Besides the patterns of argumentation, justification, and presupposition, the mechanisms of inclusion and exclusion will be at the core of the following analysis of the six areas.

CULTURE, IDENTITY, AND INDIGENEITY

Since the concepts of culture, identity, and indigeneity are so closely interrelated in the 04a-documents, I will examine them jointly.

The 04a-documents refer to the field of culture/identity/indigeneity on two levels. On the first level, culture/identity/indigeneity constitute the *goals and contents* of the demands and statements. On the second level, they are *legitimized and justified*.

The *content-oriented level* contains three key aspects: diversity, distinction, and exclusion.

Cultural Plurality

The first key aspect comprises the values diversity and plurality, seen as crucial functions of culture/identity/indigeneity. This standard motive appears in many documents, both from government and indigenous representatives, and sometimes even reappears verbatim. Government statements use plurality, diversity, and/or multiculturalism as an aim of state actions that requires no further explanations. The Brazilian representative, for example, states:

> Brazil . . . has no longer adopted policies of forced contact, neither expects that contacted people abandon their ways of life and distinc-

tiveness as indigenous peoples. On the contrary, we protect indigenous peoples' social and cultural diversity, as a core value of our national policy on the rights of indigenous peoples. (pf12regina248: 5)[7]

This document uses the protection of diversity as a unique and distinctive feature—not only in dissociation from other states, but also (relevant to election campaigns) from former governments of Brazil. This, however, changes the purpose and content of the protection of diversity: Indigenous groups become a resource for the government and for the label of diversity. Beyond that, and aside from cultural diversity, the statement considers social diversity as worthy of protection. In the name of social diversity, different standards of living, poverty, and a lack of infrastructure can be consolidated. Although the improvement of indigenous living conditions might be a (side) effect of diversity oriented politics, too, the usage of diversity as a resource contains a protectionist and patriarchal approach to indigeneity that leaves the state's power structures untouched.

In other statements, diversity is referred to as existing in close relation with other values. Spain names "the goals of social cohesion and consolidation of democratic governability," which it hopes to gain by acknowledging "ethnic and cultural diversity" (pf12maria238: 3).[8]

Documents of indigenous organizations and NGOs regard the recognition of diversity to be the basis for "peaceful coexistence between all the peoples of the world" (pf09tupac396: 1)[9] and for the "political functionality" (pf12dietrix293: 2) of indigenous communities. Cultural diversity is addressed through governmental claims and also via indigenous groups themselves: "We recommend: . . . that the Forum and the indigenous peoples support indigenous processes in different countries and that states be declared intercultural and plurinational" (pf09william123: 2; see also pf09ernesto127).[10] Indigenes are supposed to reproduce and preserve culture/identity/indigeneity by holding onto what is marked as indigenous.

Cultural Distinction

A second key aspect becomes apparent in the reference to distinction. Culture/identity/indigeneity are used to distinguish indigenous groups from the larger societies they are sharing a state with; the goal is to preserve this function:

> Indigenous peoples . . . enjoy special rights because of their cultural patterns, which distinguish them from other cultures. (pf12pablo237: 2, similar: pf09jorge195: 1)[11]

> God gives each of us, through our ancestors, *one country, one language* and *one culture,* and He reminds us not to *sell* the land that He has given

us, and not to *move* the boundaries which mark the parcels put in place by our ancestors. (pf12evariste276b: 6; italics in the original)

At this point, the concept of peoples becomes relevant again: Indigenes protest that institutions like the UNPFII or WGIP do not speak of indigenous *peoples*, thereby reproducing the colonial refusal to recognize indigenes as (distinct) peoples (pf09tupac396, pf12dalee223). In this context, indigenous representatives at the 2012 session repeatedly demanded to rename the Permanent Forum from "Indigenous Issues" to "Indigenous Peoples."[12]

Related to this is the complaint in several indigenous documents of not being officially recognized as distinct indigenous groups by their respective governments.[13] This lack of official recognition means that they cannot claim any indigenous rights on a national level.

As a sign of the cultural particularity and distinction of indigenous groups, a way of life in harmony with nature and a concept of "mother earth" is often emphasized.[14] A distinguishing feature of indigenous culture that relates to this is sustainable development and biodiversity. According to the respective documents, a special connection to nature shapes "the traditional lifestyles and culture of indigenous peoples—for example; biodiversity, conservation, and sustainable development [are] of crucial importance to indigenous peoples" (pf09eva102: 2).[15]

This mixture of strategic and nonstrategic approaches focuses on indigeneity as a distinct way of life. This is based on a concept of cultures as secluded, genuinely different, and not compatible with one another.

"Indigenous is he who lives indigenous, thinks indigenous, and is not ashamed of being indigenous" (pf09sara109: 1).[16] It is argued that a cultural, indigenous, and distinctive identity needs to be (legally) protected and respected. Also, this identity needs to reflect on the everyday life of indigenes. This demand manifests a powerful imperative for every indigenous individual: Culture/identity/indigeneity have to be actively lived and reproduced by all individuals for the collective to maintain its claim to culture/identity/indigeneity. Individual deviations from indigenous ways of life would, in this approach, fundamentally challenge the interests of the indigenous community.

In yet another approach to distinction, distinction and difference are hypostatized in a way that rejects concepts of equality. A coalition of Congolese indigenous organizations states:

> The Declaration on the Rights of Indigenous Peoples . . . is far from being implemented . . . by . . . our government that, in its constitution, preaches equality of all citizens, without admitting its war against particularism. . . . This is why we recommend . . . to apply positive discrimination against indigenous peoples according to their own politics. (pf09stephane034: 1f.)[17]

Here, the representatives accuse the government of abusing the constitutional norm of equality as a strategy to disregard distinct indigenous culture, thus promoting inequality and injustice. Instead of equality, positive discrimination in the form of particular rights is seen as mandatory in order to preserve cultural and political distinction.

The Republic of Congo accused here, claims, in turn, to implement programs for indigenes designed to improve different aspects "of their environment, thus respecting their cultures and traditions." At the same time, the government reminds the delegates that "indigenous peoples have the same rights as any other community" and that "equality of opportunity" needs to be preserved for "all inhabitants of the earth" (pf09valentine121: 2f.).[18]

France makes its understanding of distinction very clear and emphasizes, in reference to the New Caledonian Kanak people and other Melanesian groups, that it supports and pushes programs for the "protection of indigenous populations" and for their "economic and social development as well as cultural means of expression." All these measures, however, have to always be in accordance with the principles of "indivisibility . . . and equality, and its consequences" (pf09emmanuel117: 1f.).[19]

A connection of distinction and equality can be found in indigenous documents, too:

> We are all equal as human beings, but different in our culture . . . and in each people's identity. (pf09eneida092: 1)[20]

> We, the nomadic peoples or nomadic cultures, especially the Tuareg, follow a particular way of life, just as all the other peoples do. (pf09thomas135: 3)[21]

> Norway is established on the territory of two peoples—the Norwegian people and the Sami people. I fully agree that this implies that both people—the Norwegian and the Sami peoples respectively—have the same right to develop their culture and languages. (pf12egil231: 3, see also pf12pablo237: 2, pf09miguel100: 2)

According to these perspectives, peoples are equal in that they have their own culture and identity. Simultaneously, emphasis on the existence of fundamental differences remains in focus. The assumption of equivalence can neither annul the apparent deterministic boundaries between cultures, nor make them permeable—neither is it supposed to. Rather, equality serves to consolidate distinction.

Against this background, cultural destabilization, cultural threats, and cultural genocide are addressed.[22] The term cultural genocide does not refer to life and physical integrity of indigenes, but to their "survival as distinct peoples" (pf09charles071: 2). In this context, integration into majority society is seen as the biggest threat. "In several of the Caribbean islands there are people with indigenous blood line but due to the depth of the integration that has taken place over the years very few of them actually recognize and associate with their indigenous roots" (pf09charles071: 2). By refusing integration and changes, and by referring to "blood lines" and distinctions "rooted" in them, culture/identity/indigeneity are conceptualized as static, oriented toward the past, and genealogical.

Only very few instances of culture/identity/indigeneity, used as methods of distinction, can offer a dynamic understanding of culture that does not incite a partial change of cultures through their extinction; or even genocide.

> Indigenous peoples' engagement with modern technology does not mean that we have been or desire to be assimilated. Equally, recognition of our rights as Indigenous peoples must not be assessed on the basis of remaining our static in a globalising world. We cannot forgo the traditions and customs that have been handed to us by our ancestors, but nor can we be quarantined from the opportunities that arise through the development of new technologies and more efficient practices. (pf09craig112: 3 and, in almost the same words, pf09eneida092: 1)

The reference to cultural, "non-assimilated" practices is combined with openness for changes and modernity. This is supported by the findings of the participant observation: The 2012 UNPFII session was attended by indigenous representatives for whom it was normal to simultaneously use and present traditional clothes, on the one hand, and smartphones, notebooks, and tablets, on the other. Their often playful photography (by means of those modern technologies), casually documenting each other's eye-catching headdresses and clothes, displays a conscious staging of indigeneity. Different cultures are posed in this pragmatic approach not against but next to each other, thus combining progress and technology with holding onto indigenous culture.

Racism

In a third key aspect, the demand for culture/identity/indigeneity is linked to a criticism of racism and discrimination.

> Indigenous peoples . . . have historically been exposed to all forms of economic, social, cultural, and ethnic discrimination. (pf12sona262: 2)[23]

> This is why we propose . . . to respect cultural diversity and bring an end to any form of exclusion, marginalization, and racism. (pf09eneida092: 1)[24]

This third key aspect differs from the focus on diversity and distinction in a decisive way. It is not so much about preserving, protecting, and reproducing culture/identity/indigeneity. Rather, mechanisms of exclusion based on culture/identity/indigeneity are disclosed and criticized. Correspondingly, Guatemala declares:

> The goal of this public policy is to contribute to the transition from a homogenous and mono-cultural state to a plural state, so that indigenous peoples, socio-cultural groups, and citizens do not suffer from any form of racial discrimination nor social economic exclusion and that they feel their rights equally recognized in terms of their culture, ethnicity, and gender. (pf09marco132: 5)[25]

Here, cultural plurality is not used as a state's resource, but instead as a means for change in the fight against racist mechanisms of exclusion.

Some indigenous organizations claim to find culturally based mechanisms of exclusion—not only within the majority society, but also within the very cultural rights that are often the subject of indigenous demands. The indigenous women's organization *Corporación de Mujeres Mapuche Aukinko Zomo* points out that

> the State of Chile is trying to introduce a constitutional reform project regarding Indigenous Peoples called "Recognition." This limits the fundamental rights already covered by ILO Convention 169 and the Declaration on the Rights of Indigenous Peoples. This level of "Recognition" only affects aspects of culture, identity and folklore. The intention of the Chilean Government is to subordinate the international standards . . . of human rights. (pf09maria145aenes: 3f.)

The reference to culture and identity in the Chilean constitution serves to annul concrete indigenous rights, permits human rights violations, and ignores suffering. Thus, the statement argues that culture/identity/indigeneity can undermine indigenous human rights either when used as an extended, overgeneralized term or when narrowed to a folkloristic dimension.

Apart from the three key aspects discussed for the level of content, the documents contain a second, *justification-oriented level*. The strategies used to justify demands for culture/identity/indigeneity can be categorized as historical, genealogical, and transcendental argumentations.

History

In the first pattern of justification, demands for culture/identity/indigeneity are substantiated with historical references. The historical justification refers to lived, very old traditions,[26] sometimes going back "thousands of years" (pf09ghislain139: 3) or even "Millions of years" (pf09radine222: 1). It often concurs with the priority criterion; a status claim of first nation,[27] which is intended to legitimize the continued existence of a certain culture.

Some documents display the idea of indigenous cultures as the cradle of modern cultures, according to which an indigenous "ancestral and traditional culture shaped many cultures" (pf09thomas135: 3).[28] Additionally, it is assumed that the indigenous "culture created over Millions of years . . . has improved the civilized world quality of life . . . today" (pf09radine222: 1).

Furthermore, the historical argument is linked to diversity. A coalition of indigenous African organizations writes:

> Africa is the continent with the richest human and cultural diversity. Here, there is a large number of groups, communities, and peoples with different dimensions that all settled on one territory and all have their own specific language and culture. The African states, however, emerged as a result of European colonialism and usually present themselves as homogenous entities, consisting of one single people with one single language, one single culture and often one single religion. By means of their laws and practices, these states try to deny, hide, and fight ethnic and cultural diversity, which they see as a threat to national unity. This [is] the vision of the dominant ethnicity, which superimposes structurally subordinate ethnicities and which robs them of their political, socio-economic, cultural, and linguistic rights. (pf12kamira239: 1, see also pf09charles071, pf09miguel100: 2)[29]

In this argumentation, cultural identity is once again established as a resource that is attributed with an inherent value unique for Africa. European colonialism is characterized as a historical line of demarcation that distinguishes a previously fair condition from one that in a more recent state, has become poor. The time before colonialism serves as an idealized past and as a normative yardstick. This past supposedly was characterized by "ethnic and cultural diversity" and a specific "language and culture." This narrow construction of history, however—apart from its important postcolonial critique—cuts off other, less ideal historical aspects (such as inter-ethnical wars). It hypostasizes diversity as a primordial state to be reinstated. With the same selective approach, the present is marked as bad. The ideal of cultural diversity is contrasted with an alleged homogeneity, which is applied to other continents, current African national states, and European colonialism alike. In this dichotomy, everything non-indigenous is perceived as a threat to a historically justified indigenous diversity.

Genealogy

A second pattern of justification of (demands for) culture/identity/indigeneity focuses on genealogies. The historical and the genealogical pattern of justification are in a close relationship because the historical priority criterion usually refers to a direct ancestral line. The genealogical argumentation marks the character of this line even more clearly as a line of ancestry. This is mostly visible in the critique of some other indigenes' lack of "identifying with their roots" (pf09charles071: 2, see also pf09marcel111), the invocation of "our responsibility as young leaders of today to internalize the knowledge of our ancestors" (pf09gene138: 1 and, very similar, pf09jennifer101), and the wish for "our children 7 generations from now to be proud members of our respective nations" (pf09ghislain139: 3).

These approaches assume a genealogical continuity over time that is worth maintaining. Past and future generations are seen as closely connected through culture and direct blood lines. Regardless of the situation and needs of future generations, these genealogical connections are to be statically preserved and reproduced. The cultural community becomes both a refuge and a duty. Genealogy defines every individual as part of the community in both the past and the future. In the genealogical justification, culture/identity/indigeneity become a standstill, collective duty, and imperative for the individual.

Transcendence

A third pattern of justification of culture/identity/indigeneity is characterized by transcendental arguments. They are shaped either religiously, if "God's will" is cited as a reason for the right to culture/identity/indigeneity, or by reference to a given "nature":

> This is the way it is: God put us here to preserve the land. If you want to live with the land, you have to live with us. (pf09lori321EN: 1, see also pf12evariste276b: 6)

> [We want our (J. M.)] Human Right to simply exist as who we are, and to freely and naturally express our inherent nature as Indigenous Peoples. (pf12catherine263: 2)

> Our inheritance was given to us by life itself, ordained by the planet Earth to serve our purpose to the Earth in the Hemisphere renamed America's. . . . The truth of Nature does not change. (pf09radine222: 2)

The argument of indigenous closeness to nature discussed above, which is used to delimit non-indigenous, seemingly non-natural ways of life, is revaluated here. While previously the argument was about protecting close-to-nature ways of life, the transcendental justification refers to nature (or a god) in order to construct an a priori right to culture/identity/indigeneity. God and nature exhibit a transcendental character that goes along with inviolability and omitting societal, historical, and human-made processes.

Another variant of the transcendental pattern of justification strives for salvation. The argument here is that indigenous culture can make the modern world a decisively better place: "Our Indigenous knowledge of herbal medicine is effective in curing AIDS. . . . The African Nations have so much knowledge to offer the world in tackling climate change and disease" (pf09margaret052: 1).

The idea of indigenous knowledge as the basis for human salvation, in connection with fantasies of omnipotence, bears a momentum of irrationality that distinguishes the document from controversies on patent rights for herbal medicines. Meanwhile, it is based on the idea of a dynamic transculturalization: Culture/identity/indigeneity are to be protected and strengthened not as a secluded culture, but in order to improve the lives of all human beings.

The aspect of salvation attributed to indigenous cultures, however, is used not only transculturally and openly, but is also static and dichotomizing:

> The current international capitalist system in all its different forms is, by means of excessive consumerism, waste of natural resources that leads to the destruction of biodiversity, the transculturation of peoples, the threat of extinguishing our very nature, the loss of our ancient indigenous values, and the negation of the existence of our original peoples. This constitutes the most terrible threat hanging above our existence and the planet. (pf09moira089: 2, for similar statements, see pf09charles071 and pf09radine222)[30]

Along a dichotomizing boundary, two sides are portrayed homogenously and selectively. The "international capitalist system" is attributed with everything abstract, artificial, bad, and deviant that will destroy nature, values, and, eventually, the whole world. Capitalism's transculturalization, that is, its changing and mixing of cultures, is seen as a fundamental threat. On the other side, an ancient, original, indigenous culture is constructed that is seen as a, or the only, solution to save the world. Immediateness and nature legitimize culture/identity/indigeneity that has to be protected from the "other."

LANDS, TERRITORIES, AND RESOURCES

The issues of lands, territories, and resources are crucial in controversies over indigenous rights. This is evident in both indigenous statements under agenda item 04a and in reports of other UN institutions. The UN Expert Mechanism, for example, informs on the common indigenous wish to bring conflicts of land and resources to the center of attention (pf09jose085: 4). Special Rapporteur Anaya, whose job is, among other things, to receive human rights complaints from indigenous groups, confirms that the complex lands/territories/resources is a recurrent aspect of the complaints submitted (pf09jamesread087: 8).

On the *first level regarding content*, indigenous documents[31] sketch particular threats related to land conflicts. States and transnational corporations, as well as small- and medium-sized enterprises, are named as the two main culprits of land conflicts and resulting problems.[32] The companies often operate open-pit and underground mines. Other frequent reasons for complaints are joint mega projects by states and corporations such as high dams and river straightening.

The described threats to indigenes comprise two key aspects—pollution and expropriation.

Pollution

The first key aspect, pollution, is related to climate change (pf12catherine263, pf09stanely093), human rights violations,[33] direct threats to livelihood, which depends on natural resources (pf09gene138), and forced migration (pf09legb_africaucus140). The pollution of water, soil, and the environment by chemicals,[34] the exploitation of mineral resources, and the destruction of biodiversity as a result of overexploitation and monocultures (pf09ernesto127, pf09eva102) are at the center of criticism. According to the complaints, dust emitted by open-pit mining in Peru contaminates pasture and fields used for agriculture and livestock; aluminum, arsenic, iron, and zinc jeopardize fish populations and drinking water. Poisonous residues left in the soil lead to mercury poisoning (pf09alcides033). Deforestation, fertilizers in the ground, monocultures for biodiesel production, and the pollution of beaches and the Pacific (pf12evariste276a) in Bolivia are all considered a threat to indigenous livelihood. Indigenous representatives from Papua-New Guinea report "how our food sources were threatened by mine waste dumped directly into the river system and how my people were exposed to dangerous chemicals like cyanide and mercury" (pf09jethro316: 1).[35]

Displacement

The second key aspect concerns forced migration, displacement, and expropriation in favor of corporate projects. Commercial access to resources and land drives indigenes off their homeland and villages, and forces them to give up fish stock, hunting grounds, and agriculture that they depend on for their livelihood.[36] States are accused of playing an important role in these expropriations and persecutions.[37] In Colombia, for example, "the ineffectiveness of land law, Democratic Security Policy and the Colombian armed conflict" lead to criminalization and the burning of fields (pf09ana107: 1). Thus, a conscious destruction of resources is facilitated by the state.

In summary, in terms of content, concrete threats are described in order to strengthen and legitimize claims to lands/territories/resources.

Implications and effects of this become visible in more detail on the level of justification.

The *level of justification* of indigenous demands for lands/territories/resources displays four crucial patterns—individual human rights, history, genealogy, and cultural distinction.

Individual Human Rights

In the first pattern of justification, indigenous demands are legitimized by means of basic needs framed in human rights. Poisonous substances in water, food, and soil are seen as immediately life-threatening. Expropriation, militarization, and criminalization caused by land conflicts are criticized as violations of basic needs and individual human rights.[38]

History

The second pattern of justification is characterized by references to a historically prior, traditional, or long-standing use and/or ownership of the lands/territories/resources concerned. "Territorial rights to lands which indigenous peoples have lived in harmony and exercised their sovereignty for thousands of years" (pf09ghislain139: 3) and "ownership of land established through collective memories and custom law" (pf09jacqueline110: 1) are common claims in this context. They focus on traditional usage and living.[39]

In several indigenous documents, the loss of historically owned or worked lands is blamed on colonial conquest.[40] Statements criticize an ongoing colonialist attitude in land conflicts [41] and a lack of recognition of historical treaties (pf12evariste276a). Critiques of colonialism come along with demands for a "First Nation Peoples' right to their lands, territories and resources which they have traditionally owned and occupied or otherwise used" (pf12catherine263: 4). The priority criterion is to underline the historically justified claim to land.

Genealogy

A third pattern of justification makes use of a genealogical argumentation. Here, the focus lies on the land as ancestral land and on the ancestor's life on and with that land.[42] Although the historical pattern of justification refers to the (presumably ancestral) predecessors as well, the emphasis on a genealogical blood line mirrors a shift in focus. It creates the image of a distinct group precisely defined by kinship. Ancestors and their (land-bound) way of life legitimize the current way of life.

Cultural Distinction

A fourth pattern of justification points to the value of indigenous distinction in order to legitimize demands for lands/territories/resources. Cultural distinction is, once again, allocated in the special relationship[43] of indigenous groups with their lands/territories/resources. This relationship, which is mentioned by the UNDRIP as well, is described as harmonious relation between humans and nature and as respect for mother earth, which itself is to be respected.[44] The claim to lands/territories/resources is justified with a special and spiritual connection between indigenes and their land that distinguishes them from non-indigenes.

A representative of the delegation of the Holy See pleads for coexistence of distinctly indigenous and non-indigenous cultures: "Plans of extractive industries and multinational corporations, though presenting an opportunity for economic enrichment, should not come at the expense of the rights of the indigenous peoples" (pf09kuriakose134). He does not perceive multinational corporations only as a threat, but as a part of reality that has to be dealt with without undermining indigenous rights. Similar to this approach are claims to compensation payments for expropriation[45] and to indigenous participation and FPIC in questions of commercial land use.[46]

Linking cultural distinction to a deep connection to nature is a strategy in the field of pollution as well. A representative of the Arctic reports about persistent organic pollutants (POPs) that not only are a threat to health, well-being, and the environment, but also destroy the indigenous "way of life" and "cultural practices" (pf09iiite406x: 1f.). For example, traditional methods for preparing food are affected (Ibid.). A similar argument represents climate change as a threat to the distinct indigenous culture and its connection to nature.[47] While indigenes in Bolivia (pf09eneida092) and the Congo (pf09stephane034) characterize deforestation as a threat to indigenous ways of life, commercial forestation is seen as hampering "natural vegetation to take its own course of cyclic redressing system" (pf09raphael072: 2) in Bangladesh. This does not only raise the argument against interfering with nature, but also human interference with apparent natural cycles in general.

Regarding the usage of lands/territories/resources, the Indigenous Youth Caucus and other indigenous groups emphasize:

> Brothers and sisters, our Mother Earth is continuously being raped to feed the addiction of consumerism, neo-slavery and servitude. As long as we continue to murder our mother earth by means of nuclear energy, mining, and the lies of "green energy," we are killing ourselves. We are concerned with the exploitation of sacred natural elements of life. (LAWS—land, air, water, sun) Trans-national corporations are ceasing the opportunity of green-washing the illusion of helping the environment and coercing indigenous leaders to feed into the capitalist agen-

da, while strengthening the capitalist hold on our natural resources. (pf09gene138: 2)

Demands are for "a holy and complementary relation [to nature], not the predatory and patriarchal scheme that rules the world with its practices of expropriation by extractive industries with their companies, driven only by profit and greed."[48] (pf09tupac396: 2)

In this approach, a good indigenous entity is juxtaposed to a bad capitalist one. The term "green-washing" is supposed to disclose non-indigenous interaction with nature as deceptive and part of a homogeneous "capitalist agenda." Fears are stimulated by use of emotionalizing terms such as "addiction," "slavery," "killing," "predatory patriarchy," and "greed." On the other side of the dichotomy stands the indigenous community of "brothers and sisters" that exists as a solution and salvation. It symbolizes a concrete, healthy family that is holy, balanced, and close to nature. Internal contradictions, ambivalences, and dichotomous overlaps are respectively neglected or valued as a sign of "feeding the capitalist agenda."

Another argument for a land-bound distinction is expressed in the statement of a Mongolian indigenous representative. He complains about the "non-sustainable farming practices of millions of Chinese immigrants" that are destroying indigenous lands and resources (pf09tegusbayar322: 1). This rejection is aimed not only at transnational corporations and governments, but also at Chinese farmers that live in Mongolia as a "result of large-scale Chinese population transfer" (pf09tegusbayar322: 1). Chinese farmers are characterized as allochthonous immigrants that are culturally alien, ethnically distinct, and have a "wrong" relation to nature.

All these examples are based on the assumption of a binary separation between indigeneity and non-indigeneity, with governments, transnational corporations, immigrants, or capitalism in general being non-indigenous. Indigenes, on the other hand, share a distinctive feature—a close connection to nature, that is, to lands/territories/resources, which non-indigenous interference is understood as a danger to and estrangement from.

PARTICIPATION AND SELF-DETERMINATION

The issue of participation and self-determination comprises demands for free, prior, and informed consent (FPIC) as well as demands for full autonomy.

On the *first level, regarding content*, the current lack of participation and self-determination is at the center of attention of indigenous 04a documents:[49]

> Despite ... several international human rights instruments, the human rights situation of indigenous peoples in Asia remains deplorable ... especially with regards [to] ... the right of self-determination, and the principle of free, prior, informed consent in decisions that impact them. (pf12wilton224: 1)

Different claims of indigenous groups become visible in a differentiation of demands that focus on participation, self-determination, or FPIC respectively.

Participation

In the first key aspect, participation, the goal is an institutionalized indigenous decision-making body that is part of the national government. The demand for indigenous participation in government decisions is, for example, substantiated as a "supreme indigenous decision making body in the government of New Caledonia" (pf12evariste276a: 3)[50] or as "indigenous representative bodies to ... participate in the development of government policy at all levels of decision-making" (pf12geoff259).[51] These demands entail the assumption that the state is the biggest obstacle to indigenous participation.[52]

Demands targeting international decision-making aim at another level of participation. They focus on either indigenous participation in regional bodies, like ASEAN (pf09asiacaucus4a), or generally on international decisions that are relevant to indigenous groups.[53] Participation is to be implemented on all levels.[54]

Demands for participation play a role in relation to specific topics as well. These may concern national, regional, or international levels of decision-making. Especially in negotiations over climate change, indigenes demand stronger participation rights and representation.[55] They want to be treated as equal partners in working groups, meetings, and committees that discuss the Kyoto Protocol and similar agreements.

Yet another complex of topics around participation deals with the usage of lands, territories, and resources.[56] Beyond that, indigenous groups demand participation regarding development programs designed for them,[57] distribution of aid funds (pf09maria145aenes), and humanitarian operations (pf12kamira239).

Indigenous representatives claim participation in the enactment and monitoring of the UNDRIP (pf09jennifer101) and in the development of additional relevant UN mechanisms.[58] In this context, they suggest independent, international, and indigenous or mixed monitoring and report systems, as well as the employment of indigenous experts in an advisory capacity to governments (pf12santi291, pf12shane266).

Furthermore, indigenous participation in mechanisms of definition and recognition of indigeneity is brought up. In reference to the concept of self-identification, which plays an important role in the UN's working definition of indigeneity, indigenes want to decide on the status, scope, and content of indigeneity for themselves (pf09joan097). This is because, on one side, the entitlement to indigenous rights is hampered by a lack of recognition of indigeneity on a national level: "China has signed the United Nations Declaration on Rights of Indigenous Peoples without considering her 55 indigenous peoples as 'indigenous'" (pf09tegusbayar322: 2). On the other hand, an overly broad usage of indigeneity is seen as a threat to indigenous rights:

> Detrimental impacts of government control of Indigenous identification are further illustrated by the situation in Finland where the exploitation of Indigenous rights by non-Indigenous Peoples has started to emerge . . . thereby violating Sámi right to self-determination. (pf12intreabud234: 2)

> In the last few months, the State has decided to promote the creation of new Indigenous organizations, which constitute a new risk factor for the disintegration of the national Indigenous movement. (pf09ana107: 1)

Here, the representatives of the National Authority of Indigenous Government of Colombia and the Global Indigenous Youth Council claim that some groups recognized as indigenous, from their perspective, do not deserve that designation, which undermines the interest of "real" indigenous peoples.

The category of indigeneity proves to be as relevant for the issue of participation as it is disputed. It is used as a feature of distinction, but also as a political and strategic resource that can earn advantages and must be defended against other claimants. Additionally, indigeneity plays a crucial role for political cohesion that rests on the assumption of internal homogeneity and does not tolerate deviation.

Self-Determination

Aside from participation, the demand for self-determination constitutes the second key aspect. Apart from some rather unspecific demands for general self-determination, some statements refer to specific forms of sovereignty: "As sovereign First Nations . . . we continue to assert our self-determination despite the international legal framework that too often serves to undermine our absolute authority" (pf12catherine263: 1). This would include international relations to other states at eye level (pf12catherine263: 2).

On the international level—which mostly concerns external representation—demands tie membership, a right to participation, and the right to vote to the political status of a body, people, and/or nation. At this point, the two key aspects of indigenous participation and indigenous self-determination overlap.

On a national level, indigenous demands strive for comprehensive legal pluralism, that is, recognition of indigenous jurisdiction and indigenous legal systems.[59] These ought to allow for exceptions from national law if cultural reasons apply (pf09jorge195). A representative of the Yamasi claims that his group is the legitimate owner of territories between Daytona and Charleston (United States) and believes the group to be at war with the United States. He insists, "Raping an indigenous nation into US submission violates all standards of Christian warfare and UN conventions and we request that this practice be denounced by the UN and the Permanent Forum on Indigenous Issues" (pf09lori321EN: 1). A Basque representative denounces the French "refusal to recognize the Northern Basque Country from an institutional point of view. Our territory is not recognized. Even the minimalist claim for a Basque department is refused categorically"; additionally, he refers to the "solidarity between Autochthonous Peoples" (pf09mailis051: 1f.).

Including both the national and international level, the King of Polynesia makes a detailed proposal on jurisdiction:

> I would like to make a recommendation on the creation of a global indigenous tribunal to protect us, a tribunal where all indigenous peoples in the world would be represented as they are here today at the Permanent Forum. The creation of this tribunal would first be voted on by indigenous peoples and could then be recognized by the UN. It would be composed of local tribunals, also established by indigenous vote and spread among various world regions. In each country or island observers would be responsible for ensuring the implementation of the Declaration on the Rights of Indigenous Peoples. These observers would be indigenous, with a good knowledge of their country or island, and they would report to the tribunal. ... Through this means, we could ensure that all of the United Nations' instruments would be implemented. (pf12evariste276b: 5)

The demands for indigenous mechanisms have their foundation in a mistrust of non-indigenous organizations, which is explained with hundreds of years of colonization and suppression by non-indigenous governments and courts. The striving for a legal system comprised only of indigenes is, however, also related to the assumption of culturally distinct approaches. It is based on a homogenous concept of indigeneity. Additionally, it presupposes that indigenous identity includes comprehensive knowledge of indigenous issues—knowledge that non-indigenes are believed to be deficient of.

Free, Prior, and Informed Consent

The third key aspect, free, prior, and informed consent (FPIC), appears in virtually all demands for participation and self-determination.

> The right to be consulted is a prerequisite for our right to perform our right to self-determination in issues that deal with our concerns. (pf09egil099: 1)

> [The] principle of free, prior, and informed consent cannot be applied only project by project or region by region. (pf09tupac396: 3)[60]

The concept of FPIC is key in all areas. However, criticism of this concept exists as well, according to which mere mechanisms of consultation, as introduced by various countries, do not suffice at all (pf09craig112, pf12evariste276b) because they imply neither indigenous consent nor participation. In a statement by several indigenous organizations and NGOs, the FPIC-based structures of international organizations are described to be in urgent need of reform, for they do not effectively protect indigenous human rights.

> Within international bodies and processes, consensus-driven procedures are being exploited by States to the detriment of Indigenous peoples. The lowest-common-denominator among State positions often prevails. Such procedures are undermining the principles of justice, democracy, non-discrimination, respect for human rights and rule of law. (pf12jennifer260: 1)

This criticism leads back to the demands for active indigenous participation in international mechanisms and structures. It is connected to the complaint that participation in the UNPFII sessions is by no means open to all who are interested, because expenditures and expenses are high. This is why digital participation through internet livestreams should be facilitated (pf12santi291). The UN Voluntary Fund for Indigenous Peoples—the UN body that is responsible for financing indigenous representatives' travel to and participation in the UNPFII sessions—confirms this exclusion by disclosing that despite numerous grant applications, only a small number can be approved (15 percent in 2009). Likewise, the size of the fund is decreasing (pf09dalee137).[61] Trouble (as recorded in the participant observation and in explorative conversations) was also caused by a last-minute change of the 2012 session's location, as a result of which not all representatives could attend the events. The change was caused by construction at the UN site and the subsequent issuance of only one UN Secondary Pass per delegation, which, together with the UN Ground Pass, was necessary to access most of the main events. The delegates, some of whom had traveled for several days by many different means of transportation and who encountered obstacles in their visa processes, were informed of the changes only once they had arrived. Complaints were met in that some of the events were broadcasted via livestream to overflow rooms, and that Secondary Passes were not obligatory for all events any more.

Aside from the content-related level concerning participation and self-determination, the documents disclose several strategies of legitimation. They pick up on a *second level* that is *focused on justification* in these categories: cultural distinction, history, and individual human rights.

Cultural Distinction

The first pattern of justification, concerning cultural distinction, is crucial to demands for participation and self-determination. In principle, participation and self-determination are demanded in all areas that are assumed to be important to indigenes in some way. This is being related to two points. First, "indigenous peoples claim to having a collective right to self-determination is . . . based on our understanding that we are best placed to make the decisions that affect our lives and the future of our peoples" (pf09craig112: 2f.).

Second, indigenous culture, cultural diversity, indigenous legal and administrative structures, and a spiritual relationship with nature are to be preserved by means of participation and self-determination.[62]

In both cases, (re-)production of a binary separation of indigenous and non-indigenous cultures is basal. Distinct indigeneity is a resource of demands for rights that needs to be defended against others. At the same time, it is also the primary goal of demands for rights. The basic assumption here is that only indigenes know what is good for them. Indigeneity is a key category for distinction. However, its definition is disputed by all sides, including governments and indigenous groups.

History

A second pattern of justification focuses on a historical or pre-colonial existence of sovereign indigenous nations and their colonial subjugation.[63] "From the original roster of 51 members in 1945, today, there are 192 (193) members of the UN due in large part to the U.N.'s mandate for decolonization. (We believe there should be at least a dozen more added to the family of nations)" (pf12catherine263: 2). The previous existence of an independent nation is used to legitimize demands for its existence today. This approach to history raises questions as to the legitimating strength of parallelizing past and present and is also characterized by a consult of only certain historical aspects. It omits, for example, that past nations themselves might have been the result of conquering and destroying prior nations.

Individual Human Rights

In a third pattern of justification, participation and self-determination are intended to improve quality of life and to serve individual human rights. "Self-determination is 'the pillar upon which all other rights rest'" (pf09craig112: 3, see also pf12shane266). It symbolizes a right to equality (pf09saturnino189), to improved communal life (pf09tupac396), health, education, and the protection of livelihood (pf09caleen126). In questions regarding climate change, which is said to directly affect indigenes (pf12dietrix293), the right to participation is especially regarded as an expression of equality and as essential for securing quality of life and dignity.

INDIVIDUAL HUMAN RIGHTS

The insufficient protection of individual human rights comprises an important topic in indigenous 04a documents.[64] The topic pervades other areas of discussion in this chapter but warrants singular focus as well. It is often related to a demand that can be found in almost every one of the documents examined: the demand to finally implement and apply the UNDRIP and/or the ILO Convention No. 169 (as well as other international and regional human rights agreements or existing national law).

On a *content-related level*, three key aspects of individual human rights violations are addressed—economic marginalization, political and physical repression, and racist exclusion.

Economic Marginalization

The first aspect, economic marginalization, concerns the widespread poverty among indigenous populations. Indigenes are especially affected by poverty—not only in generally poorer countries (pf09celeste320, pf09wilton059), but also in wealthy nations. Canada is described as a country that,

> during its most economically productive years experienced billions in surpluses year after year, did nothing for indigenous people except to maintain the poor economic and social conditions in our communities.... Canada chose to carry out highly publicized initiatives ... not the development and sustainability of indigenous communities. (pf09ghislain139: 2)[65]

Poverty is linked to indigeneity and explained through structural discrimination and state paternalism. Further examples of indigenous poverty are the absence of infrastructure, a lack of government support in building infrastructure,[66] and a lack of housing space for indigenes.[67] Infrastructural obstacles also play a role for the enjoyment of existing national law. Aside from unaffordable court and lawyer fees (pf12evariste276a), long distances to courts and round tables as well as a lack of interpreters (pf12santi291) result in exclusion.

Hunger and insufficient nutrition are also crucial problems. They are mostly explained by subsistence farming being limited by land conflicts, forced migration, destruction of fields, climatic threats, and poisoning of groundwater and food.[68]

Yet another aspect of economic marginalization is health. Many claim that the health of indigenes is threatened by pollution of soil, drinking water, and resources, by insufficient infrastructures, impeded access to health facilities (due to a lack of infrastructure or language problems), and limited resources to fight contagious disease. Further arguments include increased mortality rates due to medically preventable illnesses and above-average suicide rates.[69]

Another result of economic marginalization is a lack of education opportunities. The indigenous documents demand rights to education for children (pf09gene138: 2), more schools (pf09stephane034), and the "right to education on all levels" (pf09saturnino189: 1).[70]

Australian documents describe a particular constellation. While demands for education are in most countries formulated by indigenes, the direction is reversed here: The Australian government requests that indigenous communities do not allow children to be "deprived of their right to education" (pf09australia115: 2). A coalition of Australian indigenes gives a complementary account, criticizing the Australian legislative proposal *Stronger Future*, which, among other things, aims at "suspending the welfare payments of impoverished Indigenous parents whose children are absent from school" (pf12shane266: 2). The document does not clarify if it criticizes the government's threat to cut welfare or compulsory school attendance. The Australian program, however, triggered discussions outside of the UNPFII, which allow the conclusion that limitations of the (human) right to education is shaped by (infra-)structural, economic, and state discrimination as well as by indigenous efforts to remain distinct (see chapter 6).

Yet another aspect of economic marginalization concerns working conditions. Indigenes are more often unemployed and discriminated against when searching and applying for jobs.[71] Additionally, they are exposed to extremely poor working conditions in some countries. This is proven by economic exploitation, violations of labor rights, illegalization of unions,[72] "inhumane conditions, both in the work place and through the industrial prison complex" (pf09gene138: 1), and by "practices analogous to slavery in countries like Bolivia and Paraguay" (pf09samuel130: 1).[73]

Repression

The diversified field of economic marginalization is accompanied by an important second aspect that can be summarized under the term of political and physical repression.

Indigenes are subject to above-average suppression by the state in several regions where arrests, police violence, and criminalization are frequent:[74] "We are surprised by the robust raids of the National Police, armed to the teeth, without a search warrant who have handcuffed us like terrorists . . . when we have simply put into practice our rights as they are recognized in the Declaration on the Rights of Indigenous Peoples" (pf12evariste276b: 6).

In this case from Polynesia, the situation is made more difficult by the fact that the rights formulated in the UNDRIP are not valid under state law and can easily be illegalized on the national level.

The subjects of criminalization or persecution are, above all, social and political protests, displaying national symbols, founding political organizations, or inciting acts of sabotage or assaults. Actions in relation to land conflicts such as land squatting are also illegalized.[75] Less frequent offenses include singing traditional songs (pf09handaire118), using traditional medicine (pf09maria145aenes, pf09marco132) or clothes (pf09marco132), or chewing coca leaves, which was illegal in Bolivia for a long time—but is now recognized as cultural practice (pf09freddy125). At times, indigenous protests are fought as terrorism (pf09william123). Detention conditions are very poor and sentences given to offending parties are often long and unjustified (pf12david335). In relation to the majority, indigenes are arrested disproportionately (pf12evariste276b) and sometimes even tortured;[76] demonstrations are crushed with excessive brutality (pf09ana107).

Militarization is another complex aspect of political and physical repression.[77] In this context, militarization means the establishment of (domestic or foreign) military bases on indigenous territory. This can lead to conflicts on land and cultural sites,[78] as well as to violence and repression. The Asia Indigenous Peoples Caucus comprehensively describes human rights violations resulting from militarization:

> Militarization is a state policy of deploying armed forces and military bases in indigenous territories, setting-up of military detachments inside or near the communities, imposing checkpoints and curfews . . . with the general effect of creating an environment of terror, massive and intense military operations including indiscriminate bombings and firing, recruitment of paramilitary forces among indigenous peoples, and many other forms of military terror. Militarization in itself is a basic human rights violation that has resulted in many serious human rights cases such as torture, illegal arrest and detention, extrajudicial killings, enforced disappearances, military rape of indigenous women including minors, . . . burning of houses and indigenous forests and destruction of community properties and resources, forcible evacuations. . . . Militarization is employed to secure state and corporate interests, and to suppress community resistance for indigenous peoples rights. (pf12windel243: 1)

Related to this are documents that present violations of indigenous rights as collateral damage resulting from governmental suppression of non-indigenous rebel groups and that demand peace talks with these groups. In India, for example, "the indigenous populations . . . are sandwiched between government forces and the naxalites. The government has set up army base in the indigenous area. . . . During each conflict the indigenous populations are the worst sufferers" (pf09minz191: 2).[79]

Wars, armed conflicts, paramilitary forces, criminal alliances, "gangs of bandits" (pf09ali192: 1), drug trafficking, and mafia-like structures are also named as direct sources of violence against which the state does not offer sufficient protection. This violence includes abductions, extortion, ransom demands, lootings, destructions, and killings.[80]

Other reports tell of displacement, expropriation, and forced migration related to wars, militarization and (para-)military disputes, or land conflicts between indigenes and states.[81]

Racism

Apart from the many forms of violence and economic marginalization, the third complex of topics addresses racism. The indigenous documents criticize state-sanctioned racism, exclusion, and structural inequality between indigenous and non-indigenous populations. The exclusion exists, for example, regarding job offers, detention, and social legislation (also see above).[82]

To counter racist and structural discrimination, justice, freedom, inclusion, equality, democracy,[83] and life "without marginalization based on one's skin color, sex, religion, or ideas"[84] are demanded (pf09eneida092: 1).

On a *second, justification-oriented level*, objections to the human rights violations described above reflect two sources of legitimation.

Individual Human Rights

The first pattern of justification is derived from the very depiction of situations of suffering and need. The basic argument here is that human rights violations are simply unacceptable.

This argument becomes clear in the following document, which expresses the demand for human rights not only for indigenes, but for every suppressed or exploited person:

> I come here to advocate for my indigenous brothers and sisters, Non-indigenous Guatemalans, Latin America, and for the world and for those of us that live in the midst of wars. . . . Daily we suffer exploitation for our labor and human rights violations. More than a thousand million people live daily with hunger, which grows as the unemployment rate does. (pf09mariana190: 1)

In this example, the point of argument is moved from an indigenous perspective to a perspective of the suppressed and marginalized people in general. Differences between parts of the population are seen less via native culture or ethnicity and more through the suffering from human rights violations. The fight to end suffering, hunger, and poverty does not need any further justification, least of all because the matters of debate are "classic" human rights, which are formally undisputed in international and regional human rights agreements.

Cultural Distinction

In a second pattern of justification of human rights, cultural distinction is used as a reference: "Life in indigenous communities has been made so miserable that over 50% of our population has been forced to live outside their communities.... Assimilation has been made the only option" (pf09ghislain139: 3). This indigenous representative from Canada outlines economic marginalization as a threat to cultural identity. There seems to be an alternative to poverty, which, however, would be tied to the challenging requirement of giving up life inside an indigenous community. Integration into the larger society is not the goal, but rather preserving cultural difference while simultaneously achieving (political, economic, and social) equality with other citizens.[85]

COLLECTIVE RIGHTS

On a *content-oriented level*, there are four kinds of references to collective rights, focusing on their general importance, their close linkage with other demands for indigenous rights, their ties to individual human rights, or their juxtaposition against individual human rights.

General Importance

Collective rights appear, first, in a general emphasis of their importance[86] — or in a general formulation of the demand for individual and collective rights.[87] "Indigenous peoples are to be considered collective rights subjects" (pf09luis108).[88]

Connection to Indigenous Demands

Second, in the first three areas of indigenous demands examined — 1) culture, identity, and indigeneity, 2) lands, territories, and resources, 3) participation and self-determination — the necessity of collective rights is implicitly or explicitly assumed. This is because collective forms of ownership, collective identity, and collective self-determination are presumed to be applicable only insufficiently if based on individual rights. "Our collective rights continue to be systematically and grossly violated, especially with regards [to] our traditional lands, territories, and resources; the right of self determination, and the principle of free, prior, informed consent" (pf12windel243: 1). Recognition of collective forms of ownership is seen as decisive for land conflicts to be successful.[89] Furthermore, this recognition plays an important role regarding the intellectual and cultural property of cultural sites, cemeteries, or knowledge of certain plants and herbs (pf09miguel100). Collective rights are understood to be crucial to the right of self-determination (pf09craig112, pf09legb_africaucus140), and, conversely, the right to self-determination is seen as the foundation of individual and collective rights (pf12shane266). "Finally, we call on the Permanent Forum to urge the Human Rights Council to end the criminalization of our collective rights: to stop militarization, genocide, ethnocide, forced displacement, detention, stigmatization, and the threatening and persecution of leaders and organizations"[90] (pf09miguel100: 2).[91]

Connection to Individual Human Rights

Third, individual human rights, human dignity and well-being, are seen as "collective progress and well-being" (pf09maria145aenes: 3). In these documents, claims for individual human rights are integrated into the demands for collective rights.

Similarly, the individual human right to education is addressed as a subject of collective rights in the form of access to bilingual, culturally sensible educational institutions. According to this, indigenous languages and indigenous perspectives on the past and the present are to be considered by educational programs. Universities worldwide are requested to establish positions for indigenous teachers, offer indigenous content, and provide scholarships and university slots for indigenous students.[92] Furthermore, indigenous access to health facilities, courts, and administrative bodies is restricted by the lack of ability many indigenes have to communicate in the culturally dominating language, coupled by a lack of use of indigenous languages within public institutions.[93] Demands for collective and individual human rights overlap in these areas.

Restriction of Individual Human Rights

At the same time, there are, fourth, explicit restrictions of individual human rights initiated by the very demand for collective rights. "Accepting artificial identities, concepts of individualism has crippled our people's ability to collectively fight our genocide in our homeland" (pf09radine222: 1). The "amerindian race" living "in the Americas" is falsely "classified as black/Negro" and "discriminated constantly in favor for European/Asian/Negro mixtures" (pf09radine222: 1). This document communicates both racist and anti-individualistic content by describing the indigenous community in delimitation from "individual artificialness" and the "mixing" with other "races."

A juxtaposition of indigenous and government statements shows a continuation of the longstanding controversy on collective rights. While Bolivia (pf09freddy125) and Venezuela (pf09moira089) acknowledge collective rights (although indigenous groups make serious reproaches against these countries), France points out that, "according to the constitutional principles of the indivisibility of the republic . . . and equality as well as its equivalence (i.e., the principle of non-discrimination), collective rights shall not have priority over individual rights" (pf09emmanuel117).[94] Australia makes demands of indigenous communities for the protection of "individuals and vulnerable groups" as well as to protect their "individual rights and freedoms" (pf09australia115: 2). Here, Australia indicates a violation of individual rights within the indigenous communities.

A possible constellation of conflict between individual and collective rights is also addressed by a representative of the UNPFII. After emphasizing the importance of connecting human rights to cultural contexts, she continues,

> I was also reminded of the internal Indigenous peoples' preparatory meeting debate in 1985 between those who believed that the UNDRIP should only reflect our collective or group rights and make no mention of our distinct individual human rights as Indigenous persons. In hindsight, this may have been a wise approach when viewed against the backdrop of the erroneous characterization by some that Indigenous human rights only attach to individuals and not to Indigenous nations, communities and peoples. On the other hand, the balanced approach taken in the final text of the UNDRIP has been and continues to be highly relevant and extremely important, for example, in relation to protecting and promoting the rights of individual Indigenous women, children and youth in the context of violence perpetrated against them. (pf12dalee223: 1)

Instead of overemphasizing collective rights, the representative points out that indigenous women and children are not sufficiently protected by collective rights alone.

In sum, references to collective rights with regard to content are connected to general or concrete demands for indigenous rights and characterized by different perspectives on individual rights that emphasize either overlapping concepts or contradictions of the two types of rights.

On the *justification-oriented level,* two key aspects are crucial.

Individual Human Rights

First, demands for collective rights are made in light of individual human rights violations and poor quality of life. From this perspective, individual human rights are violated because of individuals' affiliation with indigenous collectives, which is why they need to be supported by collective rights. Criticisms of persecution, displacement, and criminalization, as well as insufficient access to educational institutions, health care, and infrastructure are based on this assumption.

Cultural Distinction

A second key aspect of demands for collective rights focuses on preserving indigeneity and indigenous distinction. This becomes especially visible in the claim to support indigenous languages and to recognize distinct ways of life. At the same time, both patterns of justification can overlap: The preservation of cultural distinction can be tied closely to the quality of life or to the realization of individual human rights.

INTERNAL GROUP DIFFERENCES

On the *content level*, internal group differences are addressed in government documents and indigenous documents through four key aspects. These are: indigenous women, indigenous children, indigenes with disabilities, and further categories like age and class.

Indigenous Women

The first and most discussed aspect is the one of gender-specific inequalities. Several states have programs designed to support indigenous women and indigenous women's organizations. Spain claims to support the implementation of collective and individual rights of indigenous women in Latin America (pf12maria238). Peru reports having a law to promote equal opportunities for women, designed to strengthen their economic, social, and political participation in rural areas (pf09gonzalo114). The United States supports programs designed to curb violence against women and for the training of midwives in Latin America (pf09shane133). Mexico organizes workshops to create leadership positions for indigenous women within their community (pf09gabriela128). Guatemala reports successes in gender equality struggles for indigenous women (pf09marco132). In Bolivia, legislative changes are supposed to strengthen the positions of indigenous and non-indigenous women (pf09tomasa119).

All government statements and programs specifically concerned with indigenous women refer to Latin America. No government from any other region mentions women or women's rights. A second characteristic of the above statements is that they do not specify what exactly the gender equality programs aim to tackle—structures of the state and the private sector or indigenous institutions and practices.

A double exception to these two characteristics is constituted by the document submitted by the Australian delegation. After outlining the government's duties concerning gender equality, it points out the duties of the indigenous community.

> We recognize that we each have a part to play in ensuring Aboriginal and Torres Strait Islander peoples' rights are fully protected and their life outcomes are improved:
> (1) for government, by ensuring: participation ... and
> (2) for Aboriginal and Torres Strait Islander peoples, by ensuring: ... especially the right of Aboriginal and Torres Strait Islander women and children to safe and healthy lives including protection from acts of violence, other forms of harm or abuse, and [that they] are not deprived of their right to education, social and cultural development. (pf09australia115: 2)

Australia is the only government outside of Latin America to address discrimination against women and to name its actors. Responsibility for violence against indigenous women is assigned to the indigenous community, too.

Statements of indigenous and non-governmental organizations, among them various women's rights organizations, specify the spectrum of women's rights violations. They are not only from Latin America, but from regions all around the world. These documents state the special vulnerability of indigenous women. "Indigenous women experience greater levels of discrimination due to the compound effect of ethnicity, gender, class, language, and, in particular, non-represented and unrecognized status" (pf09caleen126: 1).[95]

Another point of criticism refers to a lack of mechanisms to ensure the reproductive, sexual, and general health of indigenous women.[96]

There is an often cited problem concerning sexualized violence against women and girls[97] as well as (forced) prostitution (pf09william123, pf09celeste320). Reasons for sexualized assaults are seen in militarization (pf12windel243), wars (pf09stephane034), large projects like mining (pf09jethro316), and land conflicts in which assaults are used as a means of repression (pf12sona262). Beyond this, physical violence against women is reported as a widespread problem; it is not specified, however, if this includes domestic violence.[98] Femicides, which usually go unpunished, are a form of escalated violence against indigenous women.[99]

Apart from sexual and other types of physical or psychological violence, structures of exclusion are a major problem, especially for indigenous women. One topic often mentioned in this context is the participation of women in political decisions and processes. Indigenous women's organizations demand visibility, strength, and recognition of their permanent participation in indigenous struggles.

> We, the indigenous women of Latin America, have been protagonists in all the reclaiming processes, even though our participation has not been able to be acknowledged. This is why we as indigenous women demand of the United Nations . . . to implement programs . . . so we can fortify women's organizations that strengthen already established structures. This is the only way for us indigenous women to begin to feel real and visible instead of just appearing as figures in papers and documents. (pf09eneida092: 3)[100]

> The Indigenous Women's organizations and activists are functioning *de facto* as the front of human rights documentation and monitoring efforts within communities. This presents enormous challenges that the women must bear in isolation. They are largely unrecognized and unfunded and subject to harassment, persecution, libel, slander, death threats, rape, dismemberment, maiming, destruction of property, armed forced removals, en masse displacements, and violence against their family members. (pf09womencaucus4ab: 1f.; italics in the original).

The documents prove to cover a wide spectrum of rights violations and offer hints as to the respective violators, which are mostly government and military forces. The mechanisms of defamation, isolation, and insults, however, also imply acts of violence and power struggles within the indigenous communities.

Gender-specific power relations within indigenous communities become visible via a rhetorical turn in indigenous documents: Listing women and children as victims in one line.[101] Referring to "women and children" as an entity strips the mechanisms of marginalization and oppression of their gender-specific dimension by reducing women to the level of discrimination against the allegedly weaker. This mirrors patriarchal ways of thinking when women are equated to the vulnerability and exposure of children, instead of reflecting the different mechanisms and functions of discrimination.

Indigenous Children

The situation of children and youth, however, is addressed not only in their equation with women. In the second field of discussion on internal group differences, human rights violations against children,[102] child prostitution (pf09celeste320), lack of health and educational infrastructures (pf09gene138), and the problems of juvenile delinquency and drug abuse (pf09lenny073) are on the agenda.

Indigenes with Disabilities

A third category of internal group differences, mentioned considerably less in the documents, is concerned with indigenes with disabilities. Guatemala claims to make efforts to fight discrimination based on gender, age, ethnicity, and disability (pf09marco132). Mexico demands "attention to the existing link between the rights of indigenous peoples and the exercise of the human rights of indigenous women and for the rights of indigenous people with disabilities to be addressed" (pf12gabriela242: 4).[103]

Apart from these few references by governments, there are no statements by indigenous representatives on the rights of and discriminations against indigenes with disabilities in the 04a documents. A leaflet found in the location of the 2012 UNPFII session during the participant observation was the only evidence of the topic playing a role. Although not part of the analyzed 04a document body, it is considered here because of its focus on a desideratum—and because it offers an explanation for the lack of perspective on indigenes with disabilities in the indigenous 04a documents. In the leaflet, the First Peoples Disability Network Australia (FPDN) writes,

> Aboriginal and Torres Strait Islanders with disabilities are amongst the most disadvantaged Australians yet the vast majority remain at the periphery of the disability service sector. This continues to occur for a range of reasons including the fact that the vast majority of Aboriginal and Torres Strait Islanders with disabilities do not identify as a person with disability. This is because in traditional language there was no comparable word for disability. The vast majority of Aboriginal and Torres Strait Islanders with disabilities are reluctant to take on a further negative label—particularly if they already experience discrimination based on their Aboriginality . . . despite the high prevalence of disability (at least twice that of the general population). . . . The FPDN believes there is much that the wider Australian community can learn from Aboriginal and Torres Strait Islander communities about the ways in which people with disability are valued members of their communities.[104]

In Australia, here is an apparent need for networking and support among indigenes with disabilities, their families, and their caretakers. The multiple dimensions of discrimination resulting from being indigenous and having a disability is clearly named. An explanation for the lack of indigenous discussion of the topic is seen in the particularities of indigenous languages which have no comparable word for disability. This can be interpreted to mean that people with disabilities are not stigmatized but equal members of the indigenous community. Because some forms of disability, however, make it more difficult to take part in society and handle everyday life, the absence of a word might also indicate a lack of attention to these problems and a reproduction of limitations. This can hamper special measures of support, which could be of significant importance for one's quality of life. The leaflet, however, does not answer the question of who is responsible for structures of discrimination and marginalization of indigenes with disabilities—the Australian majority society, the state or the indigenous community.

Age and Class of Indigenes

Fourth, the categories age (pf09marco132) and class (pf09jitpal067, pf09caleen126) are also mentioned sporadically when discrimination is the topic of the documents. However, neither specific constellations of problems nor concrete claims are described in detail.[105]

All in all, the spectrum of internal group differences is dominated by gender-specific approaches. These approaches are characterized almost exclusively by the fact that perpetrators are not mentioned. Thereby, this aspect significantly varies from the other areas examined, in which the state, private enterprises, or the military are mentioned as perpetrators of violence. A reason for this might be that the perpetrators of violence against women or the supporters of their exclusion might be part of the indigenous group the women belong to. The UNPFII, however, focuses mostly on raising awareness on an international level for the discrimination of indigenes by non-indigenous actors. To achieve this goal, it seems reasonable to present a homogenous identity without internal group contradictions. Following this logic, intra-indigenous conflicts are only insinuated or even omitted.

From a second, *justification-oriented* perspective of analysis, discrimination and repression are named as classic individual human rights violations against which no further justification should be required in all four content-related aspects. Beyond this, there is no reference to specific patterns of justification in the area of internal group differences.

NOTES

1. The first six sessions each had a special theme. Since 2008, there have only been special themes biannually. In the years without a special theme, general questions of the implementation of rights and recommendations are discussed.

2. The six mandated areas of the UNPFII are: 1) Economic and social development, 2) Culture, 3) Environment, 4) Education, 5) Health, and 6) Human rights. They are accompanied by the following cross-topic issues: 1) Gender and indigenous women, 2) Children and youth, 3) Millennium Development Goals, 4) Data and indicators, and, since recently, 5) the Post 2015 Agenda.

3. All UNPFII session documents are accessible on www.docip.org. See the appendix for further information.

4. The theoretical saturation is confirmed by random samples from other sessions.

5. I first assessed the material by means of qualitative content analysis; see Gläser/Laudel (2010) and Flick (2007). After this reconstruction of core aspects, I examined and interpreted the material by means of an interpretive social research approach; see Yanow/Schwartz-Shea (2006) and Rosenthal (2011). In order to find patterns of argument, implications, and mechanisms of inclusion and exclusion, selected passages were analyzed regarding their meanings, presumptions, and applications. The interpretive social research approach allows for disclosure of various meanings, latent content, implicit knowledge, and unintended effects. To prevent an intuitive approach limited to obvious or one-dimensional interpretations, and in order to facilitate intersubjective traceability, control, and transparency, the analysis was framed and given a basis by means of cooperation with an interpretation group and a participant observation—see Emerson/Fretz/Shaw (2009)—during the 2012 UNPFII session.

6. This note consists of the abbreviation for the Permanent Forum (pf), the year of the session (09 or 12), the first name of the speaker, and a number. The note reappears in the name of the pdf-document published in the UN DoCip Archive and will be used here for the identification of the documents. A complete review of all documents examined, with notes on their character and their respective author, is given in the annex.

7. Further examples are the government statements pf09gonzalo114, pf09jitpal067, pf09marcio088, pf09moira089, and pf09tomasa119.

8. In the Spanish original: "los objetivos de cohesión social y consolidación de la gobernabilidad democrática," "diversidad étnica y cultural."

9. In the Spanish original: "la coexistencia pacífica entre todos los pueblos del mundo."

10. In the Spanish original: "Recomendamos: . . . que el Foro y los pueblos indígenas apoyen los procesos indígenas en diferentes países y que se declaren estados interculturales y plurinacionales."

11. In the Spanish original: "Los pueblos indígenas . . . gozan de derechos especiales a razón de los patrones culturales propios, que los diferencian de otras culturas."

12. Source: participant observation.

13. See pf09asiacaucus4a, pf09caleen126, pf09fevzi105, pf09gene138, pf09gulnara106, pf12intreabud234, pf09joan097, pf09marcel111, pf09tegusbayar322, pf09thomas135, pf12egil231, pf09gulnara106, and pf09radine222.

14. See pf12catherine263, pf12dietrix293, pf12sona262, pf09emmanuel117, pf09eneida092, pf09freddy125, pf09gene138, pf09handaire118, pf09miguel100, pf09moira089, pf09saturnino189, pf09tegusbayar322, pf09tupac396, and pf09william123.

15. For similar argumentations, see pf12rochelle230, pf09maria145aenes, pf09moira089, pf09raphael072, and pf09samuel130.

16. In the Spanish original: "Es indígena el que vive como indígena, piensa como indígena y no se avergüenza de ser indígena." Also see pf09saturnino189, pf12shane266, pf09jitpal067, pf12dalee223, pf12regina248, and pf12leonardo228en.

17. In the French original: "La Déclaration sur les droits des Populations Autochtones . . . est loin d'être matérialisée . . . par . . . notre gouvernement qui prône dans la Constitution que tous les citoyens sont égaux et n'admet guerre de spécificité. . . . Nous adressons ainsi les recommandations . . . d'appliquer une discrimination positive pour les peuples autochtones conformément a leur politique."

18. In the French original: "dans leur milieux de vie, ceci dans le respect de leurs cultures et traditions"; "les peuples autochtones ont des droits autant que les autres communautés"; "l'égalité des chances a tous les habitants de la terre."

19. In the French original: "protection des populations autochtones"; "développement économique et social, ainsi qu'a l'expression culturelle"; "d'indivisibilité . . . d'égalité et de son corollaire."

20. In the Spanish original: "Todos somos iguales como seres humanos pero diferentes en nuestra cultura y . . . la identidad de cada pueblo."

21. In the French original: "Nous, peuples nomades ou de cultures nomades, et en particulier les Touareg, avons un mode de vie spécifique comme tous les autres peuples."

22. See pf09ali192, pf09ana107, pf09caleen126, pf09charles071, pf09ernesto127, pf09eva102, pf09gene138, pf09handaire118, pf09iiite406x, pf09lenny073, pf09mailis051, pf09radine222, pf09samuel130, pf12leonardo228en, pf09lori321EN.

23. In the Spanish original: "Los pueblos indígenas . . . han sido históricamente objeto de todas formas de discriminación económica, social, cultural y étnica."

24. In the Spanish original: "Por eso planteamos . . . respetar la diversidad cultural y terminar con toda forma de exclusión, marginamiento y racismo."

25. In the Spanish original: "El objetivo de esta política pública es contribuir al tránsito de un Estado homogéneo y monocultural hacia un Estado plural, con el fin de que los pueblos indígenas, grupos socioculturales y ciudadanos no padezcan ningún tipo de discriminación racial ni exclusión económica social y se sientan reconocidos en igualdad de derechos a partir de su cultura, etnia y género."

26. See pf09marcel111, pf09tegusbayar322, pf09jorge195: 1.

27. In pf12catherine263, pf12dietrix293, pf09gulnara106, pf09mailis051, and pf09thomas135.

28. In the French original: "culture ancestrale et originale imprègne [sic] un grand nombre de cultures."

29. In the French original: "L'Afrique est un des continent dont la diversité humaine et culturelle est la plus riche. On y trouve un grand nombre de groupes, de communautés et de peuples de différentes dimensions, établis sur un territoire et qui possèdent chacun, sa langue et sa culture spécifiques. Cependant, les Etats d'Afrique hérités du colonialisme européen, se présentent généralement comme des entités uniformes, composés d'un seul peuple, avec une seule langue, une seule culture et souvent une seule religion. Ces Etats s'efforcent alors, par leurs lois et pratiques, de nier, d'occulter et de combattre la diversité ethnique et culturelle, qu'ils considèrent comme une menace à 1'unité nationale. Cette vision [est] celle de l'ethnie dominante qui s'impose aux autres ethnies structurellement dominées et privées de leurs droits politiques, socioéconomiques, culturels et linguistiques."

30. In the Spanish original: "El actual sistema capitalista mundial, a través de sus distintas expresiones, como lo son el consumismo desmedido, el desgaste de los recursos naturales que conllevan a la destrucción de la biodiversidad, la transculturización de los pueblos que implica borrar nuestra esencia, la pérdida de nuestros valores ancestrales indígenas y la negación de la existencia de nuestros pueblos originarios, constituye la más terrible amenaza que se cierne sobre la vida y la existencia de nuestro planeta."

31. Government statements also refer comprehensively to the complex of lands/territories/resources. The representatives of Panama (pf12pablo237), Brazil (pf12regina248), Nepal (pf09jitpal067), Guatemala (pf09marco132), Congo (pf09valentine121), Venezuela (pf09moira089) and France (pf09emmanuel117) all emphasize their respect for indigenous territories—thus formally being in part diametrically opposed to indigenous accusations. The representative of Bolivia, for example, assures that his country considers the protection of nature and the environment as a matter of the state. Furthermore, he claims nationalizations of resources to be part of the struggle against private ownership and an emancipatory achievement (pf09freddy125). Bolivian indigenous groups, on the other hand, try to claim entitlement to land on private grounds (pf09eneida092).

32. Corporations are named as immediate threats in pf12catherine263, pf09jethro316, pf09mariana190, pf09samuel130, and pf09womencaucus4ab. Less often mentioned causes of land conflicts are development programs of the World Bank (pf12leonardo228en), development in general (pf09asiacaucus4a), constructions of casinos and archeological excavations (pf12santi291), and ecotourism (pf09asiacaucus4a).

33. In pf12catherine263, pf09ashley262, pf09eva102, pf09sara109, pf09stanely093, and pf09tupac396.

34. See pf09iiite406x, pf09mariana190, pf09sara109, pf12catherine263, pf09stanely093, pf09tegusbayar322.

35. Further documentation of pollution of nature and resources can be found in pf12catherine263, pf12kamira239, pf12sona262, pf12windel243, pf09ernesto127, pf09maria145aenes, pf09handaire118, pf09saturnino189, pf09marcel111, and pf09stanely093.

36. See pf12intreabud234, pf09asiacaucus4a, and pf09justa326.

37. See pf12kamira239, pf09ali192, and pf09womencaucus4ab.

38. See pf09eneida092 and pf09marcel111. Venezuela, too, points out the connection between land expropriations and other human rights violations (pf09moira089).

39. See also pf12yupo339, pf09asiacaucus4a, pf09charles071, pf09egil099, pf09jorge195, pf09legb_africaucus140, and pf09marcel111.

40. See pf12evariste276a, pf12severin344, pf09ali192, pf09caleen126, and pf09fevzi105.

41. pf12catherine263 and pf09ghislain139. For general criticisms of colonial mechanisms beyond land conflicts, see pf12catherine263, pf12dalee223, pf12dietrix293, pf12evariste276b, pf09gene138, pf09ghislain139, pf09gulnara106, pf09lori321EN, pf09mariana190, pf09miguel100, and pf09radine222.

42. See pf09catherine113, pf09maria145aenes, pf09marcel111, pf09jacqueline110, pf09tegusbayar322, and pf12sona262.

43. See pf12catherine263, pf12dietrix293, pf12sona262, and pf09jorge195.

44. See pf09eneida092, pf09maria145aenes, pf09handaire118, pf09mariana190, pf09radine222, pf09saturnino189, pf09tegusbayar322, pf09tupac396, and pf09william123. With Bolivia und Venezuela, two government representatives refer to this relationship as well (pf09freddy125, pf09moira089).

45. See, for example, bei pf09egil099, pf09jethro316, pf09stanely093, and pf09alcides033.

46. See, for example, pf12intreabud234, pf12yupo339, and pf09justa326.

47. See pf12dietrix293 and pf09eva102. Biodiversity as a basis of certain traditional practices is defended in similar ways (pf09maria145aenes).

48. In the Spanish original: "una relación sagrada y complementaria y no la schema depredadora y patriarcal que domina el mundo con sus prácticas de despojo de las industrias extractivas con sus empresas impulsadas sólo por la ganancia y la codicia."

49. See, for example, pf12evariste276a, pf09ali192, pf09ashley262, pf09catherine113, pf09gene138, pf09gulnara106, pf09marcel111, pf09sara109, pf09legb_africaucus140, and pf12dalee223.

50. In the French original: "un organisme suprême décisionnel autochtone au gouvernement de nouvelle Calédonie."

51. See also pf12geoff259, pf09gene138, pf09jennifer101, pf09miguel100, pf12evariste276b, pf12severin344, pf12geoff259, pf12kamira239, and pf09fevzi105.

52. This assumption is explicated in pf12santi291, pf12shane266, pf09ana107.

53. See, for example, pf09charles071, pf09gene138, pf09jennifer101, pf12leonardo228en, and pf12jennifer260.

54. Among others, this formulation is found in pf09celeste320 and pf09tupac396.

55. See pf12catherine263, pf12dietrix293, pf09eva102, and pf09stanely093.

56. See pf09ana107, pf09egil099, pf09handaire118, pf09iiite406x, pf09jamesread087, pf09jethro316, pf09stanely093, pf09stephane034, and pf09tegusbayar322.

57. See pf09eneida092 and, similar, pf12leonardo228en, and pf09ana107.

58. Concerning, for example, the Second International Decade of the World's Indigenous People (pf09margarita196), the World Conference on Indigenous Peoples (pf12dalee223), agendas of UN committees (pf09miguel100), and in general (pf09margarita196).

59. See pf09jorge195, pf09margarita196. The United States and Bolivia report the implementation of such a legal pluralism (pf09freddy125 and pf09shane133).

Indigenous Demands in the United Nations 143

60. In the Spanish original: "[El] principio del consentimiento libre, previo consentimiento informado no se puede aplicar en un sólo proyecto por proyecto o región por región."

61. Simultaneously, statements predominate that perceive the UNPFII as an important partner and that ask for its further support by conducting studies, offering trainings on indigenous human rights for disseminators and affected persons, paying official visits to countries, and treating key subjects (see pf09charles071, pf09catherine113, pf09craig112, pf09ghislain139, pf09gulnara106, pf09handaire118, pf09legb_africaucus140, pf09caleen126, pf09ana107, pf12albert233, pf12antti227, pf12catherine263, pf12legborsi225, pf09craig112, pf09egil099, pf09fabiana091, pf09ghislain139, pf09legb_africaucus140, pf09margarita196, and pf09stanely093).

62. See pf09ernesto127 and pf12dietrix293.

63. Most clearly in pf09fevzi105, pf09raphael072, pf09craig112, and pf12dalee223.

64. See pf09ernesto127, pf09fevzi105, pf09ghislain139, pf09iiite406x, pf09justa326, pf09legb_africaucus140, pf09margarita196, pf09mariana190, pf09miguel100, pf09minz191, pf09samuel130, pf09thomas135, pf09tomasa119, pf09tonya082, pf09wilton059, pf09womencaucus4ab, pf12catherine263, pf12dalee223, pf09jamesread087, pf12david335, pf12intreabud234, pf12jennifer260, pf12santi291, pf12sona262, and pf12windel243.

65. For similar critiques of Canada, see pf09celeste320 and pf09wilton059. For reports on poverty in other countries, see pf09ernesto127, pf09fevzi105, pf09ghislain139, pf09iiite406x, pf09justa326, pf09legb_africaucus140, pf09margarita196, pf09mariana190, pf09miguel100, pf09minz191, pf09samuel130, pf09thomas135, pf09tomasa119, pf09tonya082, pf09wilton059, pf09womencaucus4ab, pf12catherine263, pf12dalee223, pf09jamesread087, pf12david335, pf12intreabud234, pf12jennifer260, pf12santi291, pf12sona262, and pf12windel243.

66. See pf09ali192, pf12shane266, pf09ghislain139, pf09saturnino189, and pf09marcel111.

67. See pf09ghislain139, pf09jethro316, pf09lori321EN, pf09marcel111, pf12severin344, and pf09patricia163.

68. These issues are raised in pf12catherine263, pf12dalee223, pf12kamira239, pf09ana107, pf09eneida092, pf09handaire118, pf09lori321EN, pf09mariana190, pf09miguel100, pf09patricia163, pf09samuel130, pf09sara109, and pf09stephane034.

69. These problems are addressed especially in pf12evariste276b, pf12severin344, pf12shane266, pf12sona262, pf09ana107, pf09celeste320, pf09eneida092, pf09fabiana091, pf09ghislain139, pf09handaire118, pf09iiite406x, pf09lenny073, pf09lori321EN, pf09marcel111, pf09patricia163, pf09raphael072, pf09samuel130, pf09sara109, and pf09stephane034.

70. In the Spanish original: "el derecho a la educación en todos los niveles."

71. See pf09celeste320, pf09mariana190, pf09miguel100, pf12severin344, and pf09fevzi105.

72. See pf09raphael072, pf09handaire118, pf09mariana190, and pf09kuriakose134.

73. In the Spanish original: "prácticas análogas a la esclavitud en países como Bolivia y Paraguay".

74. See pf12kamira239, pf09alcides033, pf09catherine113, pf09justa326, pf09maria145aenes, pf09lori321EN, pf09mailis051, pf09marcel111, pf09miguel100, pf09patricia163, pf09tegusbayar322, pf09womencaucus4ab, pf09ernesto127, pf09samuel130, and pf12evariste276a.

75. On this especially, see pf12santi291, pf12sona262, pf09alcides033, pf09jorge195, and pf09ali192.

76. Allegations of torture are brought forward in pf09tegusbayar322, pf09mailis051 and pf09ali192.

77. See pf12catherine263, pf12windel243, pf09ana107, pf09caleen126, pf09catherine113, pf09gene138, pf09maria145aenes, pf09jethro316, pf09joan097, pf09justa326, pf09legb_africaucus140, pf09miguel100, pf09minz191, pf09samuel130, and pf09womencaucus4ab.

78. See pf12catherine263, pf12santi291, pf12windel243, pf09ernesto127, and pf09jethro316.

79. Other armed resistance and rebel groups mentioned are the National Democratic Front of the Philippines (NDFP), the Moro Islamic Liberation Front (MILF) in the Philippines, and the National Socialist Council of Nagalim (IM) in India (pf12windel243: 2).

80. See pf12windel243, pf09ali192, pf09ernesto127, pf09freddy125, pf09jethro316, pf09joan097, pf09justa326, pf09mariana190, pf09minz191, pf09patricia163, pf09stephane034, and pf09maria145aenes.

81. See pf12kamira239, pf12leonardo228en, pf12santi291, pf12sona262, pf09ali192, pf09ana107, pf09caleen126, pf09eneida092, pf09gene138, pf09maria145aenes, pf09joan097, pf09justa326, pf09kuriakose134, pf09legb_africaucus140, pf09marcel111, pf09mariana190, pf09radine222, and pf09sara109.

82. See pf12dalee223, pf12jennifer260, pf12shane266, pf09ana107, pf09caleen126, pf09dalee137, pf12geoff259, pf09gulnara106, pf09handaire118, pf09justa326, pf09marcel111, pf09miguel100, pf09patricia163, pf09samuel130, pf09sara109, pf09saturnino189, pf09tupac396, and pf09wilton059.

83. See, for example, pf12geoff259, pf09womencaucus4ab, pf09mariana190, pf09raphael072, pf12dalee223, pf12jennifer260, pf12shane266, pf09ana107, pf09caleen126, pf09dalee137.

84. In the Spanish original: "sin marginar por el color de la piel, del sexo, la religión o las ideas que tengan."

85. See also pf09wilton059, pf09fevzi105, pf09ghislain139, pf09wilton059, pf12geoff259, and pf09raphael072.

86. See pf12catherine263, pf09catherine113, pf09maria145aenes, pf09joan097, and pf09miguel100.

87. See pf12sona262, pf12david335, pf12shane266, and pf09ernesto127.

88. In the Spanish original: "Los Pueblos Indígenas sean considerados sujetos colectivos de derechos."

89. See pf12sona262, pf09jorge195, and pf09jacqueline110.

90. In the Spanish original: "Finalmente, hacemos un llamado al Foro permanente inste al Concejo de Derechos Humanos poner alto a la criminalización de nuestros derechos colectivos: cese a la militarización, genocidio, etnocidio, desplazamiento forzoso, confinamiento, estigmatización, amenazas y persecución contra líderes y organizaciones."

91. See also pf12kamira239, pf12sona262, pf09ana107, and pf09maria145aenes.

92. pf09catherine113: 5 and, similarly, pf12evariste276b and pf09eneida092. For general accounts of insufficient educational possibilities in the sense of collective rights, see pf09raphael072, pf09samuel130, pf09celeste320, pf09ghislain139, pf09handaire118, pf09lori321EN, and pf12severin344.

93. See pf09catherine113, pf09ghislain139, pf09handaire118, pf09legb_africaucus140, pf09lenny073, pf09mailis051, pf09patricia163, and pf09samuel130. States, on the other hand, point to cultural programs to support indigenous languages. See pf09freddy125, pf09gonzalo114, pf09jitpal067, pf09raimo124, pf12gabriela242, and pf12wilton224.

94. In the French original: "en vertu du principe constitutionnel d'indivisibilité de la République, d'égalité et de son corollaire (à savoir le principe de non-discrimination), des droits collectifs ne peuvent prévaloir sur les droits individuels."

95. See also pf09legb_africaucus140. For more general accounts involving the category of gender and sex, see pf09kuriakose134, pf09luis108, and pf09patricia163.

96. See pf09eneida092, pf09fabiana091, and pf09gene138.

97. See pf09ana107, pf09william123, and pf09womencaucus4ab.

98. See pf09celeste320, pf09justa326, and pf09womencaucus4ab.

99. See pf09ana107, pf12sona262, pf09gene138, pf09ghislain139, pf09kuriakose134, pf09patricia163, and pf09womencaucus4ab.

100. "Las mujeres indígenas de América Latina hemos sido protagonistas de todos los procesos reivindicativos, aunque hasta ahora no se haya podido reconocer nuestra participación. Por eso, como mujeres indígenas, exhortamos a las Naciones Unidas . . . programas . . . para que podamos consolidar organizaciones de mujeres que fortalezcan nuestras estructuras ya consolidadas. Sólo de esta manera, las mujeres indígenas podremos comenzar a sentirnos reales, visibilizadas y no simplemente figurar en papeles y documentales." See also pf09asiacaucus4a, pf09margarita196, pf09sara109, pf09thomas135, pf09william123, and pf09womencaucus4ab.

101. See, for example, pf12sona262, pf09caleen126, pf09samuel130, pf09sara109, pf09jamesread087, and pf12dalee223.

102. See pf09patricia163, pf09saturnino189, and pf12intreabud234.

103. In the Spanish original: "atención a la vinculación existente entre los derechos de los pueblos indígenas y el ejercicio de los derechos humanos de la mujer indígena y que se aborden los derechos de las personas con discapacidad indígenas."

104. Source: FDNP leaflet, found at the 2012 UNPFII session.

105. The category of class plays a role in discussions on economic marginalization in the context of individual human rights, but not as an axis of differentiation within indigenous groups.

SIX

Indigenous Rights

Culture, Identity, and Beyond

The qualitative document analysis of the UNPFII sessions documents on agenda item 04a (concerning the implementation of the UNDRIP) discloses six central and partially overlapping subject areas in which discussions on indigenous human rights take place. Each area is internally differentiated and referred to on both a content and a justification-oriented level. Table 6.1 gives an overview of the levels of content and justification of the six subject areas discussed in the documents.

Figure 6.1 demonstrates the frequency and overlapping of patterns of justification. History, cultural distinction, and individual human rights are frequent patterns of justification (see the gray fields in figure 6.1). Beyond this, there are dimensions that occur throughout both the level of content and the level of justification and that simultaneously form their own network of topics (see the black fields in figure 6.1).

These dimensions include, first, individual human rights and, second, the whole complex of culture, identity, indigeneity, and cultural distinction, which I will from now on subsume under the concept of culture. The three dominant patterns of justification and their duplications on different levels represent, in each case, different functions, meanings, possibilities, and boundaries.

CULTURE

The subject of culture serves, on the one hand, to legitimize other purposes (lands/territories/resources, participation/self-determination, individual human rights, collective rights). On the other hand, culture is itself

Table 6.1.   Dimensions of Demands for Indigenous Rights

Subject Area	Level of Content	Level of Justification
culture, identity, indigeneity	cultural plurality cultural distinction racism	history genealogy transcendence
lands, territories, resources	pollution displacement	history genealogy cultural distinction individual human rights
participation, self-determination	participation self-determination FPIC	history cultural distinction individual human rights
individual human rights	economic marginalization repression racism	cultural distinction individual human rights
collective rights	general importance connection to indigenous demands connection to individual human rights restriction of individual human rights	cultural distinction individual human rights
internal group differences	indigenous women indigenous children indigenes with disabilities age, class	individual human rights

Source: Author

content and objective of indigenous demands (culture/identity/indigeneity). Culture through an objective lens and culture as a means to an end can overlap, as becomes especially clear through the use of culture as a resource. Culture is attributed to a function—for example, culture as a contribution to humanity or to diversity—which at the same time is supposed to legitimize its reproduction. This argument is also featured in the preamble of the UNDRIP, according to which "all peoples contribute to the diversity and richness of civilizations and cultures, which constitute the common heritage of humankind" (UNDRIP, preamble). The subject area of culture is of high significance in the controversy on indigenous rights. "The threat to the survival of indigenous peoples' culture is what has motivated the claims . . . not primarily political or economic objectives. . . . In this broad sense, all the rights of indigenous peoples are cultural rights" (Wiessner 2011: 129; similarly, Pulitano 2012; Martin 2012).

Indigenous Rights: Culture, Identity, and Beyond

	Culture	History	Genealogy	Transcendence	Individual human rights
Culture, identity, indigeneity	■■■				
Lands, territories, resources					
Participation, self-determination					
Individual human rights				■■■	
Collective human rights					
Internal group differences					

Figure 6.1. Patterns of Justification for Demands for Indigenous Rights.
Source: Author

Some indigenous documents, however, point out that a culture-based argument might undermine indigenous human rights claims. This contradiction can be explained by the conceptual analysis given in chapter 2. Culture is neither empowering per se, nor repressive per se. Rather, the implications of power and emancipation that come with the recourse to culture are decisive. The concepts of culture referred to in the debates on indigenous rights move along two spectrums that give hints as to corresponding implications and meanings.

The first spectrum reaches from the pole of dichotomous cultural distinction to the pole of transcultural hybridity. Within this spectrum lie ideas of equality and hybridization models of different scope. The second spectrum spans between the poles of static culture and dynamic culture. Both spectrums overlap at different points: dynamism can coincide with transcultural hybridity as well as with the distinct development of a secluded culture. Stability can be inherent to efforts of distinction or to transcultural ideas that aim for a fixed "final state."

The three content-related levels of the subject area of culture—plurality, distinction, and racism—feature different positions in both spectrums.

The motive of cultural plurality can be related especially to the effort of distinction. If plurality serves as a resource and a distinguishing feature, it needs to be preserved (mostly) statically. Transcultural hybridity can stand in the way of the ideal of plurality.

The dimension of cultural distinction is based on an assumption of insurmountable, fundamental—and thereby, in a sense, static—differences between cultures. This is connected to efforts of keeping one's own culture "pure" and devaluing an allegedly non-indigenous transculturality. The belief that only indigenes can understand indigenes is one of the sources of demands for exclusively indigenous legal systems and monitoring mechanisms. Intra-cultural dynamics could be compatible with this approach, but not if they mean a weakening of distinction. If, in contrast, distinction is referred to as a characteristic of fundamental equality between cultural groups, this might imply an assumption of a framework of equal rights for everyone. Cultural boundaries remain untouched, however.

If culture is discussed as an axis of racism, priority lies on injustice based on cultural otherness or othering that can originate from internal and external attributions. Constellations of power between cultures are the subject of this argument. Its goal can be integration into the majority culture or equality for distinct cultural groups to be preserved. Because it aims at changing a situation characterized by inequality and racism, this argument has a dynamic component.

With regards to *individual human rights*, culture can contribute to the reproduction of inequality and human rights violations when indigenous rights are limited to a narrowly demarcated field of folklore, tradition, and customs—an approach that omits basic individual human rights and that puts culture and human rights into opposition. This conflict becomes obvious in the Chilean women's rights organization's statement discussed in chapter 5. It points out that the government ignores severe violations of human rights against indigenes under the cloak of cultural recognition (pf09maria145aenes: 3f.). Additionally, culture can even be feared to undermine collective rights:

> The culturalization of indigenous rights, which stresses cultural identity and distinctiveness over historical and legal-political aspects . . . is also highly problematic. Not only does the invocation of culture in a rights framework favor an essentialist understanding of culture; it . . . comes at the price of the right of self-determination understood as a group right. (Schulte-Tenckhoff 2012: 67)

Possible conflicts between culture and human rights become especially visible in Australia. The 04a documents indicate a serious confrontation between representatives of indigenous groups and the Australian government. The government wants to push through reforms aimed at solving problems such as alcoholism and child abuse in indigenous communities (pf09australia115), while indigenous representatives assess this as a continuation of the colonial extermination of indigenous ways of life (pf12shane266). Narrowing down the argument to the issue of culture on both sides has far-reaching implications: If the government neglects social, political, and historical reasons and inequalities and instead only understands problems as inherent to indigenous culture (see Collingwood-Whittick 2012: 126), then it perceives culture—or, more precisely, the "other's" culture—as nothing but repressive. On the other hand, if indigenous representatives conceptualize culture as a static and exclusively empowering, emancipatory framework, then everything can be justified by referring to culture—including practices that conflict with individual human rights.[1] Both approaches are insufficient and both are based on the idea of cultural incommensurability, with the only difference being the respective conclusions: assimilation or distinction.

Conflicts between culture and human rights also appear in the subject area of *internal group differences*. These become invisible when cultures are presented as externally distinct and internally homogeneous. Insisting from a collective rights perspective on the uncircumventable significance of culture for individuals (as do Taylor, Kymlicka, and also Tully 2008a: 254) tends to exhibit similar blanks. Since, however, identities are constituted in manifold ways (see chapter 3), an individual's positioning within a culture (Okin 1998a: 679f.) as well as overlapping *and* contradicting aspects in identity formations are relevant. The culture-based "argument only works well in the unrealistic situation of having a homogeneous territorially concentrated group, all of whom aspire to promote the same culture, and have the same understanding of the culture, and there are no social identities that are marginalized by the culture" (Moore 2005: 282).

This may be the reason why the subject area of internal group differences and their related human rights violations is the only one out of six core areas that does not refer to culture. If it referred to culture, conflicts between culture and individual human rights could become too visible.

This problem becomes clear in the following example: Between 1987 and 1991, the Australian Royal Commission into Aboriginal Deaths in Custody (RCIADIC) investigated the disproportionately high number of indigenous detainee deaths that occurred between 1980 and 1989. Although more than half of the imprisoned men had been sentenced for sexual or physical assaults against family members, domestic violence was valued as irrelevant in the investigation. In her evaluation of the investigation, Elena Marchetti reveals various reasons for this phenomenon (Marchetti 2008): First, indigenous women had been pressured from within the community to focus in their testimonies on indigenous land rights and self-determination. They were blamed by their communities for the men's detention because cases of domestic violence had become public. It was considered culturally and, with regard to identity politics, inappropriate to address individual rights and violence against women. Second, the commission did not actively put gender-specific or violence problems on the agenda. It assumed that indigenous women would bring up possible issues by themselves, and the commission did not want to speak "on their behalf." Third, the indigenous women were motivated intrinsically to not speak badly of their dead family members but to expose problems of the white judiciary's approach (Ibid.: 161ff.).

In this case, domestic violence against indigenous women conflicts with cultural norms and the women's interest to protect their indigenous group's identity and interests. Repressive effects are reinforced by the common assumption that "domestic violence . . . is more likely the product of Anglo-induced paternalistic values" (Zion 1992: 204). Possible conflicts between gender equality on one side, and culture/identity/indigeneity on the other, are translated into a dichotomy of indigeneity and non-indigeneity. As such they are interpreted out of focus and reproduced.[2]

The preservation of "culture as distinct" is not only a demand directed to the state and the government, but also imperative to those who live within that culture. Indigenes have to identify as indigenous and live indigenously in order to secure the reproduction of indigenous culture. The indigenous community, which can offer a safe haven and protection from a discriminatory majority society, can also mean coercion. Both aspects cannot be juxtaposed in clear distinction; rather, they determine each other. Culture can serve as a refuge if its demands are met and if culture is practiced accordingly (see also Niederauer 2014: 131f.). Inclusion and exclusion, and thus also the sense of belonging to a particular collective identity, are determined gender- and culture-specifically. In a dichotomous logic, the differentiation between belonging and not belonging becomes the only criterion. Culture evolves into everyone's duty toward the collective. Indigeneity becomes imperative not only for today's generations, but also for future generations. Questioning or challenging traditional patterns of power or inequality is more difficult if solutions remain self-referential and move full-circle back to the indigenous collective.

In this approach, the collective cannot have or publicly exhibit internal conflicts. Contradicting demands or needs because of internal mechanisms of exclusion based on gender, class, or disability potentially conflict with the imperative of indigenous identity.[3] In order to serve as an identity-constituting political resource, indigeneity has to appear homogenous and free of conflict. Simultaneously, demands for the individual related to the imperative of indigeneity are, however, characterized by internal differences.

Current efforts try to address internal heterogeneity: "Particular attention shall be paid to the rights and special needs of indigenous elders, women, youth, children and persons with disabilities in the implementation of this Declaration" (UNDRIP, Article 22.1). This sentence joins various possible axes of difference. The highly diverse mechanisms that can lead to discrimination are not named. By mixing children's physical and psychological vulnerability and women's social vulnerability, the latter is even reproduced (Okin 1989: 139). Additionally, possible conflicts between those vulnerabilities and culture, identity, and indigeneity remain untouched. If approaches remain within the performative circle of culture, identity, and indigeneity, they become a duty and solution at the same time.

In conclusion, the two subject areas of culture and individual human rights can come into (explicit and implicit) contradiction. References to culture/identity/indigeneity contribute mostly to human rights violations if used as distinction and if conceptualized statically. The more transculturally open and the more dynamic the respectively referred-to conception is, the more compatible it is with individual human rights. But even open concepts of culture can be repressive. Cross-cultural processes, through which cultures mix and dissolve, can be shaped by inequality and social hierarchy. Transculturalization can lead to forced assimilation—a central subject of indigenous criticism of state politics.

The possible conflict between culture and individual human rights is a crucial challenge for indigenous demands. On the one hand, almost all of the core subject areas include the dimension of cultural distinction, which draws on specific images of indigeneity and identity. Distinction and the indigenous identity play an important role in defining the legal subject of demands for indigenous rights, too. On the other hand, indigenous ideas, norms, and legal systems are neither static "nor is their assertion of cultural presence made in the name of an ahistorical collective essence, but in the name of living, changing, creative peoples" (Coombe 1993: 268f.). Rather, there are indigenous approaches to culture/identity/indigeneity that can adapt to the conceptual openness of UN institutions without giving up on indigeneity.[4] Yet, openness and dynamics can remain in a narrow framework if indigenous demands aim at preserving distinction in the long-term, thereby upholding a dichotomy that marks and devalues non-indigeneity as the non-authentic other (see also Horowitz 1985: 208ff.).

In conclusion, culture/identity/indigeneity and distinction offer no *sufficient* argument for demands for indigenous rights.

> At the moment, wherever there is a conflict between "local practices" and "transnational human rights standards," commentators tend to locate the source of the conflict in the "culture" or "traditions" of the group, and then look for ways in which this culture differs from "Western" culture. This tendency is exacerbated by the rhetoric of a "politics of difference," which encourages groups to press their demands in the language of respect for cultural "difference." My suggestion, however, is that we should not jump to the conclusion that cultural differences are the real source of the problem. (Kymlicka 2001a: 89)

Indeed, preserving culture and distinction is only one of three dominant patterns of justification for indigenous demands—with the other two being human rights and history.

HISTORY

History serves as a strong legitimation for demands for indigenous rights. Here, too, one has to ask for emancipatory and repressive effects and implications. Using history as a pattern of justification obtains validity by painting a certain picture of history and by showing only a certain part of it. Pointing to the (often prosperous and positively connoted) past and comparing it with the (ostensibly bad and spoiled) present produces a historiography that allows for the construction and constitution of a specific image of a culture. This approach ignores everything not fitting this dichotomy, like wars and conquests among indigenous groups (Benedict 1934: 62; Kuper 2003: 392). Using history means choosing segments from a great variety of past times, incidents, and practices, and determining what is important and what can (not) be said.

Assmann approaches the production and reproduction of history by means of his concept of cultural memory. The cultural memory makes choices, censors, suppresses, manipulates, and replaces. It does not simply refer to a given past, but it constructs this past (Assmann 1995, 2011).

Segments of the past that are chosen and assigned with importance, meaning, and objectivity shape identity in the present. They can serve to legitimate and uphold a (static) present or to reinsert a (static) past. This approach is manifested in a longing for the past:

> The road behind is a space in which Aboriginal peoples know who we are; we know our countries, families and peoples. . . . Colonial encounters have caused and continue to cause conflict, and conflict interferes with our capacity to remain connected and to reconnect with country and family. Our Aboriginal selves in relationship to country can bring us home; the dispossessed Aboriginal self confronts a space in which the only direction free of blocks and obstacles is onward and ahead. . . . What of the road behind and the Aboriginal selves? (Watson/Venne 2012: 87)

Historical patterns of justification are often linked to genealogical or transcendent patterns. These three patterns share the wish for a revival of what is imagined and objectified as original and authentic.

A central source of historical legitimation lies in the assumption that indigenous groups for a long time—some speak of "over ten thousand years" (Tully 1994: 155)—had sovereign political structures and relations to other political entities (Tully 2008a: 232). Here, too, present conceptions of indigenous sovereignty and nationality are part of the construction of a favorable past. The fact that it is very possible for other forms of society to have existed in the past is neglected (see Anaya 1996: 78f.; Kymlicka 2001b: 825f.; Moore 2005: 282ff.).

Dichotomous comparisons between the past and present lead to dichotomous assignments of guilt and innocence. Because of this, the question of who writes and who refers to which history becomes relevant. This question is a recurrent theme in indigenous criticisms of dominant narratives that omit or dismiss historical injustice done to indigenes. It is consulted, for example, in order to substantiate demands for teaching indigenous perspectives on history in schools and universities. However, these reflections are barely used when it comes to indigenous historiography.

The characteristics of historical patterns of justification become clear in the priority criterion. The priority criterion exists in three forms. First, it transports an element of having-been-there-first, a "historical continuity with pre-invasion and pre-colonial societies that developed on their territories" (Martínez Cobo 1986: para. 379ff.), or, in short, a "we were here before you" (Clifford 2007: 197). This claim of having-been-there-first is often directly linked to further demands like the claim of legitimacy: "My people were here before yours and are therefore legitimate occupiers of this land" (Canessa 2008: 353).

In its second use, the focus of the priority criterion lies on the autochthonous statement of having-been-there-always. It "carries a sense of *original or first inhabitants*. Such peoples would not only be historically prior but the first human beings to inhabit a territory" (Thornberry 2002: 38; italics in the original). Here, the criterion marks not a relational but an absolute priority.

Third, and in combination with the two other forms, the priority criterion is justified culturally by pointing to cultures and ways of life that constitute priority because they are perceived as more ancient, traditional, spiritual, or close to earth (Saugestad 2001: 43).

The priority criterion remains decisive for the definition of indigeneity — even after the revision resulting from the introduction of Asian and African groups to the international indigenous movement discussed above. The priority criterion itself is, however, a result of the cultural memory and its processes of reconstructing the past. Images of "always" or "prior" have to *choose* a historical starting point. Other historiographies have to be ignored or repelled. The hypothesis of indigenous immigration into the Americas via the Bering Strait provides an example.

> A woman from a Cree community ... was not happy about the Bering Strait theory. She pointed out that her people, and most "Indian" people, do not believe that archaeologists know anything about the origins of human life in the Americas. The idea that people first came as immigrants from Asia was, she said, absurd. It went against all that her people knew.... There had been no immigration, but an emergence. (Brody 2001: 113f.; latter ellipsis points in the original)

Surely indigenous historiography cannot be waived as a myth. Yet its appearance of naturalness and objectivity is — like any other historiography—mediated by and through present interests. Its dynamic factors can be disclosed by reflecting on the relations between past and present.

Against this background, the usage of the historical argument in order to legitimize demands for indigenous rights is not undisputed (see Pritchard 2001: 325ff.; Xanthaki 2007: 131). Accompanying conceptions of a static indigenous culture are criticized sharply (Goggin 2011). In 1993, the WGIP emphasized that indigenes do not see themselves as "the remains of traditions or customs long dead" (cited in Xanthaki 2007: 208). The static understanding of history is contrasted here with a dynamic variant. However, the historical legitimization of culture can undermine this dynamic understanding.

As a matter of fact, claims of past suffering in pursuit of compensation and recognition can be substantiated by historical argumentative patterns (Anaya 2009c: 60f.; Buchanan 2004; Kymlicka 2001b). However, history and morality are not linked intrinsically. In contrast to this, Zion argues:

> "Morality" is a charged term, alienating many because of its association with religion. International human rights law, however, deals with "self-evident" and "natural law" rights, which have the same vague content. History, on the other hand, provides a measure for the application of a morality. Deprivations of Indian rights and assaults upon their group integrity are sufficiently documented to provide guidance, and the reality of the persistence of Indians and Indian-ness must be acknowledged and protected. (Zion 1992: 212)

History alone is not a sufficient argument for current demands, however. This would constitute a one-sided criticism, characterized by two features: First, it assumes the existence of one "true" version of history. Second, it presupposes that this objectified history provides a direct deduction of moral standards. Rather, the respectively selected segments of history, as well as their effects on current moral considerations, are mediated and shaped by societal, intersubjective and subjective (negotiations over) meanings.

The question of morality depends—as even Zion implies—on the third dominant pattern of justification in indigenous demands: human suffering and violations of individual human rights.

SUFFERING AND HUMAN RIGHTS

The pattern of justification focused on *violations of individual human rights and experiences of suffering* is used in all six subject areas reconstructed in the document analysis. By making racist exclusions a subject of discussion, it plays an indirect role in the area of culture/identity/indigeneity, too.

The category of suffering needs to be understood as both subjectively and socially mediated (see also Adorno 2010: 66f.). Suffering is found on both the side of the object and the subject (the individual). Therefore, suffering cannot be reduced to an individual inwardness that is not intersubjectively comprehensible, limited to an objective setting, or condensed to an objective, static catalogue of sufferings. Suffering is a societal and a social category that can simultaneously express individual experience and make it intersubjectively comprehensible. If used as a reference in indigenous demands, it can justify the striving for "something better" and the distinction from "something worse." Nonetheless, or rather, because of its mediated character, suffering does not constitute a final or ultimate justification. This is because every effort toward finding a final justification turns out to be an effort toward a standpoint that can be (statically) related to and that needs no further legitimization, reflection, or explanation.

Suffering can exist consciously and unconsciously, and can be suppressed and exploited. It relates to experiences with social and intersubjective interaction. What exactly is seen and acknowledged as suffering is framed by historical and societal conditions. The category of suffering is not absolute, neither does it cover or explain everything. Only in consideration of its social mediation can suffering offer a possible, but not absolute, point of reference; or be used as a yardstick for criticism and a justification for the demands for human rights.

Experiences of suffering are directly linked to demands for human rights in the 04a documents. Demands for human rights can lean on internationally recognized human rights agreements, which is why most descriptions of injustices need no further justification beyond pointing to the fact that they constitute violations of essential human rights.

This recourse to human rights and their violations is, however, the basis of some demands for collective human rights, too. This is possible because of the duplicity of human rights, encompassing both a moral and a legal level. Suffering and a poor quality of life can be linked to aspects not (yet) covered by the framework of classic, legally binding human rights (they can, however, be a subject of the UNDRIP). Here, the moral dimension of human rights assumes a crucial function by allowing for legal human rights to not be seen as static scaffolding but to open the view for context, specific conditions, dynamics, expansions, and gaps in human rights. Making suffering the subject of discussion in indigenous demands for collective human rights is closely connected to such an expanding, moral-based usage of human rights. The resulting developments and implications can be marked both by emancipatory and repressive aspects—depending on their connections to other subject areas, on patterns of argument, and on concepts of culture, equality, and internal differences.

CONCLUSION

In light of these results, the common reduction of indigenous demands to collective cultural rights has to be corrected regarding two aspects.

First, big parts of demands for indigenous rights are formulated and legitimized without referring to culture. Individual human rights constitute an important alternative pattern of justification.

Second, the respective concepts of culture in demands for indigenous rights consist of assumptions, functions, and intentions so heterogeneous that they cannot be attributed to one homogenous concept of cultural rights. Repressive and emancipatory effects are, if not exclusively, then at least crucially tied to the openness and the possibilities for changes within the concepts of culture respectively referred to.

Conversely, waiving the category of culture would not constitute a viable solution. Racism and mechanisms of exclusion and oppression can be tied to cultural axes so completely that addressing culture *can* mean an extension of individual human rights; a reflection on specific dimensions of meaning, however, remains crucial.

On this basis, the effects and implications of demands for indigenous rights can be traced without ignoring experiences of oppression and suffering. Examining the concepts of indigeneity, identity, and culture does not automatically lead to the much feared erosion of solidarity:

> I am disturbed . . . by the essentialism . . . inherent in these conceptualisations of identity. . . . I also find myself in a dilemma on this issue. . . . I would find myself unable to deny the San people I have worked among their commitment to culture and identity. Instead of deconstructing what are to them key notions, my energies would be directed toward battling alongside the people I work with, uncompromisingly and, as much as possible, at their behest. (Guenther 2006: 17f.)

Yet, such an unconditional solidarity "is an act of breathtaking condescension. . . . Objectively, such an act involves contempt for the latter's intelligence" (Taylor 1994a: 70). Moreover, an examination of inherent patterns of inequality and power relations, unintended repercussions, intermediations, and the concurrence of emancipatory and repressive effects in indigenous demands does not necessarily mean to undermine them. On the contrary; a critical discussion means taking the subject of discussion seriously—something the demand for unconditional solidarity does not do.

NOTES

1. For a discussion of domestic violence against women in Australian indigenous communities, see Atkinson (1991), Payne (1990), and Marchetti (2008).

2. James Zion, who allocates gender inequality on only the non-indigenous side, also assumes that contraception is incompatible with indigenous values (Zion 1992: 199). In contrast, see Goodale (2006: 647), who mentions that the frequently cited and praised complementarity of the sexes in indigenous cultures is an idealization devoid of reality regarding gender equality.

3. See Wolff (2007) for possible escalation levels of emerging conflicts behind the homogenizing façade of shared identity.

4. For further discussions on this issue, see Guenther (2006: 18f.); Cowan (2006: 20f.); Clifford (1997: 154ff.); Robbins/Stamatopoulou (2004). In Ecuador and Peru, for example, principles founded on the rule of law, individual rights, and an improvement of the situation of women are incorporated into indigenous legal systems; see Brandt (2013).

Conclusion

Culture and Identity as Collective Human Rights?

The discussions regarding collective human rights are characterized by the fact that the relevant terms and concepts provide arguments that can be used for or against collective rights. Against this background, approaches that either support one point of view or simply add a new position to the discussion are limited. The study at hand shows that non-explicated presuppositions, ostensible matters of course, normative concepts, and contradictory constellations can and must be made the subject of discussion. Before discussing the results and drawing conclusions, I will summarize the argument outlined in the preceding chapters.

THE ANALYSIS SO FAR

In part I, the question of this study regarding the possibilities and limits of collective human rights were examined in light of communitarian and liberal approaches. The theories of Charles Taylor, Will Kymlicka, and Susan Okin proved to be central because these three researchers paradigmatically connect collective rights with culture, and they approach the question of collective cultural rights from different paradigmatic perspectives. The three theories differ in their assessment of the role of collective rights and in their basic assumptions of culture and subject constitution. Taylor underscores the value of certain cultures to individual identities. Kymlicka shares Taylor's perspective that one's culture is indispensable for individual identity. But, from a liberal perspective, he also emphasizes the danger of freedom-restricting cultural aspects. He believes these factors can be countered by the exit option. Okin, on the other hand, brings gender to the focus of attention. She expounds on the problems of culture and collective rights in light of their powerful reproduction of inequality and their restricting effect on processes of identity constitution. Both analytically and normatively, the three theories of collective rights are based on momentous, though not always explicit, concepts of culture, identity, and subject constitution.

For an analysis of collective rights, an extensive discussion of these concepts is therefore mandatory. In part II the foundation for further analytical steps was laid by elaborating on the reciprocally constituting relationship between the individual and society. The figure of the two poles existing within each other while simultaneously not dissolving into one another allows for an analytical comprehension of processes of socialization and subject constitution. By introducing the levels of culture and identity, this model is substantially extended.

Culture is characterized by constitutive contradictions that contain both emancipatory and repressive dimensions, which make its use as a yardstick for criticism difficult. Located on a level between the individual and society, culture can be a mechanism of mediation for processes of subject constitution and socialization. Culture exists within different constellations that include both the pole of the individual and the pole of society. At the same time, culture is only one of many possible mechanisms of mediation between individuals and society. If culture is not equated to society in the sense of abstract socialization, there are always alternatives to (one's) culture. Thus, dynamics, critical distance, and cultural changes become possible.

A viable concept of identity was introduced via the antinomic constellations between identity and the nonidentical, between the dynamic and static identity, and between internal and external attributions. The respective poles constitute and depend on each other. Collective identity *can* be in such a mutually constitutive relation with individual identity. Contrary to the other antinomic pairs, however, this relation is not uncircumventable, but only one of many possible mechanisms of constitution. These constellations as a whole provide the basis for acknowledging inherent contradictions in the concept of identity without the need to dissolve, to disintegrate, or to negate them. Additionally, all dimensions of the concept of identity can exhibit both emancipatory and repressive effects. To refer normatively to the category of identity is therefore only of limited use.

An analysis of liberal and communitarian concepts of collective rights, their concepts of the individual, society, identity, and culture, and their normative yardsticks of criticism provides a viable framework for the study of collective human rights. However, the entanglement of emancipatory and repressive dimensions shows that no general approach to demands for collective rights can be deduced from this framework. Rather, the discussion of concrete examples and case studies is necessary in order to disclose specific argumentative patterns and their effects. For this purpose, I conducted an empirical study of demands for indigenous rights on the international level, presented and discussed in part III. Above-average rates of unemployment, poverty, and suicide among an estimated 400 million indigenes are a clear indicator of normative relevance. The political relevance and topicality reflects in the foundation of the UNPFII, the passing of the UNDRIP, and the weight they carry within the sphere of international human rights. Indigenous movements, which, since the mid-twentieth century, have gained significantly in visibility, internationalization, and degree of organization, push demands for collective rights and the preservation of distinct identity, culture, and group structures. Setting priorities on distinction and its growing international acceptance characterizes the difference between the indigenous movement and other marginalized groups or minorities motivated by nationalism, respectively. Another characteristic is the concept of indigeneity. Indigeneity or the indigenous identity is the core of indigenous human rights documents and claims. However, its definition remains open, leading to fierce controversies on the question of who may call themselves indigenous and who may not. In this context, identity politics have immediate consequences for the agency within and the enjoyment of international law.

This special feature of the indigenous movement is reflected in statements submitted to the UNPFII sessions in 2009 and 2012 regarding the implementation of the UNDRIP. The content analysis of the documents revealed that 1) *culture*, comprised of indigeneity, identity, and distinction, and 2) *individual human rights* dominate the subject areas addressed by indigenous representatives and other stakeholders. Both topics are connected to different issues, functions, and forms that can result in both emancipatory and repressive effects. Culture and individual human rights, depending on their form, can undermine or support each other. The document analysis revealed possible frameworks, opportunities, and limits within demands for indigenous rights. At the same time, it raised several questions, which will now be addressed and synoptically discussed.

WHAT NEXT?

The discussion of demands for indigenous rights in chapter 6 demonstrates that concepts of culture and identity usually have more emancipatory potential if they allow for *dynamics* and *permeability*. This is opposed to the indigenous demand for a secluded distinction that is also to be preserved in the future. At the same time, the conceptual analysis in chapter 3 shows that identity cannot be reduced to its dynamic aspects. Static aspects, which can offer reliability, orientation, and stability—or strategic advantages in identity politics—are both normatively and constitutively important. Emphasizing dynamic aspects of collective rights can therefore not be aimed at the dissolution of stability-providing aspects of identity.

Additionally, as discussed in chapter 2, collective identities and cultures can demonstrate important instances of subject constitution and socialization and must be taken seriously. At the same time, the possibility of alternative methods of mediation between individuals and society must be kept open, for only the existence of alternative mechanisms can offer the possibility of choice. However, the demand for freedom of choice is meaningless if one does not consider the context and its (power) inequalities, a perspective that might not allow for many choices. This and other limitations of the concept of freedom of choice, however, do not allow for the reverse conclusion—that the demand for freedom of choice needs to be suspended. Rather, its context-specific conditions and obstacles need to be examined.

Certain recourses to culture and identity, however, do not permit or even actively restrict freedom of choice and alternative mechanisms of mediation, subject constitution, and socialization. This can be paradigmatically explicated in two examples. When culture is understood as a rigid category, in which inclusions and exclusions are strictly defined and regulated (be it by the state or by the indigenous administration), then the only choice—if there is a choice—is the choice to be inside or outside. The trials discussed in chapter 4, of *Canada vs. Lavell* and *Santa Clara Pueblo vs. Martinez*, demonstrate this restriction that is amplified by gendered components: Indigenous women who had married non-indigenous men were prohibited from returning to the indigenous community—even after getting a divorce. Crossing a cultural line was punished and commuting between the cultures was made impossible.

Another example is the right to indigeneity and indigenous identity *for indigenes*, which is formulated in the UNDRIP. Here, a self-referential doubling takes place—the effects of which are strongly reflected in the 04a documents. Indigenous identity becomes a means and an end at the same time. Protection, preservation, and active reproduction of the indigenous identity is, on the one hand, a central goal of indigenous demands and the UNDRIP. One reason for this goal is the conceptual peculiarity of identity: Internal identity depends on and is mediated by its external recognition. This makes a pure self-definition of one's own indigeneity—as proposed by, for example, the UNDRIP—impossible.

On the other hand, the existence of indigenous identity is a precondition for claiming the right to indigenous identity. Indigenous rights can, by definition, be claimed only by indigenes—that is, by those who identify themselves as indigenous, who are recognized as indigenous, and who "live indigenously." Thus, indigeneity becomes a resource that strengthens legal subjectivity and enhances agency within transnational and national law. Indigeneity also becomes a refuge, offering protection from racism and exclusion. At the same time, this agency is decisively limited, for it depends on being recognized as indigenous, which leads to an imperative for every individual to truly live indigenously and to reproduce indigeneity through his or her actions. In light of the variety of indigenous ways of life in different regions, in urban and rural areas, in intra-group relations that depend on age, gender, or class, in cultures so similar that the smallest differences are assigned the greatest significance—in light of this heterogeneity, definitions of indigeneity and their ensuing inclusions and exclusions are highly controversial and amplify the imperative.

This imperative is confirmed by the example of the behavior of indigenous women during the Australian Royal Commission's investigation of the deaths of detained indigenous men (see chapter 5). The aspiration to make the white judiciary's racist structures the subject of discussion resulted via the imperative of indigenous identity through the neglect of topics like domestic violence and alcoholism. It is also against this background that exogamic marriage is perceived as harmful to the indigenous group and therefore punished. The fact that this regulation was introduced by both indigenous communities (in *Santa Clara Pueblo vs. Martinez*) and state administrations (in *Canada vs. Lavell*) shows that the external constitution of indigenous identity played an important role well before the establishment of indigenous human rights. These processes of construction and the attribution of indigenous identity and its dichotomous separation from non-indigeneity began with the introduction of the "doctrine of discovery" in the fifteenth century. Demands for rights to identity, culture, and distinction have a long history, in which identity, culture, distinction, and power are closely interwoven. In order to claim these rights, indigeneity *must* be lived—by every individual.

The repressive self-reference inherent to the doubling of identity as a means and as an end is also mirrored in the invocation of future generations. They should have the opportunity to live indigenously and are thus an end of the demands. At the same time, however, referring to future generations is a means: They will have to live indigenously in order to comply with the demands and associated rights. The imperative is not only relevant for the past and for the present, but also for the future.

The fact that indigenous rights address and simultaneously turn against the individual in the form of an imperative, points to a general feature of collective rights. Collective rights are considered necessary if developments (usually marked as modern) are perceived as threats to a certain culture or collective. The goal is a targeted intervention in order to guarantee the continued existence of the community at stake. Here, an ambivalence of the term *community* becomes visible, which can be illustrated best through the history of its German translation. Following Ferdinand Tönnies's argument, the traditional translation of *community* as *Gemeinschaft* denotes an organically grown collective (Tönnies 2002). The term *Gemeinschaft*, however, became the central point of reference for National Socialism and other ultranationalist ideologies. In order to protect the concept of *Gemeinschaft* from these interpretations, *community* was subsequently translated as *Gemeinwesen*. This term is meant to have a somewhat different meaning: "A *Gemeinschaft* is something that always already exists. A member is qualified by birth rather than by effort or contribution. A *Gemeinwesen* on the other hand, has to permanently be reproduced through the efforts of its members and institutional structures" (Reese-Schäfer 2000: 29; italics added).

The conceptual distinction between *Gemeinwesen* and *Gemeinschaft*, however, has its limits. First, there is no form of community that does not require active reproduction by its members, institutions, and structures. All communities have to be actively created and kept alive by their members. This means, second, that no naturally given or even unchangeable community (*Gemeinschaft*) exists. The necessity to actively reproduce a given community is the background and the reasoning behind all demands for collective rights. Hence, it is not a particularity of indigenous rights that this reproduction, as an imperative, is directed at and against all members of a community, but a constitutive feature of collective rights. The question of how these rights and duties (may) restrict individual rights is the decisive one.

FOR BETTER OR FOR WORSE?

The categories of identity and culture can entail repressive aspects. If formulated as collective rights, these categories can even produce repressive effects and undermine individual human rights. This points to this book's initial question: What are the possibilities and limits of collective rights, and what are the conditions under which a yardstick for criticism may be formed? One possible answer to the latter question is the claim that individual rights can be used as a sufficient normative yardstick for collective rights. But this answer comes full circle, returning to the initial conflict between individual and collective human rights and, ultimately, to a binary decision between the two forms. Such a dichotomous logic is opposed to a morally open human rights system and its aspiration to "something better." An operationalized, statically set yardstick is always arbitrary and can, because of this arbitrariness and as a result of power struggles, potentially be substituted by other yardsticks. Then again, a normative yardstick that allows for a distinction between "better" and "worse" (or between "emancipatory" and "repressive") is necessary. Or else an analysis or discussion "will have little chance of digging deeper into the roots of inhumanity. It will do more damage than that: it will absolutize the difference and bar all debate about the relative virtues and demerits of coexisting forms of life. The small print is that all differences are good and worth preserving just for the fact of being different" (Bauman 2003: 106).

At this point, a reprise of Kymlicka's approach to the problem of a normative yardstick is helpful. As described in chapter 1, Kymlicka constrains his yardstick in a specific way:

> I am discussing what justice requires for minorities in the world as we know it—i.e. a world of nation-states which retain significant control

over issues of migration, internal political structures and language policies. One could (with difficulty) imagine a very different world—a world without states, or with just one world government. The rights of minorities would clearly be different in such a hypothetical world, since the power of majorities would be dramatically reduced, including their ability to impose relations of oppression and humiliation. My focus, however, is on what ethnocultural justice requires in our world. (Kymlicka 2001a: 75)

Kymlicka's argumentation for group-differentiated rights is normatively based on "the existing"—the world as we know it. However, for a substantial discussion of collective rights it is important to not lapse into an affirmation of that which exists—but to disclose repressive and emancipatory factors within "the existing" category. Kymlicka's remark can be given a productive spin if the existing is not set as a yardstick but is instead described as a social (and dynamic) context and, as such, is included in the analysis. For the case of indigenous rights, this can mean taking a closer look at the specific situations of indigenous groups within their respective states or state structures. But how can something that is supposed to point beyond the world as it exists be grasped without arbitrarily setting a normative yardstick for criticism?

Part I demonstrated that normative yardsticks are referred to in debates on collective rights at least implicitly and often explicitly. Their supposed function is that of ultimate justification. Taylor, Kymlicka, and, with a shift, Okin all highlight the category of morality in the complex constellation of individual, society, culture, and identity. Taylor designs morality as a frame in which culture and identity are constituted. According to him, this frame is so fundamental that it cannot be left behind. This figure of thought was reformulated more clearly in chapter 2 as the mutually constitutive relation between the individual and society. This relation describes the ever-present societal context of mediation that connects apparent immediateness (or objectivity or inwardness) to its societal conditionality (but not determination). This explains Taylor's close connection of individual identity and the moral frame and his emphasis of the latter (Taylor 1989b: 29ff.). At the same time (and all three authors acknowledge that fact to some extent), humans can err. Cultural views of morality, or of what is good, can change and be questioned. Morality is not simply existent or naturally given. Using different terminologies, the three authors circle around the question of how criticism can become possible and how it can turn against its own conditions of constitution.

However, part II showed that the much-debated categories of the individual, society, culture, and identity cannot fulfill the function of ultimate justification assigned to them because they are constitutively caught in relationships of mediation with each other. Likewise, they contain many levels and constellations that can be both emancipatory and repressive. The individual, society, culture, and identity all fail to provide a sufficient normative yardstick for criticism.

Can the concept of international human rights be used as a yardstick to name repressive and emancipatory aspects? "Human rights exist not to ensure human life *per se* but to protect and promote the conditions for a certain quality of life for all. In this respect, human rights are inherently normative" (Fagan 2009: 6; italics in the original).

Human rights contain an analytical distinction between a legal and a moral level. This distinction is the constitutive twofold character of universal human rights. One side of this character is codified law, such as human rights documents, treaties, and declarations passed and ratified by the UN, regional confederations of states, and states. The moral level of human rights exists in claims to more than is currently enforceable legally or by international law, but that can still serve as a strong standard to show and address suffering. Positive and moral human rights are not in opposition to each other.[1] This becomes clear especially in the fact that moral law exceeds codified law but, at the same time, is dependent on its institutionalization and implementation (Guenther 2009: 277). In accordance with this, Vernon van Dyke, who shaped the definition of subjects of collective rights (see the introduction), emphasizes that collectives have both legal and moral rights.

> By a legal right I mean a claim or an entitlement that a government is bound to uphold and does seek to uphold, at least on occasion. (If the appeal is to international law, the obligation must be accepted by more than one government.) By a moral right I mean a claim or entitlement that ought to be honored if justice is to be done or the good promoted, regardless of the attitudes and actions of any government. (van Dyke 1982: 23)

The essential function of this differentiation is clear: Moral claims to "what is good," to justice, or to "the better life"—in short: moral claims to something "better"—should be kept alive—even if they are not protected by certain governments or laws. The moral level of human rights is supposed to offer a normative yardstick that is not limited to day-to-day politics. Conversely, legal human rights are not only a method of implementation for moral claims, but also a necessary corrective, limitation, and concretization. They serve to prevent the concept of human rights from being applied to all possible grievances and suffering, thereby voiding it of meaning (Fagan 2009). The doubling of human rights into a moral and a legal dimension provides the basis for a concept of intertwined, reciprocally correcting forms of human rights. For a discussion of collective rights, however, two challenges ensue.

First, the recourse to morality does not solve the conflict between collective and individual human rights; rather; it only moves the latter to another level. Just as arguments for collective rights claim morality for groups, arguments for individual human rights use morality to prove opposite demands. Jack Donnelly, for example, says that it is the moral character of individual human rights that cannot be transferred to groups (Donnelly 1990: 41f.). Thomas Pogge argues that collective rights might be used to balance out certain disadvantages. However, with respect to the moral character of demands, the type of the legal entity at stake is completely irrelevant (Pogge 1997: 190). Meanwhile, Kymlicka sees the type of the group as the decisive criterion for moral claims. In sum, morality is used as a yardstick and a point of reference in discussions on collective rights in various ways, which is why Taylor points out that the conflict on collective rights cannot be solved by referring to morality. Rather, the conflict itself is "after all a moral issue" (Taylor 1994a: 73, see also Stapleton 1995: xxxviii).

A second challenge of morality as a yardstick lies in the question of the origin, or the source of legitimation, of morality. Some claim that the moral level of human rights stands above the law (Vismann 1998: 285) and beyond international law. This assumption of a dichotomy between morality and society raises morality to a hardly tangible, transcendent level, into theological and nature law dimensions that allegedly exist separate from society. On the other hand, without a transcendent level, human rights can be reduced and used as a tool of repression to serve political agendas (Ibid.: 301). Both one-sided uses of human rights give rise to the possibility for a yardstick that can go beyond codified human rights without referring to levels beyond society.

I will discuss this twofold challenge in recourse to Theodor W. Adorno's analysis of the relationship between immanent and transcendent criticism. (In some approaches, the latter is referred to as normative or moral criticism as well.) Different approaches to immanent and transcendent criticism circle around one central question: Is an external yardstick of criticism—in other words: an external morality—necessary, impossible, or superfluous? In a first step, I will introduce the concepts of immanent and transcendent criticism as if they were two separate procedures in order to outline their respective characteristics and boundaries. In a second step, I will examine their (internal and external) reciprocal dependency and mutual constitution.

In immanent criticism, a subject or object of critique is measured against itself—against its own term—so that the usage of external norms becomes superfluous. The immanent critique is based on the assumption that an object and its concept or definitive qualities are not identical: concepts cannot capture empirical phenomena in all their aspects, while the given phenomena fail to reflect all dimensions of a conceptual term (Adorno 2010: 107).

Immanent criticism is applied in political sciences with different nuances. First, the aspiration to approach a subject without previous knowledge or presuppositions strives for the ideal of neutrality. Trying to find normative yardsticks in the subject, and this subject's not yet developed potential, follows a similar pattern. In a third variant, points of reference such as reflectiveness and experience are sketched as foundations of immanent critique (Steinert 2007: 18). All forms of the immanent critique share the concern to not force external, subjectivist, and arbitrary yardsticks on the subject or object of analysis.

However, immanent yardsticks and contents are historically and socially contingent and can contain multiple dimensions of meaning—even simultaneously. There is no invariant, immanent content of norms, or yardstick for morality. This is related to the much discussed difficulty—if not impossibility—of approaching a situation neutrally and without any prior understanding (see Ritsert 2009: 167). Another problem lies in the narrow framework to which a purely immanent critique is reduced—similar to legal human rights, but without a moral perspective that goes beyond the given.

For these reasons, criticisms (and human rights) need something additional that is not only "different" from what exists, but, in some way or another, also "better." In this context, Adorno formulates the "categorical imperative . . . to arrange their thoughts and actions so that Auschwitz will not repeat itself, so that nothing similar will happen" (Adorno 2004: 365). Furthermore—although hardly acknowledged in discussions on the Frankfurt School—concepts of a reconciled society, individual emancipation, and (socially embedded) individual autonomy are recurrent normative yardsticks in Adorno's works (see, e.g., Adorno 1978: 115f., 247; Adorno 2001: 110ff., but also Mackenzie/Stoljar 2000b). Adorno implements some kind of transcendent criticism, which adds something external to the process of criticism. It adds something that is not necessarily already addressed by the given, or an object's concept. This addition can be a systematic theory, or the usage of norms and criteria of criticism (Ritsert 2009: 165). This addition exceeds the given and its concepts.

It is, however, impossible to assume a point of view outside of what is socially given. Everything that humans experience, think, name, define, exclude, constitute, and construct is mediated intersubjectively, subjectively, and socially. The yardsticks and points of reference in transcendent criticism do not exist outside of history or untouched by experience or society. There is no natural or God-given, abstract, pre-societal or homogenous morality. Against this background, different procedures of transcendent criticism take shape. Apart from religion, natural law, or metaphysical variants, there is a line of interpretation that refers to assumptions and norms that stand outside a given epistemological subject—but that are not set as pre-societal or invariable.

All variants of an externally added morality—that is, transcendent criticism—run the risk of being arbitrary, repressive, subjective, interchangeable, or reified.

Neither purely immanent nor purely transcendent criticism offers sufficient (and sufficiently open) criteria for a yardstick for criticism, morality, or human rights. To put it pointedly: Immanent criticism only acknowledges the object of critique or analysis, while ignoring the criticizing or analyzing subject and his or her interests and presuppositions. A merely transcendent criticism hypostatizes the criticizing subject or an objectified morality, while neglecting societal realities.

In looking for a way to combine the two extremes of immanent and transcendent criticism that does not hypostasize one and reject the other, Adorno explicates their contradictive constellation. He emphasizes, in reference to immanent and transcendent criticism,

> that these two ways belong together and are connected in a certain tension, but on the other hand, they do not dissolve in identity; ... the phenomenon has to be looked at both from the inside, according to its own demands, its own origin, and its own regularities, and also from the outside, through its functional inter-relations and the way it is perceived by humans; the meanings that it takes on in the lives of humans. These two ways of looking at the matter need to be pursued somewhat independently, trusting that, once the thought has penetrated both aspects deeply enough, they will reveal their relationship. (Adorno 2010: 219)

The immanent critique, which takes the matter or the object itself seriously, and the transcendent critique, which focuses on an object's meaning for the subjects, their experiences, and their presuppositions, collide through their respective extremes. Both poles are conflicting and simultaneously intermediated. They are reciprocally constitutive. Immanent and transcendent critiques exhibit both internal and external mediations, while constituting a strict contradiction at the same time. The limits of both sides can be picked up and developed—not by subtracting something from one of the poles, but by establishing a reflexive procedure of criticism by means of traversing the two poles.

This mediated reflexive critique differentiates from an ethic of conviction or standpoint (or ultimate justification), which raises the individual's will to meet a moral yardstick. It also differentiates from a moralistic ethic, which dichotomously opposes the individual and objectified morality without reflecting on their societal, intersubjective, and subjective mediation (Adorno 2001: 148f., 142; see also Menke 2006).

As a case and point, Adorno's imperative "to arrange their thoughts and actions so that Auschwitz will not repeat itself, so that nothing similar will happen" (see above, Adorno 2004: 365) seems to be an immanent critique that objectively results from history (Ibid.). At the same time, however, it is a subjective addition an individual can opt for or against. Simultaneously, the subjective addition is mediated through society, just as the objective result from history is subjectively mediated (Hegel 1977:

para. 75ff.). The mediated subject-object relationship permeates and connects both immanent and transcendent critique. Hence, neither critique nor morality stand outside the mediated constellation of the individual, society, culture, and identity.

The simultaneity of the impossibility and the necessity for a yardstick of critique shows very clearly that immanent and transcendent critique are in permanent tension. It is impossible to rest with one of the two poles without immediately emphasizing its counterpart. The strength of the whole constellation lies not in eliminating but in enduring their antinomy.

This mediated model of reflexive critique characterizes the constellation between a legal and a moral level of human rights. Societal, intersubjective, and subjective experiences and processes of negotiation shape both spheres. Neither of the spheres is unhistorical, pre-societal, or invariable. A reference to morality, to "the good life," or to emancipation cannot (or only repressively) be reified as a universal yardstick. At the same time, an idea of something "better" is necessary in order to transcend the given and to fill possible gaps and problems regarding the legal level of human rights.

Regarding this book's question of the possibilities and limits of collective human rights, it can be argued that, first, a distinction between emancipatory and repressive dimensions of collective human rights is necessary. Second, it is difficult to set a yardstick for this distinction. An operationalization in the form of a catalogue of norms would be reifying and, ultimately, repressive. At the same time, this difficulty allows for productive solutions. Human rights with their legal and moral levels can be consulted as a mediated and open constellation. They include both immanent and transcendent dimensions and allow for a distinction between repressive and emancipatory aspects. This distinction is indispensable for political sciences approaches that want to go beyond mere description. However, the distinction cannot be dichotomously determined, because emancipatory and repressive aspects can be closely intertwined. This is why this book examined emancipatory and repressive aspects on all levels *and* their interactions.

Another reason why human rights offer a normative, yet open framework for the analysis of collective rights lies in the fact that the former are named in the UNDRIP as a point of reference for indigenous rights. Indigenous rights and the relationship between indigenes and the state should be "based on principles of justice, democracy, respect for human rights, non-discrimination and good faith"—and the UDHR (UNDRIP, Preamble). The UNPFII documents explicitly consult human rights and dignity as normative criteria as well.

Human rights and also dignity contain a binding legal level and a moral level. In other words, they facilitate a bridging of immanent and transcendent critique.

> The concrete prospects for a life in dignity may vary considerably from individual to individual, but also from culture to culture. That basic demand, however, remains the same. . . . Accordingly, the post-1945 human rights discourse "sets" the basic principle of human dignity and declares it the goal to be achieved by human rights. In this regard, the new human rights discourse bears a "decisionist" element, because it would have been possible to opt for a different basic principle. . . . Although specific historical experiences led to this decision, these experiences made the decision in question almost inevitable. (Pollmann 2010: 43, 41 fn. 13)

Again, it becomes clear how closely immanent critique (the inevitable element) and transcendent critique (the decisionist element) are intermediated. The development of human rights and the entanglement of human rights and human dignity is a result of history, experience, and the subjective, intersubjective, and societal mediation of social processes. Different power constellations and different interests could have led to results different from the human rights system established today. However, this fact does not undermine the system's current weight.

> The first human rights declaration set a standard that inspires refugees, people who have been thrust into misery, and those who have been ostracized and humiliated. It's a standard that can give them the assurance that their suffering is not their natural destiny. The translation of the first human right into positive law gave rise to a legal duty to realize specific moral requirements, and this has become engraved into the collective memory of humanity. (Habermas 2010: 476)

Legally and morally, international human rights offer an opportunity to achieve something that is "better." Yet, human rights are no ultimate justification. They can be challenged, transformed, criticized, or abused.

IS A COLLECTIVE HUMAN RIGHT TO CULTURE AND IDENTITY "BETTER"?

An open, but not arbitrary or relativist discussion of emancipatory and repressive aspects can avoid a binary constellation of indigeneity versus non-indigeneity. With this approach, a critique of selected elements regarding demands for indigenous rights and of static concepts of history, identity, and cultural distinction does not necessarily entail an affirmation of existing structures. A reflexive critique of indigenous or other demands for collective human rights does not ignore experiences of suppression. Rather, it acknowledges these experiences by examining the functions, implications, and dimensions related to them. This shows that the concept of indigeneity contains a self-referential doubling and an imperative, and that the mere existence of culture and identity says little about their subject-constituting and agency-enabling character. Rather, internal antinomies of culture and identity can appear in various constellations. The modes in which culture and identity are referred to are shaped by how culture and identity are formulated as collective rights. If collective rights contain certain aspects of culture and identity, it is of little surprise that the groups at stake adapt these aspects as a resource and as leverage. Yet this may cut off other constitutive aspects of identity. It is important to ask in what way collective rights are supposed to reproduce (which aspects of) culture and identity and how they are connected to other claims—for example, individual human rights or the right to participate in transnational, international, and national forums.

A reflexive critique allows for the discussion of another problem related to collective and indigenous rights: the dichotomous distinction between allochthonous and autochthonous groups. This distinction depends on specific constructions of history, on cultural memory, and, above all, on dichotomous mechanisms of inclusion and exclusion. However, instead of focusing on culture, identity, and distinction, an analysis may examine experiences of suffering and the fulfillment or denial of human dignity. "One role of the robust society is to overcome both normative and cultural blindness to human suffering" (Falk 1992: 48). This approach challenges the binary distinction between ostensibly aboriginal groups and other marginalized groups like refugees, worldwide one of the most vulnerable groups.

On the other hand, a focus on human dignity and suffering does not necessarily prohibit the consideration of culture and identity. Cultures and collective identities can be emphatically discussed as modes of socialization and subject constitution. A shift in focus, however, sheds light on the fact that culture and collective identity are heterogeneous and only two of many possible instances of mediation between the individual and society. It is crucial to examine the relations of stability and dynamism, identity and the non-identical, internal and external attributions, intentional and unintentional factors, and individual and collective dimensions within the concepts of identity and culture. This makes it possible to discuss a theory and practice of collective rights that focuses on the multiplication of levels of mediation between the individual and society, as well as the (socially enabled or restricted) possibilities of exit, choice, critique, and distance—without failing to recognize the characteristics of culture and identity that are subject constituting and stabilizing.

In light of the topics discussed, culture, identity, and collective rights can only be integrated into the framework of human rights through great care. Therefore, the question of collective human rights cannot be answered dichotomously either in affirmation or refusal. Instead, an analysis that reflexively reveals the categories used and shows the emancipatory and repressive dimensions of these categories is necessary. In this way, suffering from both injustice and law can be communicated and overcome.

NOTE

1. Cornelia Vismann, however, believes that the twofold character of human rights is threatened by the UN because it blurs the line between transcendent and codified level; see Vismann (1998: 295). This argument can be countered with the assumption that human rights gain their strength from the very connection of the two levels; see Clapham (2006: 99f.). For a discussion of the relevance of morality in law, see Menke/Pollmann (2007: 25ff.); Raz (1988: 265ff.); Lohmann (1998); Bobbio (1996).

Appendix

UNPFII Documents

SOURCES

Documents of the 2009 session, agenda item 04a, 8th UNPFII conference (pf09name). Online path: www.docip.org > Permanent Forum 2009: statements

Documents of the 2012 session, agenda item 04a, 11th UNPFII conference (pf12name). Online path: www.docip.org > Permanent Forum 2012: statements

KEY

Name of document: Organization(s) [type of organization(s)], presenting representative [or n. n., "no name"]. Type of document.

pf09alcides033: Comunidad Indígena de Jancos San Pablo-Cajamarca (Peru) [indigenous organization], presented by Alcides Chiquilín. Intervención.

pf09ali192: Mbororo Social and Cultural Development Association (MBOSCUDA) (Kamerun) [indigenous organization], presented by Ali Aii Shatu. Statement.

pf09ana107: National Authority of Indigenous Government (ONIC) of Colombia [indigenous organization], presented by Ana Manuela Ochoa Arias. Statement.

pf09ashley262: Grand Council of the Crees (Eeyou Istchee), Inuit Circumpolar Council, Assembly of First Nations, Québec Native Women, First Nations Summit, Assembly of First Nations of Québec and Labrador (AFNQL), First Peoples Human Rights Coalition, Indigenous World Association, Canadian Friends Service Committee (Quakers) [indigenous organizations and NGOs], presented by Ashley Iserhoff, Deputy Grand Chief, Grand Council of the Crees (Eeyou Istchee). Joint Statement.

pf09asiacaucus4a: Asian Indigenous Women's Network [indigenous organization], presented by Eleanor Dictaan-Bang-Oa. Statement.

pf09australia115: Australian Government, Australian Human Rights Commission, Aboriginal and Torres Strait Islander organisations [government, indigenous organizations and NGOs], presented by [n. n.]. Joint Statement.

pf09birgitte090: International Labor Organization [UN institution], presented by Birgitte Feiring. Statement.

pf09caleen126: La Red Xicana Indígena, Member ENLACE-North (Continental Network Indigenous Women), Winnemem Wintu Tribe, Na Koa Ikaika Ka Lahui Hawaii, The Indigenous Worlds Association, Bansa Adat Alifuru, Touaregh Tribal People (Niger), Coordinadora de las Organizaciones Indígenas de la Cuenca Amazónica (COICA), California Indian Heritage Council, Lipan Apache Women's Defence, Lipan Apache Band of Texas, Centro sin Fronteras, Chicago, International Indigenous Women's Network (FIMI), Cómision de Instrumentos Internacionales del Enlace Continental de Mujeres Indígenas, Coalición de mujeres de Ocosingo Chiapas, Las Huellas del Jaguar Chiapas, Corporación de mujeres mapuche de Aukinko Zomo Chile [indigenous organizations and NGOs], presented by Chief Caleen Sisk-Franco. Collective statement on unrecognized and unrepresented peoples.

pf09catherine113: Pacific Caucus [indigenous organization], presented by Catherine Davis. Intervention.

pf09celeste320: Native Women's Association of Canada [indigenous organization], presented by Celeste McKay, director of Human Rights and International Affairs. Statement.

pf09charles071: Indigenous people of Dominica located in the Eastern Caribbean [indigenous organization], presented by Charles Williams, chief. Statement.

pf09craig112: National Native Title Council, Foundation for Aboriginal and Islander Research Action, Marninwarntikura Women's Resource Centre, New South Wales Aboriginal Land Council, Human Rights and Equal Opportunity Commission, National Indigenous Higher Education Network, Aboriginal and Torres Strait Islander Women's Legal and Advocacy Service Aboriginal Corporation, Aboriginal Legal Rights Movement, Bullana, The Poche Centre for Indigenous Health, National Indigenous Youth Movement of Australia, Aboriginal Legal Service of Western Australia Inc., National Aboriginal Community Controlled Health Organisation, Indigenous Peoples Organisation Network Youth Delegation [indigenous organizations and NGOs], presented by Craig Cromelin. Joint Intervention.

pf09dalee137: Board of Trustees of the United Nations Voluntary Fund for Indigenous Populations [UN institution], presented by Dalee Sambo Dorough. Statement.

pf09dolores094: Spain (PM) [government], presented by Dolores Martín, directora del programa indígena de la agencia española de cooperación internacional para el desarrollo. Intervención.

pf09egil099: Sami Parliament in Norway [indigenous organization], presented by Egil Olli, president. Statement.

pf09emmanuel117: France (PM) [government], presented by Emmanuel Lebrun-Damiens, réprésentant. Intervention.

pf09eneida092: Coordinadora de Organizaciones Indígenas, Campesinas y Comunidades Interculturales de Bolivia [indigenous organization], presented by Eneida Charupa. Propuesta.

pf09erica098: Greece (PM) [government], presented by Erica-Irene Daes, representative. Statement.

pf09ernesto127: Movimiento de Autoridades Indígenas de Colombia [indigenous organization], presented by Ernesto Ramiro Estacio, senador indígena de Colombia. Intervención.

pf09eva102: Denmark (Delegation) [government], presented by Eva Raabyemagle. Statement.

pf09fabiana091: Comisión Económica para América Latina y el Caribe [UN institution], presented by Fabiana del Popolo. Statement.

pf09fevzi105: Mejlis (Parliament) of the Crimean Tatar People [indigenous organization], presented by Fevzi Amzayev, deputy head, Foreign Relations Division. Statement.

pf09freddy125: Bolivia (PM) [government], presented by Freddy Mamani Machaca, segundo secretario. Discurso.

pf09gabriela128: Mexico (Delegation) [government], presented by Gabriela Garduzo. Intervención.

pf09gene138: Indigenous Youth Caucus [indigenous organization], presented by Gene Henry. Intervention.

pf09ghislain139: Assembly of First Nations of Québec and Labrador [indigenous organization], presented by Ghislain Picard, chief. Statement.

pf09gonzalo114: Peru (PM) [government], presented by Gonzalo Gutiérrez, embajador, representante permanente. Intervención.

pf09gulnara106: TAMAYNUT Organization (Marokko), Ogiek Cultural Initiatives Programmes (Kenia), Parakuyo Women Development Fund, Pastoralists Indigenous Community Development Organization (Tanzania), Foundation for Research and Support of Indigenous Peoples of Crimea (Ukraine), United Confederation of Taino People (Boriken, Puerto Rico), Asociación de Mujeres Waorani de la Amazonia Ecuatoriana (Ecuador), Rapa Nui Parliament (Osterinsel), Federación Única de Trabajadores Pueblos Originarios de Chuquisaca (Bolivien), Tuvalu Climate Action Network (Tuvalu), Bangsa Adat Alifuru (Maluku), Eagle Clan Arawaks (Barbados, Guyana), International Indian Treaty Council — participants of "Project Access Global Capacity Training" [indigenous organizations], presented by Gulnara Abbasova. Intervention.

pf09handaire118: Coordination Autochtone Frankophone [indigenous organization], presented by Handaine Mohamed. Declaración.

pf09iiite406x: Island Sustainability Alliance C. I. Inc (Pacific Island Peoples), International Indian Treaty Council, Akiak Native Community (Alaska), Alaska Intertribal Council, Native Village of Savoonga (Alaska), Alaska Community Action on Toxics, Resist Environmental Destruction on Indigenous Lands (Alaska), Native Women's Association of Canada, National Congress of American Indians (Alaska Region)—participants of "Indigenous Peoples Caucus for the Stockholm Convention COP 4 High Level Segment in Geneva" [indigenous organizations], presented by Andrea Carmen. Joint Statement.

pf09jacqueline110: Cordillera Peoples Alliance, Asia Pacific Indigenous Youth Network, Asia Indigenous Peoples Pact [indigenous organizations], presented by Jacqueline K. Carino. Intervention.

pf09jamesread087: Special Rapporteur on the Situation of the Human Rights and Fundamental Freedoms of Indigenous Peoples [UN institution], presented by James Anaya. Statement.

pf09jarmo095: Finland (PM) [government], presented by Jarmo Viinanen, ambassador, permanent representative. Statement.

pf09jennifer101: Asia Pacific Indigenous Youth Network [indigenous organizations], presented by Jennifer Awingan. Collective statement of the National Indigenous Youth Conference in the Philippines.

pf09jethro316: Akali Tange Association (Porgera, Enga Province, Papua-Neuguinea), supported by Asia Caucus, Pacific Caucus, Western Shoshone Defense Project (Nevada, USA), Peoples Earth, Society for Threatened Peoples International (ECOSOC), Indigenous Peoples Link [indigenous organizations and NGOs], presented by Jethro Tulin, executive officer. Intervention.

pf09jitpal067: National Foundation for Development of Indigenous Nationalities (Nepal) [government], presented by Jitpal Kirat, vice-president. Statement.

pf09joan097: Asia Caucus, Asia Indigenous Peoples Pact [indigenous organizations], presented by Joan Carling. Statement.

pf09jorge195: Indigenous World Association, Asociación Argentina de Abogados en Derecho Indígena, Coordinación de Organizaciones Mapuches de Neuquen [indigenous organizations], presented by Jorge Nahuel, Nilo Cayugueo, Dario Duch. Declaración conjunta.

pf09jose085: Mecanismo de Expertos sobre los Derechos de los Pueblos Indígenas [UN institution], presented by José Carlos Morales, vice-president. Informe.

pf09justa326: Land Is Life, Confederación de Mujeres Indígenas de Bolivia, Nacionalidad Waorani de Ecuador, Fundación para la Promoción del Conocimiento Indígena, Dewan Adat Papua (Papua Customary Council), Comitê Intertribal, El Molo Eco-Tourism Rights and Development Forum (The El Molo Forum), Nacionalidad Zapara de la Amazonia Ecuatoriana, Maasai Women for Education and Economic Development, Society for Indigenous Development (Manipur), Mainyoito Pastoralists Integrated Development Organisation, Indigenous Women's Network on Biodiversity of Abya Yala, Asia Pacific Indigenous Youth Network [indigenous organizations and NGOs], presented by Justa Cabrera. Intervención conjunta.

pf09kuriakose134: The Holy See Delegation [church], presented by Kuriakose Bharanikulangara, counsellor of the permanent observer. Statement.

pf09legb_africaucus140: African Caucus, Indigenous Peoples of Africa Coordinating Committee [indigenous organizations], presented by Legborsi Saro Pyagbara. Statement.

pf09lenny073: Flying Eagle Woman Fund, Fundación Rigoberta Mencha Tum [indigenous organizations], presented by Lenny Foster. Joint Intervention.

pf09lori321EN: Yamasi People [indigenous organization], presented by Lori Johnston. Request.

pf09luis108: Fondo para el desarrollo de los pueblos indígenas de América Latina y el Caribe [international organization], presented by Luis Evelis Andrada Casama, president. Intervención.

pf09mailis051: Northern Basque Country (Delegation) [indigenous organization], presented by Mailys Iriart. Speech.

pf09marcel111: Traversée en Terre Touarègue [indigenous organization], presented by Marcel Fortuné, president. Intervention.

pf09marcio088: Brazil [government], presented by Marcio Augusto Freitas Almeira, répresentant. Statement.

pf09marco132: Guatemala (PM), Comisión Presidencial contra la Discriminación y el Racismo contra los Pueblos Indígenas en Guatemala [government], presented by Marco Antonio Curuchich. Intervención.

pf09margaret052: Retrieve Foundation (Ireland), for Credo Mutwa, Spiritual Leader of the Zulu Nation and South Africa [indigenous organization], presented by Margaret Connolly, Indigenous Irish Spiritual Leader. Statement.

pf09margarita196: Enlace Continental de Mujeres Indígenas [indigenous organization], presented by Margarita Gutierrez. Intervención.

pf09maria145aenes: Corporación de Mujeres Mapuche Aukinko Zomo, Member of Mesa de Trabajo Mapuche sobre Derechos Colectivos and Enlace Continental de Mujeres Indígenas [indigenous organization], presented by Guido Conejeros Meliman and María Isabel Curihuentro Llancaleo. Intervención.

pf09mariana190: MayaVision Organization, Seven Generation Foundation, Guatemala Caucus (International Touaregue, Global Indig-

Appendix

enous Initiative at URI, Consejo Mam, Consejo Mayan Quiche, Tonatierra, Local SEIU 721, Central American Caucus, Caucus of Latin American Women, Banagra Adat Alifum (Malucu), Seventh Generations Fund, CEDHUNS (Panama), Comité Salvadoreño para el Reconocimiento de Pueblos Indígenas (El Salvador), La Red Xicana Indígena [indigenous organizations], presented by Mariana Francisco Xuncax. Speech.

pf09miguel100: Caucus de Abya Yala [indigenous organization], presented by Miguel Palacín. Declaración.

pf09minz191: Jharkhand Indigenous Youth for Action, Mandary Literary Council [indigenous organizations and NGOs], presented by Abhay Sagar Minz, Meenakshi Manda. Joint Statement.

pf09moira089: Venezuela (PM) [government], presented by Moira Mendez. Intervención.

pf09patricia163: Consultoría de los Pueblos Indígenas en el Norte de México, Comisión Internacional del Arte de los Pueblos Indígenas, Unificación y Lucha Triqui, Pueblo de Guásimas-Belem, Río Yaqui [indigenous organizations and NGOs], presented by Patricia Susana Rivera Reyes. Declaración colectiva.

pf09radine222: Foundation for Indigenous Americans of Anasazi Heritage [indigenous organization], presented by Radine Harrison-Jennings. Intervention.

pf09raimo124: Norway, Ministry of Labor and Social Inclusion [government], presented by Raimo Valle, state secretary. Statement.

pf09raphael072: Society of Zo-Ram Vengtu, Zo-mi National Congress, Zo-mi Inkuan, Chin Community, Bawm Social Council of Bangladesh, Bawm-Zo Indigenous People of Bangladesh [indigenous organizations], presented by Raphael Thangmawia, Zo-Reunification Organisation. Joint Statement.

pf09samuel130: Caucus Latinoamericano [indigenous organization], presented by Samuel Carpintero. Intervención.

pf09sara109: Organización de Jóvenes Emberá y Wounaan de Panamá [indigenous organization], presented by Sara Omi Casamá. Intervención.

pf09saturnino189: Movimiento de Acción y Resistencia Indígena [indigenous organization], presented by Saturnino Dionisio Sic Sapon. Intervención.

pf09shane133: USA (Delegation) [government], presented by Shane Christenson. Statement.

pf09stanely093: Kalina people in Suriname [indigenous organization], presented by Stanley Liauw Angie. Statement.

pf09stephane034: Action Communautaire pour la Promotion des Défavourisés Batwa, Centre d'Accompagnement des Autochtones

Pygmées et Minoritaires Vulnérables [indigenous organizations], presented by Stephane Ilandu Bulambo. Communication.

pf09tegusbayar322: Indigenous Mongolian people in China [indigenous organization], presented by Tegusbayar. Statement.

pf09thomas135: Caucus Nomade Touareg [indigenous organization], presented by Thomas Fortune. Declaración.

pf09tomasa119: Bolivia [government], presented by Tomasa Yarhui, senator. Intervención.

pf09tonya082: UNPFII [UN institution], presented by Tonya Gonnella Frichner, expert member, North America region. Intervention.

pf09tupac396: TONATIERRA, Yaotachcauh, Tlahtokan Nahaucalli, Izkalotlan Áztlan, Territorios de las Naciones O'otham, Abya Yala del Norte [indigenous organizations], presented by Tupac Enrique Acosta. Declaración.

pf09valentine121: Congo [government], presented by Valentin Mavoungou. Declaración.

pf09william123: Cónclave Mundial de Iglesias Evangélicas Indígenas/ World Caucus of Indigenous Churches, Consejo Mundial de Iglesias/World Council of Churches, Consejo Nacional de Iglesias de Filipinas, Consejo de Pueblos Indígenas Evangélicos del Ecuador, Consejo Nacional de Iglesias de Australia, Consejo Latinoamericano de Iglesias, Iglesia Evangélica Luterana Boliviana, Iglesia Evangélica Metodista en Bolivia, Confederación de Pueblos, Organizaciones, Comunidades e Iglesias Indígenas Evangélicas del Chimborazo (Ecuador) [church and indigenous organizations], presented by William Chela. Declaración conjunta.

pf09wilton059: International Organization of Indigenous Resource Development, Assembly of First Nations of Canada, Assembly of First Nations Quebec and Labrador, Quebec Native Women's Association, Native Women's Association of Canada, Amnesty International, Metis Native Council [indigenous organizations and NGOs], presented by Wilton Littlechild. Joint Statement.

pf09womencaucus4ab: Global Indigenous Women's Caucus [indigenous organization], presented by [n. n.]. Statement.

pf12albert233: International Labor Organization, Office for the United Nations [UN institution], presented by Albert K. Barume, senior specialist on Indigenous and Tribal Peoples' Issues. Statement.

pf12antti227: Office of the High Commissioner for Human Rights [UN institution], presented by Chief Antti Korkeakivi, Indigenous Peoples and Minorities Section. Statement.

pf12berndette226: New Zealand (PM) [government], presented by Bernadette Cavanagh, deputy permanent representative. Statement.

pf12catherine263: Pacific Caucus [indigenous organization], presented by Catherine Davis. Statement.

pf12dalee223: United Nations Permanent Forum on Indigenous Issues [UN institution], presented by Dalee Sambo Dorough, member of the UNPFII. Introductory remarks.

pf12david335: Consejo Nacional de Ayllus y Markas del Qullasuyu (Bolivia) [indigenous organization], presented by David Crispin. Discurso.

pf12dietrix293: Kamakakuokalani Center for Hawaiian Studies (Hawai'i), Tuvalu Climate Change Network (Tuvalu), Aotearoa Indigenous Rights Trust (Aotearoa, New Zealand), The Koani Foundation (Hawai'i), Aupuni Hawai'i (Hawai'i), Clan Hitorangi - Rapa Nui (Rapa Nui), Kobe Oser (West Papua), Hale O Haumea (Hawai'i), Queensland Cultural Heritage and Native Title Management (Australia), Gugu Badhun Limited (Australia), Foundation for Indigenous Recovery and Development Australia, National Indigenous Higher Education Network (Australia), Te Rinanga o Te Rarawa (Aotearoa/New Zealand) [indigenous organizations and NGOs], presented by Dietrix Jon Ulukoa Duhaylonsod. Joint Statement.

pf12egil231: Sami Parliament of Norway [indigenous organization], presented by Egil Olli, president. Statement.

pf12evariste276a: Organisation de l'Union Nationale du Peuple Kanak de nouvelle Calédonie [indigenous organization], presented by Évariste Wayaridri. Intervention.

pf12evariste276b: Te Taata Maohi No Maohi Nui Tahiti (Polynesia) [indigenous organization], presented by Temataru Tetuaura, king of Polynesia. Statement.

pf12gabriela242: Mexico (Delegation) [government], presented by Gabriela Garduza Estrada, directora de Asuntos Internacionales de la Comisión Nacional para el Desarrollo de los Pueblos Indígenas (CDI). Intervención.

pf12geoff259: New South Wales Aboriginal Land Council [indigenous organization], presented by Craig Cromelin, councillor for the Wiradjuri Region, member of the Ngiyampaa Peoples. Intervention.

pf12intreabud234: Global Indigenous Youth Council [indigenous organization], presented by Intreabud Ricky Tran. Statement.

pf12jennifer260: Grand Council of the Crees (Eeyou Istchee), Assembly of First Nations, Canadian Friends Service Committee (Quakers), Amnesty International, International Indian Treaty Council, Africa Indigenous Peoples Climate Change Network, Union of British Columbia Indian Chiefs, Chiefs of Ontario, Treaty Four First Nations, Mainyoito Pastoralists Integrated Development Organization, First Peoples Human Rights Coalition [indigenous organizations and NGOs], presented by Jennifer Preston. Joint Statement.

pf12kamira239: Caucus Africain, Congres Mondiale Amazigh [indigenous organizations], presented by Kamira Nait Sid. Declaración.

pf12legborsi225: Board of Trustees of the United Nations Voluntary Fund for Indigenous Populations [UN institution], presented by Legborsi Saro Pyagbara. Statement.

pf12leonardo228en: Indian Law Resource Center [indigenous organization], presented by Leonardo Crippa, senior attorney. Statement.

pf12maria238: Spain (PM) [government], presented by María Victoria Wulff, directora del programa indígena de la agencia española de cooperación internacional para el desarrollo. Intervención.

pf12pablo237: Panama (PM) [government], presented by Pablo Antonio Thalassinos, S.E. embajador. Intervención.

pf12regina248: Brazil (PM) [government], presented by Regina Maria Cordeiro Dunlop, H.E. ambassador. Statement.

pf12rochelle230: UNESCO [UN institution], presented by Rochelle Roca-Hachem. Intervention.

pf12santi291: Hitorangi Indigenous Community [indigenous organization], presented by Santi Hitorangi. Statement.

pf12severin344: Association pour l'integration et le developpement durable au Burandi [indigenous organization], presented by Séverin Sindizera, directeur général. Intervention.

pf12shane266: Aboriginal and Torres Strait Islander Unit Anti-Discrimination Commission Qld, Gugu Badhun Limited, Gamarada Indigenous Healing and Life Training, Foundation for Indigenous Recovery and Development Australia, National Aboriginal and Torres Strait Islander Legal Service, Secretariat of National Aboriginal and Islander Child Care, Turkindi Indigenous Information Network, Western Australian Aboriginal Legal Service, Aboriginal Rights Coalition [indigenous organizations and NGOs], presented by Shane Duffy, Indigenous Peoples Organisation Network of Australia. Joint Intervention.

pf12sona262: Enlace continental de Mujeres Indígenas de las Américas, Member of Foro Internacional de Mujeres Indígenas, Asociación de los Derechos de la Mujer y el Desarrollo [indigenous organizations], presented by Sonia Enriquez Vidal. Intervención.

pf12wilton224: Expert Mechanism on the Rights of Indigenous Peoples [UN institution], presented by Wilton Littlechild. Statement.

pf12windel243: Asia Indigenous Peoples Caucus [indigenous organization], presented by Windel Bolinget. Intervention.

pf12yupo339: Ainu Association of Hokkaido [indigenous organization], presented by Yupo Abe. Statement.

References

Abdelal, Rawi, Yoshiko M. Herrera, Alastair Iain Johnston, and Rose McDermott. 2006. "Identity as a Variable." *Perspectives on Politics* 4 (4): 695–711.

Addis, Adeno. 1997. "On Human Diversity and the Limits of Toleration." In *Ethnicity and Group Rights*. Edited by Ian Shapiro and Will Kymlicka, 112–53. New York: New York University Press.

Adorno, Theodor W. 1956a. "Gesellschaft." In *Soziologische Exkurse: Nach Vorträgen und Diskussionen*. Edited by Institut für Sozialforschung, 22–39. Frankfurt am Main: Europäische Verlagsanstalt.

———. 1956b. "Gruppe." In *Soziologische Exkurse: Nach Vorträgen und Diskussionen*. Edited by Institut für Sozialforschung, 55–69. Frankfurt am Main: Europäische Verlagsanstalt.

———. 1978. *Minima Moralia: Reflections on a Damaged Life*. Translated by Edmund Jephcott. London: Verso.

———. 1982. "Subject and Object." In *The Essential Frankfurt School Reader*. Edited by Andrew Arato and Eike Gebhardt, 497–511. New York: Continuum.

———. 2001. *Problems of Moral Philosophy*. Translated by Thomas Schröder and Rodney Livingstone. Stanford, CA: Stanford University Press.

———. 2002. *Introduction to Sociology*. Translated by Christoph Gödde and Edmund Jephcott. Stanford, CA: Stanford University Press.

———. 2004. *Negative Dialectics*. Translated by E. B. Ashton. London: Routledge.

———. 2008. *Lectures on Negative Dialectics: Fragments of a Lecture Course 1965/1966*. Translated by Rolf Tiedemann and Rodney Livingstone. Cambridge: Polity.

———. 2010. *Einführung in die Dialektik: Nachgelassene Schriften*. Berlin: Suhrkamp.

African Commission's Working Group on Indigenous Populations/Communities. 2009. *Report*. Adopted by the African Commission on Human and Peoples' Rights, November 2003. Reprinted in *International Human Rights and Indigenous Peoples*. Edited by S. James Anaya, 32–35.

Alexandrowicz, Charles Henry. 1967. *Introduction to the History of the Law of Nations in the East Indies*. London: Oxford University Press.

Al-Hibri, Azizah Y. 1999. "Is Western Patriarchal Feminism Good for Third World/Minority Women?" In *Is Multiculturalism Bad for Women?* Edited by Joshua Cohen, Matthew Howard, and Martha Nussbaum, 41–46. Princeton, NJ: Princeton University Press.

Allen, Steve, and Alexandra Xanthaki, eds. 2011. *Reflections on the UN Declaration on the Rights of Indigenous Peoples*. Oxford: Hart Publishing.

Alston, Philip, ed. 2005. *Non-State Actors and Human Rights*. Oxford and New York: Oxford University Press.

American Anthropological Association, Executive Board. 1947. "Statement on Human Rights." *American Anthropologist* 49 (4/1): 539–43.

Anaya, S. James. 1996. *Indigenous Peoples in International Law*. Oxford: Oxford University Press.

———. 1997. "On Justifying Special Ethnic Group Rights: Comments on Pogge." In *Ethnicity and Group Rights*. Edited by Ian Shapiro and Will Kymlicka, 222–31. New York: New York University Press.

———. 2009a. "Indigenous Peoples and the International System: Introduction." In *International Human Rights and Indigenous Peoples*. Edited by S. James Anaya, 1–54. New York: Aspen Publishers.

———. 2009b. "The United Nations Declaration on the Rights of Indigenous Peoples." In *International Human Rights and Indigenous Peoples*. Edited by S. James Anaya, 55–132. New York: Aspen Publishers.

———. 2009c. "Why There Should Not Have to Be a Declaration on the Rights of Indigenous Peoples." Talk at the Congress of Americanists, July 2006. Reprinted in *International Human Rights and Indigenous Peoples*. Edited by S. James Anaya, 58–63. New York: Aspen Publishers.

Anaya, S. James, and Siegfried Wiessner. 2009. "The UN Declaration on the Rights of Indigenous Peoples: Towards Re-empowerment." In *International Human Rights and Indigenous Peoples*. Edited by S. James Anaya, 99–102. New York: Aspen Publishers.

Anderson, Benedict. 1983. *Imagined Communities: Reflections on the Origin and Spread of Nationalism*. London and New York: Verso.

Andreopoulos, George J., Zehra F. Kabasakal Arat, and Peter H. Juviler, eds. 2006. *Non-state actors in the Human Rights Universe*. Bloomfield, IL: Kumarian Press.

An-Na'im, Abdullahi Ahmed. 1999a. "The Cultural Mediation of Human Rights. The Al-Arqam Case in Malaysia." In *The East Asian Challenge for Human Rights*. Edited by Joanne Bauer and Daniel Bell, 147–68. Cambridge and New York: Cambridge University Press.

———. 1999b. "Promises We Should All Keep in Common Cause." In *Is Multiculturalism Bad for Women?* Edited by Joshua Cohen, Matthew Howard, and Martha Nussbaum, 59–64. Princeton, NJ: Princeton University Press.

Antweiler, Christoph. 2007. *Was ist den Menschen gemeinsam? Über Kultur und Kulturen*. Darmstadt: Wissenschaftliche Buchgesellschaft.

Appiah, Kwame Anthony. 1994. "Identity, Authenticity, Survival. Multicultural Societies and Social Reproduction." In *Multiculturalism: Examining the Politics of Recognition*. Edited by Charles Taylor, 149–63. Princeton, NJ: Princeton University Press.

Archambault, Caroline S. 2011. "Ethnographic Empathy and the Social Context of Rights: 'Rescuing' Maasai Girls from Early Marriage." *American Anthropologist* 113 (4): 632–43.

Assmann, Jan. 1995. "Collective Memory and Cultural Identity." *New German Critique* (65): 125–33.

———. 2011. *Cultural Memory and Early Civilization: Writing, Remembrance, and Political Imagination*. Cambridge: Cambridge University Press.

Atkinson, Judy. 1991. "'Stinkin Thinkin': Alcohol, Violence and Government Responses." *Aboriginal Law Bulletin* 2 (51): 4–6.

Avanza, Martina, and Gilles Laferté. 2005. "Dépasser la 'construction des identités'? Identification, image sociale, appartenance." *Genèsis* 61: 134–52.

Bachmann-Medick, Doris. 2016. *Cultural Turns: New Orientations in the Study of Culture*. Berlin: de Gruyter.

Bakhtin, Mikhail Mikhaïlovich. 1994. *The Dialogic Imagination: Four Essays*. Austin: University of Texas Press.

Bal, Mieke. 2009. "Becoming of the World versus Identity Politics." *Nordlit: Tidsskrift i litteratur og kultur* (24): 9–30.

Bandow, Doug. 2008. "Human Rights in Danger? Myths and Realities in the UN." *Friedrich-Naumann-Stiftung Occasional Paper* 45.

Banting, Keith G., and Will Kymlicka, eds. 2006. *Multiculturalism and the Welfare State. Recognition and Redistribution in Contemporary Democracies*. Oxford: Oxford University Press.

Barnard, Alan. 2004. "Indigenous Peoples: A Response to Justin Kenrick and Jerome Lewis." *Anthropology Today* 20 (5): 19.

Barnard, Alan, and Justin Kenrick, eds. 2001. *Africa's Indigenous Peoples. "First Peoples" or "Marginalized Minorities"?* Edinburgh: Centre of African Studies, University of Edinburgh.

Bassel, Leah. 2012. *Refugee Women: Beyond Gender versus Culture*. London and New York: Routledge.

Batstone, David B. 1991. *From Conquest to Struggle. Jesus of Nazareth in Latin America*. Albany: State University of New York Press.
Bauman, Zygmunt. 2003. *Community: Seeking Safety in an Insecure World*. Cambridge: Polity Press.
Bedorf, Thomas. 2010. *Verkennende Anerkennung. Über Identität und Politik*. Frankfurt am Main: Suhrkamp.
Bell, Daniel. 1980. *The Winding Passage: Sociological Essays and Journeys*. Cambridge: Abt Books.
Bell, Diane. 1992. "Considering Gender: Are Human Rights for Women, Too? An Australian Case." In *Human Rights in Cross-Cultural Perspectives: A Quest for Consensus*. Edited by Abdullahi Ahmed An-Na'im, 339–62. Philadelphia: University of Pennsylvania Press.
Benedict, Ruth. 1934. *Patterns of Culture*. Boston and New York: Houghton Mifflin.
Benhabib, Seyla. 2002. *The Claims of Culture: Equality and Diversity in the Global Era*. Princeton, NJ: Princeton University Press.
Benhabib, Seyla, and Drucilla Cornell. 1987. "Introduction: Beyond the Politics of Gender." In *Feminism as Critique: Essays on the Politics of Gender in Late-Capitalist Societies*. Edited by Seyla Benhabib and Drucilla Cornell, 1–15. Cambridge: Polity Press.
Benjamin, Jessica. 1988. *The Bonds of Love. Psychoanalysis, Feminism, and the Problem of Domination*. New York: Pantheon Books.
Berlin, Isaiah. 2002. "Two Concepts of Liberty." In *Liberty*, 166–217. Oxford: Oxford University Press.
Berting, Jan, Peter R. Baehr, J. Herman Burgers, Cees Flinterman, Barbara de Klerk, Rob Kroes, Cornelius A. van Minnen, and Koo VanderWal, eds. 1990. *Human Rights in a Pluralist World: Individuals and Collectivities*. Westport, CT, and London: Meckler.
Bhabha, Homi K. 1994. *The Location of Culture*. London and New York: Routledge.
———. 1999. "Liberalism's Sacred Cow." In *Is Multiculturalism Bad for Women?* Edited by Joshua Cohen, Matthew Howard, and Martha Nussbaum, 79–84. Princeton, NJ: Princeton University Press.
Bloch, Anne-Christine. 1995. "Minorities and Indigenous Peoples." In *Economic, Social and Cultural Rights: A Textbook*, edited by Asbjørn Eide, Catarina Krause, and Allan Rosas, 309–21. Dordrecht: Martinus Nijhoff.
Bobbio, Norberto. 1996. *The Age of Rights*. Cambridge, UK: Polity Press; Blackwell.
Borelli, Silvia, and Federico Lenzerini, eds. 2012. *Cultural Heritage, Cultural Rights, Cultural Diversity: New Developments in International Law*. Leiden: Martinus Nijhoff Publishers.
Brandt, Hans-Jürgen, ed. 2013. *Cambios en la justicia comunitaria y factores de influencia*. Lima: Instituto de Defensa Legal.
Brightman, Robert. 1995. "Forget Culture: Replacement, Transcendence, Relexification." *Cultural Anthropology* 10 (4): 509–46.
Brody, Hugh. 2001. *The Other Side of Eden. Hunters, Farmers, and the Shaping of the World*. New York: North Point Press.
Brölmann, Catherine, Rene Lefeber, and Marjoleine Zieck, eds. 1993. *Peoples and Minorities in International Law*. Dordrecht: Martinus Nijhoff.
Brownlie, Ian. 1992. *Treaties and Indigenous Peoples: The Robb Lectures*. Oxford and New York: Clarendon Press; Oxford University Press.
Brubaker, Rogers, and Frederick Cooper. 2000. "Beyond 'Identity.'" *Theory and Society* 29 (1): 1–47.
Brumann, Christoph. 1999. "Writing for Culture: Why a Successful Concept Should Not Be Discarded." *Current Anthropology* 40 (S1): S1–S27.
Buchanan, Allen. 2004. *Justice, Legitimacy, and Self-Determination: Moral Foundations for International Law*. Oxford and New York: Oxford University Press.
Butler, Judith. 1990. *Gender Trouble: Feminism and the Subversion of Identity*. New York: Routledge.
———. 1993. *Bodies that Matter: On the Discursive Limits of Sex*. New York: Routledge.

References

Calhoun, Craig J. 1994. "Social Theory and the Politics of Identity." In *Social Theory and the Politics of Identity*. Edited by Craig J. Calhoun, 9–36. Oxford and Cambridge: Blackwell.

Canessa, Andrew. 2006. "Todos somos indigenas: Towards a New Language of National Political Identity." *Bulletin of Latin American Research* 25 (2): 241–63.

———. 2007. "Who Is Indigenous? Self-Identification, Indigeneity, and Claims to Justice in Contemporary Bolivia." *Urban Anthropology and Studies of Cultural Systems and World Economic Development* 36 (3): 195–237.

———. 2008. "The Past Is Not Another Country: Exploring Indigenous Histories in Bolivia." *History and Anthropology* 19 (4): 353–69.

Capotorti, Francesco. 1979. *Study on the Rights of Persons Belonging to Ethnic, Religious and Linguistic Minorities*. New York: United Nations Pub.

Cerulo, Karen A. 1997. "Identity Construction: New Issues, New Directions" *Annual Review of Sociology* 23: 385–409.

Chandler, David. 2002. *From Kosovo to Kabul: Human Rights and International Intervention*. London and Ann Arbor: Pluto Press.

Chapman, Chris. 2011. "Transitional Justice and the Rights of Minorities and Indigenous Peoples." In *Identities in Transition: Challenges for Transitional Justice in Divided Societies*. Edited by Paige Arthur, 251–70. Cambridge: Cambridge University Press.

Charters, Claire, and Rodolfo Stavenhagen, eds. 2009. *Making the Declaration Work: The United Nations Declaration on the Rights of Indigenous Peoples*. Copenhagen, and New Brunswick, NJ: IWGIA, Distributors Transaction Publisher, Central Books.

Chodorow, Nancy J. 1978. *The Reproduction of Mothering: Psychoanalysis and the Sociology of Gender*. Berkeley: University of California Press.

Clapham, Andrew. 2006. *Human Rights Obligations of Non-State Actors*. Oxford and New York: Oxford University Press.

Clifford, James. 1997. *Routes: Travel and Translation in the Late Twentieth Century*. Cambridge: Harvard University Press.

———. 2007. "Varieties of Indigenous Experience: Diaspora, Homelands, Sovereignties." In *Indigenous Experience Today*. Edited by Marisol de la Cadena and Orin Starn, 197–223. Oxford and New York: Berg.

Cohen, Joshua, Matthew Howard, and Martha C. Nussbaum, eds. 1999. *Is Multiculturalism Bad for Women?* Princeton, NJ: Princeton University Press.

Collingwood-Whittick, Sheila. 2012. "Australia's Northern Territory Intervention and Indigenous Rights on Language, Education and Culture: An Ethnocidal Solution to Aboriginal 'Dysfunction'?" In *Indigenous Rights: In the Age of the UN Declaration*. Edited by Elvira Pulitano, 110–42. Cambridge: Cambridge University Press.

Conklin, Beth A. 1997. "Body Paint, Feathers, and VCRs: Aesthetics and Authenticity in Amazonian Activism." *American Ethnologist* 24 (4): 711–37.

Coombe, Rosemary J. 1993. "The Property of Culture and the Politics of Possessing Identity: Native Claims in the Cultural Appropriation Controversy." *Canadian Journal of Law and Jurisprudence* 6 (2): 249–85.

Cowan, Jane K. 2006. "Culture and Rights after *Culture and Rights*." *American Anthropologist* 108 (1): 9–24.

Cowan, Jane K., Marie-Bénédicte Dembour, and Richard Wilson. 2001a. "Introduction." In *Culture and Rights: Anthropological Perspectives*. Edited by Jane K. Cowan, Marie-Bénédicte Dembour, and Richard Wilson, 1–26. Cambridge and New York: Cambridge University Press.

———. 2001b. *Culture and Rights: Anthropological Perspectives*. Cambridge and New York: Cambridge University Press.

Crawford, James. 1988a. "Some Conclusions." In *The Rights of Peoples*. Edited by James Crawford, 159–77. Oxford and New York: Clarendon Press; Oxford University Press.

Crawford, James, ed. 1988b. *The Rights of Peoples*. Oxford and New York: Clarendon Press; Oxford University Press.

Cristescu, Aureliu. 1981. *The Right to Self-Determination. Historical and Current Developments on the Basis of United Nations Instruments.* New York: United Nations Pub.
Daes, Erica-Irene A. 1993. "Some Considerations on the Right of Indigenous Peoples to Self-Determination." *Transnational Law and Contemporary Problems* 3 (1): 1–12.
———. 1996. *Working Paper on the Concept of Indigenous Peoples.* UN Doc E/CN 4/Sub 2/AC 4/1996/2.
———. 2001. "Indigenous Peoples and Their Relationship to Land." Final working paper. UN Doc E/CN.4/Sub.2/2001/21, http://www.unhchr.ch/Huridocda/Huridoca.nsf/0/78d418c307faa00bc1256a9900496f2b/$FILE/G0114179.pdf, accessed March 25, 2013.
Dallmayr, Fred R. 2010. "Introduction." In *Comparative Political Theory: An Introduction.* Edited by Fred R. Dallmayr, 3–6. New York: Palgrave Macmillan.
Danielsen, Dan, and Karen Engle, eds. 1995. *After Identity: A Reader in Law and Culture.* New York and London: Routledge.
Deitelhoff, Nicole. 2009. "Grenzen der Verständigung? Kulturelle Fragmentierung im Regieren jenseits des Nationalstaats." In *Was bleibt vom Staat?: Demokratie, Recht und Verfassung im globalen Zeitalter,* edited by Nicole Deitelhoff and Jens Steffek, 187–220. Frankfurt am Main and New York: Campus.
Dench, Geoff. 2003. *Minorities in the Open Society.* New Brunswick: Transaction Publishers.
Deng, Francis M., Sadikiel Kimaro, Terrence Lyons, Donald Rothchild, and I. William Zartman. 1996. *Sovereignty as Responsibility: Conflict Management in Africa.* Washington, DC: Brookings Institution.
Derrida, Jacques. 1976. *Of Grammatology.* Baltimore and London: Johns Hopkins University Press.
———. 1992. "The Other Heading: Memories, Responses, and Responsibilities." In *The Other Heading: Reflections on Today's Europe,* 4–83. Bloomington: Indiana University Press.
———. 1998. *Monolingualism of the Other: Or the Prosthesis of Origin.* Stanford, CA: Stanford University Press.
DESA/UNPFII. 2009. *State of the World's Indigenous Peoples.* New York: United Nations Pub.
Diner, Dan, and Seyla Benhabib, eds. 1988. *Zivilisationsbruch: Denken nach Auschwitz.* Frankfurt am Main: Fischer Taschenbuch Verlag.
Dinstein, Yoram. 1976. "Collective Human Rights of Peoples and Minorities." *The International and Comparative Law Quarterly* 25 (1): 102–20.
Donders, Yvonne M. 2002. *Towards a Right to Cultural Identity?* Antwerpen: Intersentia.
Donnelly, Jack. 1990. "Human Rights, Individual Rights and Collective Rights." In *Human Rights in a Pluralist World: Individuals and Collectivities.* Edited by Jan Berting et al., 39–62. Westport, CT, and London: Meckler.
———. 2006. "Human Rights." In *The Oxford Handbook of Political Theory.* Edited by John S. Dryzek, Bonnie Honig, and Anne Phillips, 601–20. Oxford and New York: Oxford University Press.
Eide, Asbjørn. 1986. "United Nations Action on the Rights of Indigenous Populations." In *The Rights of Indigenous Peoples in International Law: Workshop Report.* Edited by Ruth Thompson, Ruth, 11–33. Saskatoon: University of Saskatchewan Native Law Centre.
———. 1995. "Cultural Rights as Individual Human Rights." In *Economic, Social and Cultural Rights: A Textbook.* Edited by Asbjørn Eide, Catarina Krause, and Allan Rosas, 229–41. Dordrecht: Martinus Nijhoff.
Eisenberg, Avigail. 2003. "Diversity and Equality. Three Approaches to Cultural and Sexual Difference." *Journal of Political Philosophy* 11 (1): 41–64.
Emerson, Robert M., Rachel I. Fretz, and Linda L. Shaw. 2009. "Participant Observation and Fieldnotes." In *Handbook of Ethnography.* Edited by Paul Atkinson, Amanda Coffey, Sara Delamont, John Lofland, and Lyn Lofland, 325–68. Los Angeles: Sage.
Erikson, Erik H. 1968. *Identity: Youth and Crisis.* New York: Norton.

Errico, Stefania. 2009. "The Draft UN Declaration on the Rights of Indigenous Peoples: An Overview." In *International Human Rights and Indigenous Peoples*. Edited by S. James Anaya, 63–70. New York: Aspen Publishers.
Etzioni, Amitai. 1993. *The Spirit of Community: Rights, Responsibilities and the Communitarian Agenda*. New York: Crown Publishers.
———. 1996. "The Responsive Community: A Communitarian Perspective." Presidential Address, American Sociological Association, August 20, 1995. *American Sociological Review* 61 (1): 1–11.
———. 1997. *The New Golden Rule: Community and Morality in a Democratic Society*. New York: Basic Books.
Fagan, Andrew. 2009. *Human Rights: Confronting Myths and Misunderstandings*. Cheltenham, Northampton, UK: Edward Elgar.
Falk, Richard. 1992. "Cultural Foundations for the International Protection of Human Rights." In *Human Rights in Cross-Cultural Perspectives: A Quest for Consensus*. Edited by Abdullahi Ahmed An-Na'im, 43–64. Philadelphia: University of Pennsylvania Press.
Fanon, Frantz. 1986. *Black Skin, White Masks*. London: Pluto Press.
Fearon, James. 1999. "What Is Identity (As We Now Use the Word)?" Manuscript, Stanford University.
Finnemore, Martha, and Kathryn Sikkink. 1998. "International Norm Dynamics and Political Change." *International Organization* 52 (4): 887–917.
Flick, Uwe. 2007. *Qualitative Sozialforschung: Eine Einführung*. Reinbek bei Hamburg: Rowohlt Taschenbuch Verlag.
Flinterman, Cees. 1990. "Three Generations of Human Rights." In *Human Rights in a Pluralist World: Individuals and Collectivities*. Edited by Jan Berting et al., 75–82. Westport, CT, and London: Meckler.
Forst, Rainer. 1994a. "Kommunitarismus und Liberalismus: Stationen einer Debatte." In *Kommunitarismus: Eine Debatte über die moralischen Grundlagen moderner Gesellschaften*. Edited by Axel Honneth, 181–212. Frankfurt am Main and New York: Campus.
———. 1994b. *Kontexte der Gerechtigkeit: Politische Philosophie jenseits von Liberalismus und Kommunitarismus*. Frankfurt am Main: Suhrkamp.
Foucault, Michel. 1984. "Nietzsche, Genealogy, History." In *The Foucault Reader*. Edited by Paul Rabinow, 76–100. New York: Pantheon Books.
Francioni, Francesco, and Martin Scheinin, eds. 2008. *Cultural Human Rights*. Boston: Martinus Nijhoff Publishers.
Fredericks, Bronwyn. 2010. "Reempowering Ourselves: Australian Aboriginal Women." *Signs: Journal of Women in Culture and Society* 35 (3): 546–50.
Gesellschaft für bedrohte Völker. n.d. "Indigene Völker und ihr Menschenrechtsschutz zentriert auf die ILO-Konvention Nr. 169." Dossier. http://www.gfbv.it/3dossier/diritto/ilo169-pd.html, accessed March 27, 2013.
Gilman, Sander L. 1999. "'Barbaric' Rituals." In *Is Multiculturalism Bad for Women?* Edited by Joshua Cohen, Matthew Howard, and Martha Nussbaum, 53–58. Princeton, NJ: Princeton University Press.
Gilroy, Paul. 1993. *The Black Atlantic: Modernity and Double Consciousness*. Cambridge, MA: Harvard University Press.
Gläser, Jochen, and Grit Laudel. 2010. *Experteninterviews und qualitative Inhaltsanalyse: Als Instrumente rekonstruierender Untersuchungen*. Wiesbaden: VS Verlag für Sozialwissenschaften.
Gleason, Philip. 1983. "Identifying Identity: A Semantic History." *The Journal of American History* 69 (4): 910–31.
Goffman, Erving. 1963. *Stigma: Notes on the Management of Spoiled Identity*. Englewood Cliffs, NJ: Prentice-Hall.
Goggin, Sean. 2011. "Human Rights and 'Primitive' Culture: Misrepresentations of Indigenous Life." *The International Journal of Human Rights* 15 (6): 873–86.

Goodale, Marc. 2006. "Reclaiming Modernity: Indigenous Cosmopolitanism and the Coming of the Second Revolution in Bolivia." *American Ethnologist* 33 (4): 634–49.
Gray, Andrew. 1997. *Indigenous Rights and Development: Self-Determination in an Amazonian Community*. Providence, RI: Berghahn Books.
Griffin, James. 2008. *On Human Rights*. Oxford: Oxford University Press.
Guenther, Mathias. 2006. "The Concept of Indigeneity: Response to Alan Barnard: Kalahari Revisionism, Vienna and the 'Indigenous Peoples' Debate." *Social Anthropology* 14 (1): 17–19.
Habermas, Jürgen. 1974. "On Social Identity." *Telos* (19): 91–103.
———. 1975. "Moral development and Ego Identity." *Telos* (24): 41–55.
———. 1979. "Historical Materialism and the Development of Normative Structures." In *Communication and the Evolution of Society*, 95–129. London: Heinemann.
———. 1994. "Struggles for Recognition in the Democratic Constitutional State." In *Multiculturalism: Examining the Politics of Recognition*. Edited by Charles Taylor, 107–48. Princeton, NJ: Princeton University Press.
———. 2010. "The Concept of Human Dignity and the Realistic Utopia of Human Rights." *Metaphilosophy* 41 (4): 464–80.
Hall, Gillette, and Harry Anthony Patrinos. 2012. *Indigenous Peoples, Poverty, and Development*. New York: Cambridge University Press.
Hall, Stuart. 1992a. "The Question of Cultural Identity." In *Modernity and Its Futures*. Edited by Stuart Hall, David Held, and Anthony McGrew, 273–316. Cambridge, UK: Polity Press.
———. 1992b. "The West and the Rest. Discourse and Power." In *Formations of Modernity*. Edited by Stuart Hall and Bram Grieben, 185–227. Cambridge, UK: Polity Press.
———. 1996a. "Introduction: Who Needs 'Identity'?" In *Questions of Cultural Identity*. Edited by Stuart Hall and Paul du Gay, 1–17. London, Thousand Oaks (CA), and New Delhi: Sage.
———. 1996b. "New Ethnicities." In *Critical Dialogues in Cultural Studies*. Edited by David Morley and Kuan-Hsing Chen, 442–51. London and New York: Routledge.
———. 1997. "The Local and the Global: Globalization and Ethnicity." In *Dangerous Liaisons: Gender, Nation, and Postcolonial Perspectives*. Edited by Anne McClintock, Aamir Mufti, and Ella Shohat, 173–87. Minneapolis and London: University of Minnesota Press.
———. 2000. "Conclusion: The Multi-Cultural Question." In *Un/settled Multiculturalisms: Diasporas, Entanglements, Transruptions*. Edited by Barnor Hesse, 209–41. London: Zed Books.
Hall, Stuart, and Paul du Gay, eds. 1996. *Questions of Cultural Identity*. London, Thousand Oaks (CA), and New Delhi: Sage.
Hegel, Georg Wilhelm Friedrich. 1977. *Phenomenology of Spirit*. Translated by Arnold Vincent Miller and John N. Findlay. Oxford: Oxford University Press.
———. 2010. *The Science of Logic*. Translated by George Giovanni. Cambridge: Cambridge University Press.
Heintze, Hans-Joachim, ed. 1998a. "Moderner Minderheitenschutz. Rechtliche oder politische Absicherung?" *50. Jahrestag der UN-Menschenrechtserklärung*. Bonn: Dietz.
———. 1998b. "Rechtliche oder politische Absicherung von Minderheiten? Eine Einführung in die Thematik." In *Moderner Minderheitenschutz: Rechtliche oder politische Absicherung? Zum 50. Jahrestag der UN-Menschenrechtserklärung*. Edited by Hans-Joachim Heintze, 14–54. Bonn: Dietz.
Henrich, Dieter. 1979. "Identität: Begriffe, Probleme, Grenzen." In *Identität*. Edited by Odo Marquard and Karlheinz Stierle, 133–86. München: Wilhelm Fink Verlag.
Hirschman, Albert O. 1970. *Exit, Voice, and Loyalty: Responses to Decline in Firms, Organizations, and States*. Cambridge, MA: Harvard University Press.
Hobsbawm, Eric J., and Terence Ranger, eds. 1992. *The Invention of Tradition*. Cambridge: Cambridge University Press.

Hodgson, Dorothy L. 2002. "Introduction: Comparative Perspectives on the Indigenous Rights Movement in Africa and the Americas." *American Anthropologist* 104 (4): 1037–49.

———. 2009. "Becoming Indigenous in Africa." *African Studies Review* 52 (3): 1–32.

Hofstätter, Peter R. 1959. *Einführung in die Sozialpsychologie*. Stuttgart: Kröner.

Holder, Cindy L., and Jeff J. Corntassel. 2002. "Indigenous Peoples and Multicultural Citizenship: Bridging Collective and Individual Rights." *Human Rights Quarterly* 24 (1): 126–51.

Honig, Bonnie. 1999. "My Culture Made Me Do It." In *Is Multiculturalism Bad for Women?* Edited by Joshua Cohen, Matthew Howard, and Martha Nussbaum, 35–40. Princeton, NJ: Princeton University Press.

Horowitz, Donald L. 1985. *Ethnic Groups in Conflict*. Berkeley, Los Angeles, and London: University of California Press.

Human Rights Council. 2008. "Protect, Respect and Remedy: A Framework for Business and Human Rights." *Report of the Special Representative of the Secretary-General on the Issue of Human Rights and Transnational Corporations and Other Business Enterprises, John Ruggie*. A/HRC/8/5, http://www.reports-and-materials.org/sites/default/files/reports-and-materials/Ruggie-report-7-Apr-2008.pdf, accessed October 5, 2015.

IFAD. n. d. "Statistics and Key Facts about Indigenous Peoples." http://www.ruralpovertyportal.org/topic/statistics/tags/, accessed November 13, 2012.

Igoe, Jim. 2006. "Becoming Indigenous Peoples: Difference, Inequality, and the Globalization of East African Identity Politics." *African Affairs* 105 (420): 399–420.

Jaggar, Alison M. 2009. "Okin and the Challenge of Essentialism." In *Toward a Humanist Justice: The Political Philosophy of Susan Moller Okin*. Edited by Debra Satz and Rob Reich, 166–80. Oxford and New York: Oxford University Press.

Jenkins, Richard. 2008. *Social Identity*. London and New York: Routledge.

Jennings, Francis. 1976. *The Invasion of America: Indians, Colonialism, and the Cant of Conquest*. New York and London: W. W. Norton & Company.

Jones, Peter. 1999. "Human Rights, Group Rights and Peoples' Rights." *Human Rights Quarterly* 21 (1): 80–107.

———. 2000. "Individuals, Communities and Human Rights." *Review of International Studies* 26 (5): 199–215.

Kahane, David. 2003. "Dispute Resolution and the Politics of Cultural Generalization." *Negotiation Journal* 19 (1): 5–27.

Kenrick, Justin, and Jerome Lewis. 2004. "Indigenous Peoples' Rights and the Politics of the Term 'Indigenous.'" *Anthropology Today* 20 (2): 4–9.

Kingsbury, Benedict. 1998. "'Indigenous Peoples' in International Law: A Constructivist Approach to the Asian Controversy." *The American Journal of International Law* 92 (3): 414–57.

Krennerich, Michael. 2013. *Soziale Menschenrechte: Zwischen Recht und Politik*. Schwalbach am Taunus: Wochenschau-Verlag.

Kroeber, Arnold L., and Talcott Parsons. 1958. "The Concepts of Culture and of Social System." *American Sociological Review* 23: 582–83.

Kukathas, Chandran. 1992. "Are There Any Cultural Rights?" *Political Theory* 20 (1): 105–39.

———. 2009. "The Dilemma of a Dutiful Daughter." In *Toward a Humanist Justice: The Political Philosophy of Susan Moller Okin*. Edited by Debra Satz and Rob Reich, 181–200. Oxford and New York: Oxford University Press.

Kuper, Adam. 2003. "The Return of the Native." *Current Anthropology* 44 (3): 389–95.

Kymlicka, Will. 1988. "Liberalism and Communitarianism." *Canadian Journal of Philosophy* 18 (2): 181–204.

———. 1991. "Liberalism and the Politicization of Ethnicity." *Canadian Journal of Law and Jurisprudence* 4 (2): 239–56.

———. 1994. "Communitarianism, Liberalism, and Superliberalism." *Critical Review* (New York), 8 (2): 263–84.

———. 1995a. "Misunderstanding Nationalism." *Dissent* 42 (Winter): 130–37.

——. 1995b. *Multicultural Citizenship: A Liberal Theory of Minority Rights*. Oxford: Oxford University Press.
——. 1997. *States, Nations and Cultures*. Assen: Van Gorcum.
——. 1998. "American Multiculturalism in the International Arena." *Dissent* 45 (Fall): 73–79.
——. 1999. "Liberal Complacencies." In *Is Multiculturalism Bad for Women?* Edited by Joshua Cohen, Matthew Howard, and Martha Nussbaum, 31–34. Princeton, NJ: Princeton University Press.
——. 2001a. "Human Rights and Ethnocultural Justice." In *Politics in the Vernacular: Nationalism, Multiculturalism, and Citizenship*, 69–90. Oxford and New York: Oxford University Press.
——. 2001b. "Theorizing Indigenous Rights." In *Politics in the Vernacular: Nationalism, Multiculturalism, and Citizenship*, 120–32. Oxford and New York: Oxford University Press.
——. 2002. *Contemporary Political Philosophy. An Introduction*. New York: Oxford University Press.
——. 2007. *Multicultural Odysseys: Navigating the New International Politics of Diversity*. Oxford: Oxford University Press.
——. 2011a. "Beyond the Indigenous/Minority Dichotomy?" In *Reflections on the UN Declaration on the Rights of Indigenous Peoples*. Edited by Steve Allen and Alexandra Xanthaki, 183–208. Oxford: Hart Publishing.
——. 2011b. "Transitional Justice, Federalism, and the Accommodation of Minority Nationalism." In *Identities in Transition: Challenges for Transitional Justice in Divided Societies*, edited by Paige Arthur, 303–33. Cambridge: Cambridge University Press.
Laclau, Ernesto, and Chantal Mouffe. 2001. *Hegemony and Socialist Strategy: Towards a Radical Democratic Politics*. London and New York: Verso.
Langbaum, Robert. 1977. *The Mysteries of Identity: A Theme in Modern Literature*. New York: Oxford University Press.
Lauren, Paul Gordon. 2011. *The Evolution of International Human Rights. Visions Seen*. Philadelphia: University of Pennsylvania Press.
Lindley, Marc Frank. 1926. *The Acquisition and Government of Backward Territory in International Law: Being a Treatise on the Law and Practice Relating to Colonial Expansion*. London: Longmans, Green & Co.
Lohmann, Georg. 1998. "Menschenrechte zwischen Moral und Recht." In *Philosophie der Menschenrechte*. Edited by Stefan Gosepath and Georg Lohmann, 62–95. Frankfurt am Main: Suhrkamp.
——. 2004. "'Kollektive' Menschenrechte zum Schutz von Minderheiten?" In *Anthropologie, Ethik, Politik: Grundfragen der praktischen Philosophie der Gegenwart*. Edited by Thomas Rentsch, 92–107. Dresden: Thelem.
MacIntyre, Alasdair C. 1984. *After Virtue: A Study in Moral Theory*. Notre Dame, IN: University of Notre Dame Press.
Mackenzie, Catriona, and Natalie Stoljar. 2000a. "Introduction: Autonomy Refigured." In *Relational Autonomy: Feminist Perspectives on Autonomy, Agency, and the Social Self*. Edited by Catriona Mackenzie and Natalie Stoljar, 3–31. New York: Oxford University Press.
Mackenzie, Catriona, and Natalie Stoljar, eds. 2000b. *Relational Autonomy: Feminist Perspectives on Autonomy, Agency, and the Social Self*. New York: Oxford University Press.
Mackenzie, William James Millar. 1978. *Political Identity*. New York: St. Martin's Press.
Malešević, Siniša. 2006. *Identity as Ideology: Understanding Ethnicity and Nationalism*. Basingstoke, UK: Palgrave Macmillan.
Marchart, Oliver. 2010. *Die politische Differenz: Zum Denken des Politischen bei Nancy, Lefort, Badiou, Laclau und Agamben*. Berlin: Suhrkamp.
Marchetti, Elena. 2008. "Intersectional Race and Gender Analyses: Why Legal Processes Just Don't Get It." *Social & Legal Studies* 17 (2): 155–74.

Margalit, Avishai, and Moshe Halbertal. 1994. "Liberalism and the Right to Culture." *Social Research* 61 (3): 491–510.
Marks, Greg C. 1991. "Indigenous Peoples in International Law: The Significance of Francisco de Vitoria and Bartolomé de las Casas." *Australian Yearbook of International Law* 13: 1–51.
Martin, Kathleen J. 2012. "Traditional Responsibility and Spiritual Relatives: Protection of Indigenous Rights to Land and Sacred Places." In *Indigenous Rights: In the Age of the UN Declaration*. Edited by Elvira Pulitano, 198–227. Cambridge: Cambridge University Press.
Martín Alcoff, Linda. 2003. "Introduction. Identities: Modern and Postmodern." In *Identities: Race, Class, Gender, and Nationality*. Edited by Linda Martín Alcoff and Eduardo Mendieta, 1–8. Malden: Blackwell.
Martínez, Alfonso Miguel. 1999. *Human Rights of Indigenous Peoples: Study on Treaties, Agreements and Other Constructive Arrangements between States and Indigenous Populations: Final Report by the Special Rapporteur*. E/CN 4/Sub 2/1999/20.
Martínez Cobo, José. 1986. *Study of the Problem of Discrimination against Indigenous Populations: Final Report by the Special Rapporteur*. UN Doc. E/CN 4/Sub 2/1986/7.
Maynard, John. 2007. *Fight for Liberty and Freedom: The Origins of Australian Aboriginal Activism*. Canberra: Aboriginal Studies Press.
McDonald, Michael. 1991. "Should Communities Have Rights? Reflections on Liberal Individualism." *Canadian Journal of Law and Jurisprudence* 4 (2): 217–37.
McGinness, Joe. 1991. *Son of Alyandabu: My Fight for Aboriginal Rights*. St Lucia, and Portland, OR: University of Queensland Press.
Mead, George Herbert. 1979. *Mind, Self, and Society: From the Standpoint of a Social Behaviorist*. Chicago: University of Chicago Press.
Meentzen, Angela. 2007. *Staatliche Indigena-Politik in Lateinamerika im Vergleich: Mexiko, Guatemala, Ekuador, Peru und Bolivien*. Peru: Konrad-Adenauer-Stiftung.
Melucci, Alberto. 1995. "The Process of Collective Identity." In *Social Movements and Culture*. Edited by Hank Johnston and Bert Klandermans, 41–63. Minneapolis: University of Minnesota Press.
Mende, Janne. 2011a. *Begründungsmuster weiblicher Genitalverstümmelung: Zur Vermittlung von Kulturrelativismus und Universalismus*. Bielefeld: Transcript.
———. 2011b. "Kultur, Volk und Rasse: Die deutsche Ethnologie im Nationalsozialismus und ihre Aufarbeitung." *Anthropos* 106 (2): 529–45.
Menke, Christoph. 2006. *Reflections of Equality*. Stanford, CA: Stanford University Press.
Menke, Christoph, and Arnd Pollmann. 2007. *Philosophie der Menschenrechte: Zur Einführung*. Hamburg: Junius.
Messer, Ellen. 1997. "Pluralist Approaches to Human Rights." *Journal of Anthropological Research* 53 (3): 293–317.
Mohanty, Chandra Talpade. 1997. "Under Western Eyes: Feminist Scholarship and Colonial Discourses." In *Dangerous Liaisons: Gender, Nation, and Postcolonial Perspectives*. Edited by Anne McClintock, Aamir Mufti, and Ella Shohat, 255–77. Minneapolis and London: University of Minnesota Press.
Montaigne, Michel de. 2008. *Les essais*. Livre 2. Mérignac: Guy de Pernon.
Moore, Margaret. 2005. "Internal Minorities and Indigenous Self-Determination." In *Minorities within Minorities: Equality, Rights and Diversity*. Edited by Avigail I. Eisenberg and Jeff Spinner-Halev, 271–93. Cambridge: Cambridge University Press.
Morgan, Rhiannon. 2011. *Transforming Law and Institution: Indigenous Peoples, the United Nations and Human Rights*. Burlington, VT: Ashgate.
Morsink, Johannes. 1999. *The Universal Declaration of Human Rights: Origins, Drafting, and Intent*. Philadelphia: University of Pennsylvania Press.
Mouffe, Chantal. 1995. "Democratic Politics and the Question of Identity." In *The Identity in Question*. Edited by John Rajchman, 33–46. New York and London: Routledge.
Mountford, Charles P. 1976. *Nomads of the Australian Desert*. Adelaide: Rigby.

Müller, Stefan. 2011. *Logik, Widerspruch und Vermittlung: Aspekte der Dialektik in den Sozialwissenschaften*. Wiesbaden: VS Verlag für Sozialwissenschaften.
Nafziger, James A. R., Robert Kirkwood Paterson, and Alison Dundes Renteln, eds. 2010. *Cultural Law*. Cambridge: Cambridge University Press.
Nagengast, Carole. 1997. "Women, Minorities, and Indigenous Peoples." *Journal of Anthropological Research* 53 (3): 349–69.
Nagle, John. 2009. *Multiculturalism's Double-Bind: Creating Inclusivity, Cosmopolitanism and Difference*. Farnham, Surrey, and Burlington, VT: Ashgate.
Nancy, Jean-Luc. 2013. *Être singulier pluriel*. Paris: Galilée.
Nathan, Dev, Govind Kelkar, and Pierre Walter. 2004. *Globalization and Indigenous Peoples in Asia: Changing the Local-Global Interface*. New Delhi, and Thousand Oaks, CA: Sage.
Neidhardt, Friedhelm. 1986. "'Kultur und Gesellschaft': Einige Anmerkungen zum Sonderheft." *Kölner Zeitschrift für Soziologie und Sozialpsychologie* 27 (Sonderheft Kultur und Gesellschaft): 10–18.
Neier, Aryeh. 2012. *The International Human Rights Movement: A History*. Princeton, NJ: Princeton University Press.
Newman, Dwight G. 2006/2007. "Theorizing Collective Indigenous Rights." *American Indian Law Review* 31 (2): 273–89.
Niederauer, Martin. 2014. *Die Widerständigkeiten des Jazz: Sozialgeschichte und Improvisation unter den Imperativen der Kulturindustrie*. Frankfurt am Main: Peter Lang.
Niethammer, Lutz. 2000. *Kollektive Identität: Heimliche Quellen einer unheimlichen Konjunktur*. Reinbek bei Hamburg: Rowohlt.
Niezen, Ronald. 2003. *The Origins of Indigenism: Human Rights and the Politics of Identity*. Berkeley and Los Angeles: University of California Press.
Nunner-Winkler, Gertrud. 2002. "Identität und Moral." In *Transitorische Identität: Der Prozesscharakter des modernen Selbst*. Edited by Jürgen Straub and Joachim Renn, 56–84. Frankfurt am Main and New York: Campus.
Nussbaum, Martha C. 1999. "A Plea for Difficulty." In *Is Multiculturalism Bad for Women?* Edited by Joshua Cohen, Matthew Howard, and Martha C. Nussbaum, 105–14. Princeton, NJ: Princeton University Press.
Okin, Susan Moller. 1989. *Justice, Gender, and the Family*. New York: Basic Books.
———. 1998a. "Feminism and Multiculturalism: Some Tensions." *Ethics* 108 (4): 661–84.
———. 1998b. "Feminism, Women's Human Rights, and Cultural Differences." *Hypatia* 13 (2): 32–52.
———. 1998c. "Konflikte zwischen Grundrechten. Frauenrechte und die Probleme religiöser und kultureller Unterschiede." In *Philosophie der Menschenrechte*. Edited by Stefan Gosepath and Georg Lohmann, 310–42. Frankfurt am Main: Suhrkamp.
———. 1999a. "Is Multiculturalism Bad for Women?" In *Is Multiculturalism Bad for Women?* Edited by Joshua Cohen, Matthew Howard, and Martha C. Nussbaum, 7–24. Princeton, NJ: Princeton University Press.
———. 1999b. "Reply." In *Is Multiculturalism Bad for Women?* Edited by Joshua Cohen, Matthew Howard, and Martha C. Nussbaum, 115–31. Princeton, NJ: Princeton University Press.
———. 2002. "'Mistresses of their own destiny': Group Rights, Gender, and Realistic Rights of Exit." *Ethics* 112 (2): 205–30.
Oliveira, Adolfo de. 2009. "Introduction: Decolonising Approaches to Indigenous Rights." In *Decolonising Indigenous Rights*. Edited by Adolfo de Oliveira, 1–16. New York and London: Routledge.
Parekh, Bhikhu. 1999. "A Varied Moral World." In *Is Multiculturalism Bad for Women?* Edited by Joshua Cohen, Matthew Howard, and Martha C. Nussbaum, 69–75. Princeton, NJ: Princeton University Press.
Parkipuny, Moringe ole. 1989. "The Human Rights Situation of Indigenous Peoples in Africa." *Fourth World Journal* 4 (1): 1–4.

Payne, Sharon. 1990. "Aboriginal Women and the Criminal Justice System." *Aboriginal Law Bulletin* 2 (46): 9–11.
Pelican, Michaela. 2009. "Complexities of Indigeneity and Autochthony: An African Example." *American Ethnologist* 36 (1): 52–65.
Peters, Julie, and Andrea Wolper, eds. 1995. *Women's Rights, Human Rights: International Feminist Perspectives*. New York: Routledge.
Phillips, Anne. 2007. *Multiculturalism without Culture*. Princeton, NJ: Princeton University Press.
Pogge, Thomas W. 1997. "Group Rights and Ethnicity." In *Ethnicity and Group Rights*. Edited by Ian Shapiro and Will Kymlicka, 187–221. New York: New York University Press.
Poletta, Francesa, and James M. Jasper. 2001. "Collective Identity and Social Movements." *Annual Review of Sociology* 27: 283–305.
Pollmann, Arnd. 2010. "Menschenwürde nach der Barbarei: Zu den Folgen eines gewaltsamen Umbruchs in der Geschichte der Menschenrechte." *Zeitschrift für Menschenrechte* 4 (1): 26–45.
Pörksen, Uwe. 1995. *Plastic Words: The Tyranny of a Modular Language*. University Park: Pennsylvania State University Press.
Post, Robert. 1999. "Between Norms and Choices." In *Is Multiculturalism Bad for Women?* Edited by Joshua Cohen, Matthew Howard, and Martha C. Nussbaum, 65–68. Princeton, NJ: Princeton University Press.
Pritchard, Sarah. 1998. "Working Group on Indigenous Populations: Mandate, Standard-Setting Activities and Future Perspectives." In *Indigenous Peoples, the United Nations and Human Rights*. Edited by Sarah Pritchard, 40–64. London: Zed Books; Federation Press.
———. 2001. *Der völkerrechtliche Minderheitenschutz. Historische und neuere Entwicklungen*. Berlin: Duncker & Humblot.
Pulitano, Elvira. 2012. "Indigenous Rights and International Law. An Introduction. " In *Indigenous Rights: In the Age of the UN Declaration*. Edited by Elvira Pulitano, 1–30. Cambridge: Cambridge University Press.
Ranger, Terence. 1992. "The Invention of Tradition in Colonial Africa." In *The Invention of Tradition*. Edited by Eric J. Hobsbawm and Terence Ranger. Cambridge: Cambridge University Press.
Rawls, John. 1971. *A Theory of Justice*. Cambridge, MA: Belknap Press of Harvard University Press.
———. 1985. "Justice as Fairness: Political Not Metaphysical." *Philosophy and Public Affairs* 14 (3): 223–51.
Raz, Joseph. 1988. *The Morality of Freedom*. Oxford: Oxford University Press.
———. 1996. "Multiculturalism: A Liberal Perspective." In *Ethics in the Public Domain: Essays in the Morality of Law and Politics*, 170–91. Oxford: Clarendon Press.
———. 1999. "How Perfect Should One Be? And Whose Culture Is?" In *Is Multiculturalism Bad for Women?* Edited by Joshua Cohen, Matthew Howard, and Martha C. Nussbaum, 95–99. Princeton, NJ: Princeton University Press.
Reckwitz, Andreas. 2000. *Die Transformation der Kulturtheorien: Zur Entwicklung eines Theorieprogramms*. Weilerswist: Velbrück.
———. 2001. "Multikulturalismustheorien und der Kulturbegriff. Vom Homogenitätsmodell zum Modell kultureller Interferenzen." *Berliner Journal für Soziologie* 11 (2): 179–200.
———. 2002. "Toward a Theory of Social Practices: A Development in Culturalist Theorizing." *European Journal of Social Theory* 5 (2): 243–63.
———. 2006. *Das hybride Subjekt: Eine Theorie der Subjektkulturen von der bürgerlichen Moderne zur Postmoderne*. Weilerswist: Velbrück.
Reese-Schäfer, Walter. 2000. *Politische Theorie heute. Neuere Tendenzen und Entwicklungen*. München, Wien: Oldenbourg.
———. 2001. *Kommunitarismus*. Frankfurt am Main and New York: Campus.

Reus-Smit, Christian. 2001. "Human Rights and the Social Construction of Sovereignty." *Review of International Studies* 27 (4): 519–38.
———. 2004. "Society, Power, and Ethics." In *The Politics of International Law*. Edited by Christian Reus-Smit, 272–90. Cambridge and New York: Cambridge University Press.
Richards, Patricia. 2005. "The Politics of Gender, Human Rights, and Being Indigenous in Chile." *Gender & Society* 19 (2): 199–220.
Riedel, Eibe. 2004. "Der internationale Menschenrechtsschutz. Eine Einführung." In *Menschenrechte: Dokumente und Deklarationen*. Edited by Ludwig Watzal, 11–40. Bonn: Bundeszentrale für Politische Bildung.
Rimbaud, Arthur. 1972. *Oeuvres complètes*. Édition établie, présentée et annotée par Antoine Adam. Paris: Gallimard.
Ritsert, Jürgen. 1997. "Das Nichtidentische bei Adorno. Substanz- oder Problembegriff?" *Zeitschrift für Kritische Theorie* 3 (4): 29–51.
———. 2001. *Soziologie des Individuums: Eine Einführung*. Darmstadt: Wissenschaftliche Buchgesellschaft.
———. 2004. *Sozialphilosophie und Gesellschaftstheorie*. Münster: Westfälisches Dampfboot.
———. 2009. "Der Mythos der nicht-normativen Kritik. Oder:Wie misst man die herrschenden Verhältnisse an ihrem Begriff?" In *Probleme der Dialektik heute*. Edited by Stefan Müller, 161–76. Wiesbaden: VS Verlag für Sozialwissenschaften.
———. 2011. *Moderne Dialektik und die Dialektik der Moderne*. Münster: Monsenstein und Vannerdat.
Robbins, Bruce, and Elsa Stamatopoulou. 2004. "Reflections on Culture and Cultural Rights." *The South Atlantic Quarterly* 103 (2–3): 419–34.
Rodríguez-Piñero, Luis. 2005. *Indigenous Peoples, Postcolonialism, and International Law. The ILO Regime, 1919–1989*. Oxford and New York: Oxford University Press.
Rorty, Richard. 1993. "Human Rights, Sentimentality and Universality." In *On Human Rights: The Oxford Amnesty Lectures 1993*. Edited by Stephen Shute and Susan Hurley, 111–34. New York: Basic Books.
Rosa, Hartmut. 1998. *Identität und kulturelle Praxis: Politische Philosophie nach Charles Taylor*. Frankfurt am Main, New York: Campus.
Rosas, Allan. 1995a. "The Right of Self-Determination." In *Economic, Social and Cultural Rights: A Textbook*, edited by Asbjørn Eide, Catarina Krause, and Allan Rosas, 79–87. Dordrecht: Martinus Nijhoff.
———. 1995b. "So-Called Rights of the Third Generation." In *Economic, Social and Cultural Rights: A Textbook*. Edited by Asbjørn Eide, Catarina Krause, and Allan Rosas, 243–46. Dordrecht: Martinus Nijhoff.
Rosenthal, Gabriele. 2011. *Interpretative Sozialforschung. Eine Einführung*. Weinheim, München: Juventa-Verlag.
Roy Burman, B. K., and B. G. Verghese. 1998: *Aspiring to Be. The Tribal/Indigenous Condition*. Delhi: Konark Publishers.
Sahlins, Marshall. 1999. "Two or Three Things that I Know about Culture." *The Journal of the Royal Anthropological Institute* 5 (3): 399–421.
Said, Edward W. 1978. *Orientalism*. New York: Pantheon Books.
———. 1994. *Culture and Imperialism*. New York: Vintage Books.
Sandel, Michael J. 1982. *Liberalism and the Limits of Justice*. Cambridge and New York: Cambridge University Press.
Sanders, Douglas. 1991. "Collective Rights." *Human Rights Quarterly* 13 (3): 368–86.
Sassen, Saskia. 1999. "Culture beyond Gender." In *Is Multiculturalism Bad for Women?* Edited by Joshua Cohen, Matthew Howard, and Martha C. Nussbaum, 76–78. Princeton, NJ: Princeton University Press.
Saugestad, Sidsel. 2001. *The Inconvenient Indigenous: Remote Area Development in Botswana, Donor Assistance and the First People of the Kalahari*. Uppsala: Nordic Africa Institute.
Schimmelfennig, Frank. 2008. *Internationale Politik*. Paderborn: Schöningh.

Schmitz, Kenneth L. 1991. "The Unity of Human Nature and the Diversity of Cultures." In *Relations between Cultures*. Edited by George McLean and John Kromkowski, 305–22. Washington, DC: Council for Research in Values and Philosophy.
Schopenhauer, Arthur. 1995. *The World as Will and Idea*. London: Dent.
Schulte-Tenckhoff, Isabelle. 2012: "Treaties, Peoplehood, and Self-Determination: Understanding the Language of Indigenous Rights." In *Indigenous Rights: In the Age of the UN Declaration*. Edited by Elvira Pulitano, 64–86. Cambridge: Cambridge University Press.
Schweppenhäuser, Gerhard. 2005. *Die Antinomie des Universalismus: Zum moralphilosophischen Diskurs der Moderne*. Würzburg: Königshausen & Neumann.
Scott, John. 1990. *A Matter of Record: Documentary Sources in Social Research*. Cambridge, UK, and Cambridge, MA: Polity Press; Blackwell.
Selznick, Philip. 1992. *The Moral Commonwealth: Social Theory and the Promise of Community*. Berkeley: University of California Press.
Sen, Amartya. 1999. *Development as Freedom*. New York: Anchor Books.
———. 2007. *Identity and Violence: The Illusion of Destiny*. New York: Norton.
Shachar, Ayelet. 2009. "What We Owe Women." In *Toward a Humanist Justice: The Political Philosophy of Susan Moller Okin*. Edited by Debra Satz and Rob Reich, 143–65. Oxford and New York: Oxford University Press.
Shue, Henry. 2004. "Thickening Convergence: Human Rights and Cultural Diversity." In *The Ethics of Assistance: Morality and the Distant Needy*. Edited by Deen K. Chatterjee, 217–41. Cambridge: Cambridge University Press.
Sieder, Rachel, and Jessica Witchell. 2001. "Advancing Indigenous Claims through the Law. Reflections on the Guatemalan Peace Process." In *Culture and Rights: Anthropological Perspectives*. Edited by Jane K. Cowan, Marie-Bénédicte Dembour, and Richard Wilson, 201–25. Cambridge and New York: Cambridge University Press.
Speed, Shannon. 2006. "At the Crossroads of Human Rights and Anthropology: Toward a Critically Engaged Activist Research." *American Anthropologist* 108 (1): 66–76.
Spinner-Halev, Jeff. 2001. "Feminism, Multiculturalism, Oppression, and the State." *Ethics* 112 (1): 84–113.
Spivak, Gayatri Chakravorty. 1988. *In Other Worlds: Essays in Cultural Politics*. New York: Routledge.
———. 1999. *A Critique of Postcolonial Reason: Toward a History of the Vanishing Present*. Cambridge, MA: Harvard University Press.
Spivak, Gayatri Chakravorty, Sara Danius, and Stefan Jonsson. 1993. "An Interview with Gayatri Chakravorty Spivak." *Boundary 2* 20 (2): 24–50.
Stamatopoulou, Elsa. 2007. *Cultural Rights in International Law*. Leiden and Boston: Martinus Nijhoff Publishers.
Stapleton, Julia. 1995. "Introduction." In *Group Rights: Perspectives since 1900*. Edited by Julia Stapleton, ix-xxxix. Bristol, UK: Thoemmes.
Stavenhagen, Rodolfo. 1990. "The Right to Cultural Identity." In *Human Rights in a Pluralist World: Individuals and Collectivities*. Edited by Jan Berting et al., 255–58. Westport, CT, and London: Meckler.
———. 1995. "Cultural Rights and Universal Human Rights." In *Economic, Social and Cultural Rights: A Textbook*, edited by Asbjørn Eide, Catarina Krause, and Allan Rosas, 63–78. Dordrecht: Martinus Nijhoff.
———. 2009. "Making the Declaration Work." In *Making the Declaration Work: The United Nations Declaration on the Rights of Indigenous Peoples*. Edited by Claire Charters and Rodolfo Stavenhagen, 352–71. Copenhagen, and New Brunswick, NJ: IWGIA, Distributors Transaction Publisher, Central Books.
Steinert, Heinz. 2007. *Das Verhängnis der Gesellschaft und das Glück der Erkenntnis: Dialektik der Aufklärung als Forschungsprogramm*. Münster: Westfälisches Dampfboot.
Stephens, Carolyn, Clive Nettleton, John Porter, Ruth Willis, and Stephanie Clark. 2005. "Indigenous Peoples' Health—Why Are They behind Everyone, Everywhere?" *The Lancet* 366 (9479): 10–13.

Straub, Jürgen. 1998. "Personale und kollektive Identität: Zur Analyse eines theoretischen Begriffs." In *Identitäten: Erinnerung, Geschichte, Identität 3*. Edited by Aleida Assmann and Heidrun Friese, 73–104. Frankfurt am Main: Suhrkamp.
Strauss, Anselm L. 1959. *Mirrors and Masks: The Search for Identity*. New Brunswick, NJ: Transaction Publishers.
Suzman, James. 2003. "Response to Adam Kuper: The Return of the Native." *Current Anthropology* 44 (3): 399–400.
Svensson, Tom G. 1992. "Right to Self-Determination: A Basic Human Right concerning Cultural Survival: The Case of the Sami and the Scandinavian State." In *Human Rights in Cross-Cultural Perspectives: A Quest for Consensus*. Edited by Abdullahi Ahmed An-Na'im, 363–84. Philadelphia: University of Pennsylvania Press.
Tamir, Yael. 1993. *Liberal Nationalism*. Princeton, NJ: Princeton University Press.
———. 1999. "Siding with the Underdogs." In *Is Multiculturalism Bad for Women?* Edited by Joshua Cohen, Matthew Howard, and Martha C. Nussbaum, 47–52. Princeton, NJ: Princeton University Press.
Taylor, Charles. 1975. *Hegel*. Cambridge: Cambridge University Press.
———. 1985. "What's Wrong with Negative Liberty." In *Philosophy and the Human Sciences*. Cambridge and New York: Cambridge University Press.
———. 1989a. "Cross Purposes: The Liberal-Communitarian Debate." In *Liberalism and the Moral Life*. Edited by Nancy L. Rosenblum, 159–82. Cambridge, MA: Harvard University Press.
———. 1989b. *Sources of the Self: The Making of the Modern Identity*. Cambridge, MA: Harvard University Press.
———. 1993. "Why Do Nations Have to Become States?" In *Reconciling the Solitudes: Essays on Canadian Federalism and Nationalism*. Edited by Guy Laforest, 40–58. Montreal: McGill-Queen's University Press.
———. 1994a. "The Politics of Recognition." In *Multiculturalism: Examining the Politics of Recognition*. Edited by Charles Taylor, 25–73. Princeton, NJ: Princeton University Press.
———. 1994b. "Reply and Re-Articulation: Charles Taylor Replies." In *Philosophy in an Age of Pluralism: The Philosophy of Charles Taylor in Question*. Edited by James Tully, 211–57. Cambridge: Cambridge University Press.
Thapan, Meenakshi, ed. 2005. *Transnational Migration and the Politics of Identity*. New Delhi and Thousand Oaks, CA: Sage.
Thompson, Richard H. 1997. "Ethnic Minorities and the Case for Collective Rights." *American Anthropologist* 99 (4): 786–98.
Thornberry, Patrick. 1991. *International Law and the Rights of Minorities*. Oxford: Clarendon Press.
———. 2002. *Indigenous Peoples and Human Rights*. Manchester: Manchester University Press.
Thornberry, Patrick, and María Amor Martín Estébanez. 2004. *Minority Rights in Europe. A Review of the Work and Standards of the Council of Europe*. Strasbourg, and Croton-on-Hudson, NY: Council of Europe Publishing and Manhattan Pub. Co.
Tomuschat, Christian. 2008. *Human Rights: Between Idealism and Realism*. Oxford and New York: Oxford University Press.
Tönnies, Ferdinand. 2002. *Community and Society: Gemeinschaft und Gesellschaft*. Mineola, NY: Dover Publications.
Trigger, David S. 1992. *Whitefella Comin': Aboriginal Responses to Colonialism in Northern Australia*. Cambridge: Cambridge University Press.
Tully, James. 1994. "Aboriginal Property and Western Theory: Recovering a Middle Ground." *Social Philosophy and Policy* 11 (2): 153–80.
———. 2008a. "The Negotiation of Reconciliation." In *Public Philosophy in a New Key*. Vol. I, *Democracy and Civic Freedom*, 223–56. Cambridge: Cambridge University Press.

———. 2008b. "The Struggles of Indigenous Peoples for and of Freedom." In *Public Philosophy in a New Key*. Vol. I, *Democracy and Civic Freedom*, 257–88. Cambridge: Cambridge University Press.

Tyson, Adam D. 2010. *Decentralization and Adat Revivalism in Indonesia. The Politics of Becoming Indigenous*. London and New York: Routledge.

UNESCO. 1995. *Our Creative Diversity: Report of the World Commission on Culture and Development*. Paris: UNESCO Publishing.

Unger, Roberto Mangabeira. 1986. *The Critical Legal Studies Movement*. Cambridge, MA: Harvard University Press.

United Nations Department of Public Information. 2011. *Basic Facts about the United Nations*. New York: United Nations Pub.

Valencia-Weber, Gloria, and Christine P. Zuni. 1995. "Domestic Violence and Tribal Protection of Indigenous Women in the United States." *St. John's Law Review* 69: 69–170.

van Cott, Donna Lee. 1995. *Indigenous Peoples and Democracy in Latin America*. New York: St. Martin's Press.

van Dyke, Vernon. 1982. "Collective Entities and Moral Rights: Problems in Liberal-Democratic Thought." *The Journal of Politics* 44 (1): 21–40.

VanderWal, Koo. 1990. "Collective Human Rights: A Western View." In *Human Rights in a Pluralist World: Individuals and Collectivities*. Edited by Jan Berting et al., 83–98. Westport, CT, and London: Meckler.

Vasak, Karel. 1979. "For the Third Generationof Human Rights: The Rights of Solidarity." Talk at the International Institute of Human Rights, 10. Study Session.

Vertovec, Steven. 2001. "Transnationalism and Identity." *Journal of Ethnic and Migration Studies* 27 (4): 573–82.

Vismann, Cornelia. 1998. "Menschenrechte: Instanz des Sprechens—Instrument der Politik. In *Demokratischer Experimentalismus: Politik in der komplexen Gesellschaft*. Edited by Hauke Brunkhorst, 279–304. Frankfurt am Main: Suhrkamp.

Waldron, Jeremy. 2002. "Indigeneity? First Peoples and Last Occupancy." Quentin-Baxter Memorial Lecture, http://www2.law.columbia.edu/faculty_franke/ThursdayLunch/Waldron.facultylunch.indigeneity.pdf, accessed November 13, 2012.

Walzer, Michael. 2009. *Spheres of Justice: A Defense of Pluralism and Equality*. New York: Basic Books.

Watson, Irene, and Sharon Venne. 2012. "Talking Up Indigenous Peoples' Original Intent in a Space Dominated by State Interventions." In *Indigenous Rights: In the Age of the UN Declaration*. Edited by Elvira Pulitano, 87–109. Cambridge: Cambridge University Press.

Weiss, Thomas G. 2005. "Governance, Good Governance and Global Governance. Conceptual and Actual Challenges." 2000. Reprinted in *The Global Governance Reader*. Edited by Rorden Wilkinson, 68–88. London and New York: Routledge.

Welsch, Wolfgang. 2005. "Auf dem Weg zu transkulturellen Gesellschaften." In *Differenzen anders denken: Bausteine zu einer Kulturtheorie der Transdifferenz*. Edited by Lars Allolio-Näcke, Britta Kalscheuer, and Arne Manzeschke, 314–41. Frankfurt am Main, New York: Campus.

Wendt, Alexander E. 1987. "The Agent-Structure Problem in International Relations Theory." *International Organization* 41 (3): 335–70.

Werbner, Pnina. 2001. "The Limits of Cultural Hybridity: On Ritual Monsters, Poetic Licence and Contested Postcolonial Purifications." *The Journal of the Royal Anthropological Institute* 7 (1): 133–52.

Whelan, Daniel J., and Jack Donnelly. 2007. "The West, Economic and Social Rights, and the Global Human Rights Regime: Setting the Record Straight." *Human Rights Quarterly* 29 (4): 908–49.

Wiessner, Siegfried. 2008. "Indigenous Sovereignty: A Reassessment in Light of the UN Declaration on the Rights of Indigenous Peoples." *Vanderbilt Journal of Transnational Law* 41 (4): 1141–76.

———. 2011. "The Cultural Rights of Indigenous Peoples: Achievements and Continuing Challenges. *European Journal of International Law* 22 (1): 121–40.
Wilmer, Franke. 1993. *The Indigenous Voice in World Politics: Since Time Immemorial.* Newbury Park, CA: Sage.
Wolff, Jonas. 2007. "(De-)Mobilising the Marginalised: A Comparison of the Argentine Piqueteros and Ecuador's Indigenous Movement." *Journal of Latin American Studies* 39 (01): 1–29.
Xanthaki, Alexandra. 2007. *Indigenous Rights and United Nations Standards. Self-Determination, Culture and Land*. Cambridge: Cambridge University Press.
Yanow, Dvora, and Peregrine Schwartz-Shea. 2006. *Interpretation and Method: Empirical Research Methods and the Interpretive Turn*. Armonk, NY: Sharpe.
Yashar, Deborah J. 2005. *Contesting Citizenship in Latin America: The Rise of Indigenous Movements and the Postliberal Challenge*. Cambridge and New York: Cambridge University Press.
Yasuaki, Onuma. 1999. "Toward an Intercivilizational Approach to Human Rights." In *The East Asian Challenge for Human Rights*. Edited by Joanne R. Bauer and Daniel Bell, 103–23. Cambridge and New York: Cambridge University Press.
Young, Iris Marion. 1994. "Gender as Seriality: Thinking about Women as a Social Collective." *Signs: Journal of Women in Culture and Society* 19 (3): 713–38.
———. 1997. "Deferring Group Representation." In *Ethnicity and Group Rights*. Edited by Ian Shapiro and Will Kymlicka, 349–476. New York: New York University Press.
Zakaria, Fareed, and Kuan Yew Lee. 1994. "Culture Is Destiny: A Conversation with Lee Kuan Yew." *Foreign Affairs* 73 (2): 109–26.
Zion, James W. 1992. "North American Indian Perspectives on Human Rights." In *Human Rights in Cross-Cultural Perspectives: A Quest for Consensus*. Edited by Abdullahi Ahmed An-Na'im, 191–220. Philadelphia: University of Pennsylvania Press.

Index

Aborigines, 55, 91, 94, 136, 138, 151–152. *See also* Australia
acculturation, 8, 35, 36, 63, 66, 81, 89, 96, 100, 114, 132, 150, 153
Adorno, Theodor W., 49, 50, 51, 57, 65, 66, 67–68, 69–70, 72, 83, 156, 169, 170, 171; East Africa, 93; South Africa, 93
age, 135, 138, 139, 148, 164
agency, 22, 23, 26, 36, 40, 51, 59, 69, 72, 73, 74, 77, 84n8, 87, 88, 108, 162, 164, 173
agriculture, 119
allochthonous, 9, 31, 35, 97, 98, 105n9, 122, 174. *See also* autochthonous
America : the Americas, 89, 91, 133, 155; Canada, 25, 29, 91, 105n5, 128, 132; Central America, 92; North America, 92, 101; South America, 91, 92, 105n2, 131, 135, 136, 137; United States of America, 63, 91, 92, 105n2, 105n5, 125, 135, 142n59
American Anthropological Association, 4
Anaya, James, 90, 92, 96, 98, 103, 105n10, 118. *See also* Special Rapporteur on the Rights of Indigenous Peoples
ancestry, 9, 25, 26, 31, 97, 98, 105n7, 113, 116–117, 120, 147, 148, 154. *See also* future generations; heritage; priority criterion
Arctic, 92, 121
armed conflict, 119, 131. *See also* war
armed groups, 130–131, 144n79
Asia, 92, 105n2, 123, 155
Association of Southeast Asian Nations (ASEAN), 123
Australia, 89, 91, 105n2, 105n5, 134, 136, 138, 150. *See also* Aborigines

Australian Aboriginal Progressive Association, 91
Australian Royal Commission into Aboriginal Deaths in Custody (RCIADIC), 151, 165
authenticity, 23
autochthonous, 8, 9, 31, 35, 97, 125, 155, 174. *See also* allochthonous
autonomy, 10, 20, 26, 33, 50, 51, 53, 54, 55, 56, 60, 69, 74, 76, 99, 122, 170

Barabaig, 93
biodiversity, 112, 118, 119
Black Power Movement, 73
Bolivia, 105n3, 119, 121, 129, 130, 134, 135, 141n31, 142n44, 142n59, 143n73
Brazil, 105n3, 110, 111, 141n31
business corporations, 102, 119, 121, 122, 139, 141n32

capitalism, 10, 80, 118, 122
the Caribbean, 92, 113
children, 37, 39, 85n12, 103, 104, 116, 129, 134, 135, 136, 137, 139n2, 148, 152
citizenship, 97
Civil Rights Movement, 31, 63
civil society, 44, 107
class, 135, 136, 139, 145n105, 148, 152, 164
climate change, 117, 119, 121, 123, 127. *See also* environment; pollution
Cobo-report, 91–92, 95, 96, 99, 102, 155
colonialism, 31, 89–90, 94, 116, 120, 141n29, 157, 165. *See also* doctrine of discovery; postcolonialism
communitarianism, 10, 11, 16, 19–21, 20, 21–28, 32, 37, 44, 44n2, 49, 54
community, 5, 6, 8, 10, 15, 16, 17, 19, 21, 22, 24, 25, 26, 28, 29, 35, 43, 45n6, 49,

205

Index

55, 56, 57, 81, 99, 100, 103, 105n7, 112, 113, 117, 122, 130, 132, 133, 135, 136, 138, 151, 152, 155, 164, 165–166
consent, 76, 101, 122, 123, 125, 126, 133, 143n60. *See also* consultation
constitutive outside, 67, 68, 84n6
consultation, 126. *See also* consent
Convention No. 107. *See* International Labour Organization Convention No. 107
Convention No. 169. *See* International Labour Organization Convention No. 169
cosmopolitanism, 80
Council of the Iroquois Confederacy, 91
criminalization, 119, 120, 129, 130, 133, 135. *See also* detention
critique : immanent critique, 169–170, 171, 173; moral critique. *See* critique, transcendent critique ; normative critique; critique, transcendent critique ; reflexive critique, 171, 172, 173, 174; transcendent critique, 171, 172, 173. *See also* yardstick, normative
cultural relativism, 4–5, 13n5, 14n12, 16, 112, 173. *See also* universalism
culture: cultural ethnocide, 114; cultural hybridity, 47, 58, 59, 149; cultural memory, 154, 155; customary law, 2, 3, 98; customs, 29, 56, 90, 98, 99, 101, 114, 150, 156; diversity, 3, 54, 70, 110, 110–111, 114, 116, 127, 147; transculturation, 118, 153. *See also* distinction; multiculturalism

decent work. *See* labor
Declaration of Human Rights (1789), 1, 2, 3, 4, 6, 13n3, 104, 172
Declaration of Independence, 2
deconstruction, 53, 66, 67, 158. *See also* Derrida, Jacques
democracy, 6–7, 28, 43, 77, 80–81, 82, 104, 111, 119, 126, 131, 172
Derrida, Jacques, 58, 66, 67, 68, 69–70, 72, 83, 84n6, 85n13

detention, 41, 129, 130, 131, 132, 151. *See also* criminalization
development, 1, 3, 4, 5, 6, 7, 17, 23, 26, 31, 37, 39, 41, 45n8, 54, 63, 77, 79, 87, 90, 93, 94, 95, 96, 99, 103, 105n2, 107, 112, 113, 123, 128, 136, 139n2, 141n32, 157, 165, 173
deviation, 60, 69, 76, 81, 112, 124
dialectics, 66, 70
dignity, 4, 15, 22, 23, 24, 73, 127, 133, 172–173, 174
disability, 138, 152
discrimination, 7, 8, 9, 10, 14n8, 40, 89, 91, 97, 98, 104, 112, 113, 114, 115, 126, 128, 129, 131, 134, 136, 137, 138, 139, 140n17, 144n94, 152, 172
displacement, 70, 102, 119, 131, 132, 135, 137, 148. *See also* relocation
distinction, 3, 7, 9, 10, 22, 23, 27, 30, 31, 31–32, 33, 34, 35, 40, 45n7, 47, 51, 56, 58, 60, 64, 74, 75, 80, 81, 82, 84n8, 95, 96, 97, 100, 102, 110, 111, 112, 113, 113–114, 114, 120, 121, 122, 124, 127, 132, 135, 147, 148, 149–150, 150, 152, 153, 156, 162, 163, 165, 166, 168, 172, 173, 174. *See also* culture
doctrine of discovery, 90, 165
domestic violence, 95, 136, 151, 152, 158n1, 165. *See also* gender

Economic and Social Council (ECOSOC), 91, 92, 108
ecotourism, 141n32
education, 14n8, 41, 69, 71, 89, 98, 127, 129, 133, 135, 136, 137, 139n2, 144n92
environment, 6, 89, 101, 113, 119, 121, 130, 139n2, 141n31. *See also* climate change; pollution
erga omnes, 3
ethnicity. *See* identity
ethnocide. *See* culture
Eurocentrism, 67, 82
Europe, 67, 69, 90; Eastern Europe, 63, 92
exclusion, 63, 78, 82, 95, 97, 102, 103, 107, 110, 114–115, 126, 128, 131, 136, 139, 140n5, 141n24, 141n25, 152, 156, 158, 164, 174

exit option, 9, 40–41, 43, 161. *See also* free will; freedom of choice
Expert Mechanism on the Rights of Indigenous Peoples, 93
expropriation, 89–90, 101, 119, 120, 121, 122, 131, 142n38
extractive industry, 119, 121, 121–122, 136

family, 6, 30, 34, 37, 38, 39, 40, 43, 45n5, 57, 79, 81, 105n7, 122, 127, 137, 151, 154
feminism, 37, 39, 104
First Peoples Disability Network Australia, 138
forced contact, 110
forced migration. *See* displacement
France, 113, 134
free, prior and informed consent. *See* consent
free will, 53. *See also* exit option; freedom of choice
freedom of choice, 15, 99, 163, 164. *See also* exit option; free will
future generations, 25, 26, 95, 98, 99, 117, 152, 165. *See also* ancestry, heritage

Gemeinschaft. *See* community
Gemeinwesen. *See* community
gender, 9, 10, 14n10, 37, 37–38, 39, 40, 41, 42, 43, 47, 64, 71, 73, 75, 103, 104, 115, 135–136, 136, 137, 138, 139, 139n2, 144n95, 151–152, 159n2, 161, 164. *See also* domestic violence
genocide, 1, 14n8, 113, 114, 132, 133
global society, 80
global governance, 12
good governance, 104
group-differentiated rights, 29, 30, 31, 32, 35, 36, 43, 82, 167

Habermas, Jürgen, 73, 77, 78, 79, 80, 80–81, 82, 85n13, 173
Hadzabe, 93
health care, 89, 135
Hegel, G.W.F., 22, 23, 51, 68, 73, 84n6, 84n8, 171

heritage, 9, 25, 98, 147. *See also* ancestry; future generations; priority criterion
Holocaust, 2
Human Rights Committee. *See* United Nations Human Rights Committee
human rights duties, 5, 173
human rights generations, 6
humanitarianism, 3, 123
hunter-gatherers, 93, 94

identity: collective identity, 20, 23, 27, 32, 39, 47, 56, 63, 75–76, 77–80, 80, 81–83, 84, 84n10, 85n13, 98, 132, 152, 162, 174; dialogical identity, 23, 73, 74; ethnic identity, 30, 31, 33, 95; indigenous identity, 125, 152, 153, 162, 164–165; individual identity, 15, 23, 24, 29, 30, 36, 42, 43, 45n5, 47, 58, 63, 71, 74, 75, 77, 78, 79, 80, 82, 161, 162, 167; rational identity, 78
illiteracy, 89
imperative, 39, 58, 112, 117, 152, 164–166, 170, 171, 173
intellectual property, 89
International Bill of Human Rights, 2
International Convention on Elimination of all Forms of Discrimination against Women, 9
International Covenant on Civil and Political Rights, 2, 8, 103
International Covenant on Economic, Social and Cultural Rights, 2
International Decade of the World's Indigenous People, 93, 142n58
International Fund for Agricultural Development, 105n1
International Indian Treaty Council, 91
International Labour Organization (ILO), 90, 92, 97, 98, 99, 108, 115, 128
International Labour Organization Convention No. 107, 90–91, 92
International Labour Organization Convention No. 169, 92, 97, 98, 99, 108, 115, 128
international law, 1, 2, 3, 5, 8, 12, 16, 93, 95, 96, 97, 98, 102, 103, 162, 168, 169
International Work Group for Indigenous Affairs, 91, 96, 110
ius cogens, 3

Kymlicka, Will, 11, 14n9, 16, 21, 29, 30–34, 34, 35, 35–36, 37, 39, 40, 43, 44, 44n1, 45n8, 45n9, 47, 48, 52, 54, 56, 58, 61n4, 65, 82, 84n5, 105n8, 151, 153, 154, 156, 161, 166–167, 168

labor, 39, 89, 90, 100, 129, 131
lands, 95, 101–102, 103, 105, 105n7, 110, 118, 119, 120, 121, 122, 123, 132, 141n31, 147, 148. *See also* resources
language, 3, 6, 8, 9, 13n2, 22, 25, 26, 28, 29, 31, 33, 44n4, 56, 77, 94, 98, 99, 103, 105n7, 111, 113, 116, 129, 133, 135, 136, 138, 144n93, 153, 166
Las Casas, Bartolomé de, 90
law cases: Canada (Attorney General) vs. Lavell, 103, 164, 165; Cayuga Indians case, 90; Delgamuukw vs. British Columbia, 102; Eastern Greenland case, 90; Island of Palmas case, 90; Kitok vs. Sweden, 103; Santa Clara Pueblo vs. Martinez, 103, 164, 165; Sandra Lovelace vs. Canada, 103; West Sahara case, 91
League of Nations, 7, 91
liberalism, 11, 16, 19, 20, 37, 43, 43–44, 44n2, 49, 54, 82
liberty, 19, 22, 23, 24, 28, 32, 36, 39, 44, 70
livestock, 119

Maasai, 93
Martínez Cobo, Jose R., 91, 95, 101, 102, 155. *See also* Special Rapporteur on the Rights of Indigenous Peoples
master-slave parable, 73
migration, 30, 31, 34, 35, 119, 128, 131, 166
military, 101, 102, 130, 131, 137, 139. *See also* armed groups
mining. *See* extractive industry
minority, 1, 5, 6–8, 8, 10, 25, 31, 34, 35, 36, 39, 45n8, 56, 76, 82, 96
monoculture, 119
moral, 1, 3, 4, 12, 13, 15, 16, 20, 22–23, 24, 26, 26–27, 28, 37, 38, 39, 47, 54, 55, 56, 58, 70, 72, 77, 79, 80, 81, 93, 156, 157, 167, 168–169, 170, 171, 172, 173

mother earth, 112, 121
multiculturalism, 21, 36, 81, 110. *See also* culture

National Indian Youth Council, 105n2
national socialism, 6–7, 61n3, 165
natural law, 1, 156, 170
nature, 10, 51, 52, 56, 58, 61n3, 66, 68, 69, 112, 117, 118, 121, 122, 127, 141n31, 142n35, 169
New Caledonian Kanak, 113
New Zealand, 105n5
norms, 2, 3, 9, 12, 29, 33, 41, 43, 54, 56, 71, 79, 80, 96, 98, 107, 108, 152, 153, 169, 170, 172

Okin, Susan Moller, 11, 16, 21, 35, 36, 37, 37–38, 39, 40, 40–42, 42, 42–43, 43, 44, 47, 48, 52, 54, 59, 65, 81, 151, 152, 161, 167

Pacific, 92, 119
participation, 40, 63, 77, 90, 91, 92, 101, 110, 121, 122, 123, 124, 125, 126, 127, 132, 135, 136, 137, 147, 148. *See also* self-determination
pastoralists, 93
Pastoralists Indigenous NGO's Forum (PINGO), 93
peace, 3, 6, 8, 130
persistent organic pollutants, 121
pollution, 119, 121, 129, 142n35, 148. *See also* climate change; environment
postcolonialism, 84n7, 116. *See also* colonialism
poverty, 71, 111, 128, 132, 162
power, 3, 4, 5, 22, 23, 31, 34, 37, 39, 40, 42, 43, 47, 51, 52, 54, 58, 60, 67, 70, 71, 72, 74, 76, 90, 95, 96, 100, 101–102, 111, 137, 149, 150, 152, 158, 163, 165, 166, 173
priority criterion, 94–95, 115, 116, 120, 155
private sphere, 34, 38, 39, 40, 41, 43, 81
property, 89, 101, 102, 132, 137
prostitution, 89, 136, 137
protest, 112, 130
psychoanalysis, 37, 84n1, 85n12

public sphere, 81
Pufendorf, Samuel von, 90

reflection, 23, 50, 59–60, 69, 71, 76, 81, 82, 84n8, 154, 156, 158
reflexivity. *See* reflection
refugees, 31, 173, 174
religion, 3, 5, 8, 9, 41, 42, 45n5, 64, 71, 105n7, 116, 131, 141n29, 144n84, 156, 170
relocation, 25, 69, 70, 81, 89, 101, 102, 110, 119, 128, 131, 132, 135, 136, 137, 148, 153. *See also* displacement
resources, 97, 101–102, 102, 103, 110, 118, 119, 119–120, 120, 121, 122, 123, 129, 130, 132, 141n31, 142n35, 147, 148. *See also* lands
responsibility, 3, 99, 116, 136
Russian Federation, 92, 105n5

sabotage, 130
Sami, 113, 124
San, 97, 158
secession, 30, 97, 99, 100
self-determination, 7, 26, 28, 31, 53, 72, 96, 97, 99–100, 103, 104, 105, 110, 122–123, 124, 125, 126, 127, 132, 147, 148, 150, 151. *See also* participation
self-government, 35, 90, 99, 100, 104
slavery, 90, 121, 122, 129
solidarity, 8, 24, 43, 125, 158
sovereignty, 3, 5, 10, 99, 100, 102, 120, 124, 154
Special Rapporteur on the Rights of Indigenous Peoples, 93, 96, 108. *See also* Anaya, James; Martínez Cobo, Jose R.
spiritual relationship, 101, 102, 127
state, 2, 3, 4, 5, 6, 8, 10, 15, 30, 31, 33, 34, 35, 36, 38, 43, 45n5, 45n8, 47, 56, 57, 60, 64, 71, 78, 79, 80–81, 82, 84n5, 87, 90, 92, 96, 97, 98, 99–100, 101, 102, 104, 105n2, 107, 110, 111, 112, 115, 116, 119, 123, 124, 126, 128, 129, 130, 131, 135, 136, 138, 139, 141n31, 144n93, 149, 152, 153, 164, 165, 166, 167, 168, 172
state violence, 129, 130

subject constitution, 29, 43, 44, 55, 161–162, 163, 164, 171, 174
sustainability, 4, 128
symbolic interactionism, 22, 84n1

Taylor, Charles, 11, 16, 21–25, 25, 26, 26–28, 28, 29, 37, 39, 40, 43, 44, 44n2, 44n4–45n7, 45n12, 47, 48, 49, 52, 54, 56, 58, 61n4, 65, 73, 81, 151, 158, 161, 167, 168
terra nullius, 90, 91, 102
territory. *See* lands
terrorism, 129, 130
torture, 130
Tuareg, 113

UNESCO Convention against Discrimination in Education, 14n8
UNESCO Declaration of the Principles of International Cultural Co-Operation, 14n8
United Nations, 1, 2, 3–4, 6, 7, 8, 9, 12, 13n3, 14n7, 14n8, 88, 89, 91, 92, 98, 105n4, 108, 123, 125, 137
United Nations Charter, 3, 104
United Nations Commission on Human Rights, 14n7, 93, 105n4
United Nations Conference on Discrimination against Indigenous Populations in the Americas, 91
United Nations Convention on the Prevention and Punishment of the Crime of Genocide, 14n8
United Nations Decade for Women, 9
United Nations Declaration on the Rights of Indigenous Peoples, 1, 12, 89, 93, 98–105, 108, 109, 121, 123, 128, 130, 134, 147, 152, 157, 162–163, 164, 172
United Nations Declaration on the Rights of Persons Belonging to National or Ethnic, Religious and Linguistic Minorities, 8
United Nations Economic and Social Council, 91, 92, 108, 180
United Nations Educational, Scientific and Cultural Organization, 6, 10, 14n8

United Nations General Assembly, 92, 93
United Nations Human Rights Committee, 10, 103
United Nations Permanent Forum on Indigenous Issues, 12, 88, 92–93, 94, 96, 99, 105n1, 108, 109, 112, 114, 126, 129, 134, 138, 139, 139n2, 139n3, 140n5, 143n61, 145n104, 147, 162, 163, 172
United Nations Security Council, 3
United Nations Sub-Commission on Prevention of Discrimination and Protection of Minorities, 7, 8, 91
United Nations World Conference on Human Rights, 3, 6, 92
Universal Declaration of Human Rights (1948), 1, 2, 3, 4, 6, 13n3, 104, 172
universalism, 1, 5, 13n5, 27, 37, 82. *See also* cultural relativism

Vitoria, Francisco de, 90

war, 4, 6, 89, 112, 116, 125, 131, 136, 154. *See also* armed conflict
water, 101, 119, 120, 121, 128, 129
welfare, 44, 129
working conditions. *See* labor
Working Group on Indigenous Populations, 91–93, 95, 96, 102, 112, 156, 187, 198
World Bank, 141n32
World Conference on Human Rights, 3, 6, 92
World Council of Indigenous Peoples, 91
World War I, 6
World War II, 1, 6–7, 61n3
Wounded Knee, 105n2

yardstick, normative, 13, 25, 27, 28, 33, 34, 36, 42, 43, 44, 48, 54, 55, 60, 69, 83, 84, 102, 103, 116, 157, 162, 166, 167–168, 168–169, 169–170, 171, 172. *See also* critique